TELLING OUR TALES

# TELLING OUR TALES

*Stories and Storytelling for all Ages*

Jeanette Ross

SKINNER HOUSE BOOKS
Boston

First edition ©1994, this edition ©2002 by Jeanette Ross. Published by Skinner House Books. Skinner House Books is an imprint of the Unitarian Universalist Association, a liberal religious organization with more than 1,000 congregations in the United States and Canada. 25 Beacon Street, Boston, MA 02108. All rights reserved.

ISBN 1-55896-434-7

Printed in Canada

Text design by Terry Bain. Cover design by Kathryn Sky-Peck.

05 04 03 02

6 5 4 3 2 1

Library of Congress Cataloging-in-Publication Data

Ross, Jeanette.
  Telling our tales : stories and storytelling for all ages / Jeanette Ross.
  —2nd ed.
     p.   cm.
  Includes bibliographical references.
  ISBN 1-55896-434-7 (alk. paper)
  1. Tales. 2. Storytelling. 3. Folklore—Performance. I. Title.
GR76 .R67 2002                                          398.2—dc21
                                                        2002021042

# CONTENTS

INTRODUCTION    vii

CREATION AND OTHER BEGINNINGS
*In the Beginning*    3
*Ares*    8
*The Chicken Stars*    11
*Etana Ascends to Heaven*    15
*The Miraculous Birth of Abraham*    21
*Coyote Creates*    25
*How the Devil Helped*    29
*Mother of the Dark*    33

THE WISE AND HEROIC
*Brave John and Marie*    41
*Seven Most Obedient Sons*    50
*What Sun Wanted*    55
*Na Ha Calls Down the Storm*    60
*How Wisdom Scattered*    66
*Glooscap and Baby*    71
*What We Learned from the Devil*    77
*The Power of the Question*    82
*The Quarrel*    87

FINDING OUR PLACE
*Most Precious*    93
*Lady Green of the Speaking Tree*    102
*Good From Bad*    110
*Better Rude Than Sorry*    115
*Water of Life*    123

*Shaydoola*  129
*Of Course*  134
*The Lesson*  141

FAMILIAR TALES AND CHARACTERS
*I'll Never Be Old*  147
*Written in Gold*  153
*Witling's Treasure*  159
*Legend of the Great Tuber*  166
*No Stranger at the Door*  174
*Second Shepherd's Play*  178
*Mighty Red Riding Hood*  182
*Moshe's Miraculous Shirt*  186

FROM THE KIDS
*How Blondes Came to Be Known as Airheads*  193
*Our Heroine Eva Kneva*  197
*Sharing the Well*  202
*Saving Stone Monster*  209
*Back to Reality*  216

STORYTELLER'S SECRETS
*Telling Tales*  227
*Create Your Own Story*  256

BIBLIOGRAPHY
291

# INTRODUCTION

"We are all connected," say the Lakota and Crow people in prayer. "The eight-legged, six-legged, four-legged, two-legged, those who crawl on grandmother earth. . . ." And we are not only connected; we are very much alike. My friend Tom Bray, home-spun philosopher and sculptor, insists that individual differences, even within the average family, are greater than collective differences between one culture and another. Enter any room full of children and the old truth emerges again. As different as we may appear to be, we have common needs, concerns, and tasks in life. And like it or not, we are all connected.

We have seen the rediscovery of folkways and folk truths in regions as diverse as China, Russia, northern Europe, Mexico, and the United States, with a subsequent reinvigoration of many art forms, from dance to visual art to storytelling. At the same time, the investigations of physics suggest that from the subatomic level to the farthest reaches we can imagine, every vibrating speck of existence is connected to every other.

Humans and subatomic particles both demonstrate a tendency to move in ways that are habitual but not precisely predictable.

We move, in families and societies, within shells that aren't easily broken, and yet when we break out, when we transcend the ordinary rounds, there is a sudden release of energy, we could even say ecstasy. Attempting to describe these tendencies, the observer of physical law resorts to metaphor, what Albert Einstein called convenient fictions. Which brings us directly back to storytelling. Physicist Fritjof Capra says that all living things are engaged in self-maintenance, self-renewal, and self-transcendence. This elegantly summarizes the messages embedded in stories all around the world.

Although most of us now learn stories from books, this has its perils. Print has an authority quite different from the gift of story delivered directly by another person. A story in print is the property of someone else. Storytellers, by contrast, can reexperience and reinvent what they are sharing. Jon Norstog, a longtime resident at Window Rock, Arizona, tells of a Navajo singer and philosopher, Mr. Quinton, who has studied the Bible and world religions, and concludes that because Coyote and Jesus are the same kind of being, in the last days Coyote will also come back.

There are many ways for any story to be told and much borrowing, from traders moving along the "Silk Road," to village markets in Pakistan to any school playground. Storytellers are performers. In telling stories, acting them out, turning them into our own ritual and rhyme and dance, we connect ourselves to the experience of others. To participate in the story lifts it from being cute, strange, the life of someone quite different, to being felt at the story's core. The goal of a story is not its literal truth or some vivid representation of quaint beliefs once accepted as true. Rather, we use the emotional experience of a story to test out the consequences of a particular course or action and to consider what might be possible, what great deeds we might ourselves pursue. We have a safe adventure in a short time.

Children appreciate a large amount of awe, the strange and new. As we get older, the yearning to imagine is counterbalanced and stifled by the desire to be certain. Although we wonder and allow all things to be possible at one age, usually midchildhood, we soon build walls against the uncertain, protect ourselves with explanations against the unlikely, and declare stories of magical occurrence to be fairy tales for children only. Too easily, adults exchange "I wonder!" for "I wonder why?" and demand a factual answer that eliminates the wonder. Psychologist James Hillman has said that the sin of our time is literalism, a demand that something must have happened in order to be true. Recently, religious historian Karen Armstrong has pointed out how modernism exerts a tyranny of the factual that intimidates traditional cultures.

Mythologist Joseph Campbell says that stories create a coherent universe with a place for every sparrow, every orphan child. Yet perils abound. We are all vulnerable. Like Job, each of us must be reconciled to a world in which we are broken and healed by the same forces. Many stories (including the Book of Job) have a satisfying roundness, where the innocent, weak, and ignorant are eventually triumphant despite trials and betrayals along the way. Myths and folk tales like these are especially appropriate to cultures that honor the myth of individuality, the conviction (psychiatrist E. E. Hadley calls it a delusion) that each person has fixed principles and capacities that allow for free choice among a wide range of options. The story of Jack and the Beanstalk, for instance, could describe the way we must assert ourselves against enormous obstacles and authorities if we are to thrive. Certainly the giant and Jack are not living in community! The forest surrounding Sleeping Beauty and Red Riding Hood can similarly be seen as the dangerous world we must enter, alone, in order to reach another equivalent of a happy ending. Hillman approves of such stories, which he says relieve us of our guilt so that we too can go on and experience the growth that comes only after breaking rules, surviving life's many big and small betrayals.

Just as common in the European tradition are stories of small kindnesses rewarded along the path of adventure. In this collection, "Water of Life" incorporates several subtle understandings about the dangers encountered in the great life task, particularly those of succumbing to greed and envy, along with a suspicion that paradise (in this case the remarkable water of life) may be much closer to home than we first believe.

The Chinese tale included here, from a collection approved by the People's Republic, has a different underlying assumption, suggesting that we are "saved" by living in community rather than by embarking on a personal quest. The wisdom of nomadic people is honored in the Arawak creation story, which suggests that paradise is no single place and that the imposing of artificial limits or laws can lead only to calamity. The Azerbaijan tale of Shaydoola has a moral more in keeping with agricultural people; the fool who wanders off, leaving spouse and children to tend the land, deserves only what grace he has earned.

## STORY TYPES

In the most straightforward sense, a story is a recollection of an event or events, a retelling. The word derives from the Latin word *historia*, which comes from the Greek word for wisdom.

Although wisdom derives from history, our oldest visual records illustrate how soon we humans went beyond a description of past events to express an idealized, imagined past as well as wishes and intentions for the future. Ancient drawings and crafted objects suggested powerful narratives not limited by the past, thus the term *tale* for a narrative true or imagined. There is an implied meaning to such narration; a tale reveals more than it says.

One of the most complex and profound forms of story, the myth, is also one of the oldest. I define myth by its large reverberatory power, as a story that is particularly false but generally true. The story of Etana and the eagle is recorded on clay tablets and illustrated in official Sumerian cylinder seals often enough that we know it was a favorite in several different cultures. A myth is a story that explains something important—what it means to be good or heroic, how to become a contributing member of a functioning society—and it illustrates how something important may have been discovered or made available. The story "What Sun Wanted" comes from the peaceful Arawak people, who had no cultural or religious hierarchy that might refashion a story for their own agenda. The moral of the story—that the best control is no control—seems appropriate for a people who lacked weapons or strategies for aggression when Columbus encountered them.

Those stories we call myth were often the narrative parts of religious ceremonies. At weddings and feasts in Japan a thousand years ago, villagers would act out stories of the Buddha's helping them get a good harvest, a long life, a big family. In medieval England, guilds of craftsmen performed stories from the Bible to accompany holy days; the story version of the "Second Shepherd's Play" is an example of an invented, performed comic myth. In the same spirit on a different continent, "The Lesson," based upon a story fragment in *Tales of Uncle Remus*, could easily be a warning about the cost of assimilating into what is perceived to be a richer society.

Mythological time, that distant time in which the world was established, often contains humanized animals and animalized humans. It is a time when tremendously important change is possible. The story of Ares moves from the earliest age, the innocent egotism of the first human, to an age of self-awareness and sense of place in a much larger universe. This transition takes place without punishment for the sin of gaining such knowledge, without a loss of paradise. The story "How Wisdom Scattered" extends the moral of "Ares," reminding young listeners that maintaining respect for elders does not preclude the possibility of finding wisdom on one's own. The age of myth-making has not ended. "What We Learned from the Devil" is an Americanized African story suggesting that nowadays we are more likely to learn from the Devil than from our ancestors.

Folklorists sometimes speak of living myth as stories whose assumptions and events are accepted without question. The sacred texts of one culture or age become the mythology of another. It is easier to identify the assumptions imbedded in someone else's mythology than one's own (an identification limited, of course, by our biases and understandings). Early twentieth-century observers like Thomas Mann suggested that the blending of bird, deer, bull, and human found in ancient mythology shows that the ego of earlier peoples was less defined, more connected to all life, uncomplicated by a linear time line or time divisions. Today's folklorists guard against romantic projections into past, simpler lives and instead see folkloric and tribal behavior in youth cultures, opera traditions, and Wall Street.

Indo-European stories often reward adventurers with wealth and prestige. They suggest that innocent, even foolish children who persevere will be rewarded, while those who act selfishly and impatiently will ultimately suffer. Russian folk myth has a character known as Koschei the Deathless, once a creator-god of great power and cruelty. After the advent of Christian belief, Koschei emerges from a dark cavern or castle to walk the land, punishing or rewarding on a whim. But even his gifts have a cost. In "I'll Never Be Old," Koschei's female equivalent illustrates the losses associated with self-indulgence.

Christian scholars have added another worthwhile term to the study of myth—*kerygma*, the core of truth within a story available whether or not we accept literally the events through which the myth is told. Those who do not accept the existence of devils, for instance, still find a psychological truth in the story of Jesus' temptation in the wilderness. The story "Better Rude Than Sorry" places a strong-willed orphan in a harsh, demonic environment in order to demonstrate the destructive power of silence and the potential healing power available even in these circumstances. The reality of a spirit world in this tale is not emphasized or dismissed, simply accepted. Another story, "The Power of the Question," based upon the intertestamental "Testament of

Solomon," gives a child's eye view of a person believed to have magical powers. It shows us an adult using power wisely.

Although there is much diffusion of story elements around the world, there are no essential kinds of story. Myths of creation, of earth and its beings, are central to Judaism and Christianity, while China's three great religions (Buddhism, Confucianism, and Taoism), with their deep understanding of human relationship and purpose, have only the most rudimentary of creation stories. Instead, they have earthy, compelling moral tales like "The Quarrel" (I have borrowed from a Japanese version, but many other variants exist), "Seven Most Obedient Sons," and "Of Course!" Asia also abounds in wonder tales, filled with dragons, demons, and magical transformations. "The Chicken Stars," from Thailand, makes a virtue of self-sacrifice. A wonder tale from Brazil, "Mother of the Dark," combines several story fragments with archeological evidence to provide a playful contrast as well as an earthy young goddess-creator.

A flurry of nineteenth-century language investigation (on the ancestor language of many European and Asian peoples) stimulated the investigations of cultural habits that came to be called folklore. These can be practices among contemporary, even print-oriented people: urban legends, family traditions, and schoolyard-play songs are examples. Folk tales, then, are orally transmitted stories that may be silly or serious, keepers of morality, fantasy, jokes too clever to forget, or all of the above. Tales also contain, in their repetitions and elaborations, our love of ritual and ceremony, the rhythms and returns that suggest an orderly universe.

Fairytales are stories with a plot, often elaborate tales that have been carried around the world until they are a blend of local, historical, and literary traditions. Many have magical events and characters (permutations of earlier gods, demons, and heroes, perhaps) that Celtic people called fairies. These were some of the first collected by the Grimm brothers, Andrew Lang, and others, thus are some of the best-known tales for people of Indo-European descent. The story "Good from Bad," about the brothers Fitzer and Spitzer, is based upon the intersection between a magical fairyland and the land of our ordinary concerns.

One more term: A *legend* is a story about a heroic ancestor, one for whom we may or may not find historic evidence. Legends have been retold by so many generations that they say more about the tellers than the original subject. This collection includes three legendary figures in very different styles. Glooscap, the legendary founder of the Passamaquoddy people, has the innocent obsessiveness of other trickster heroes among Native Americans. His story hints at the human cost of spending all one's time fighting the good fight. The story of Na Ha, bringer of storms, comes from the extreme southern tip of South America; this hero is an example of sacrifice for the greater good described in solemn, noble terms. His story incorporates the admiration of individual powers, including magical powers, which is typical of hunting communities. Somewhere in between the naive hero-progenitor Glooscap and the self-sacrificing Na Ha is the hero in the Crow Indian story of the creation of earth. Coyote succeeds by leading a team effort, then offers good, if rudimentary, advice before leaving his creations to continue on their own.

Legends have a wish-fulfillment quality about them. Nightmares are a manifestation of our doubt that we can face that which frightens us. Heroes of traditional legend triumph over demons and dangers. They comfort and strengthen us. More importantly, they are compassionate beings we can admire and emulate. Coyote, for instance, is a wise fool who now is seen in modern dress, enjoying contemporary pleasures. Like us, he is capable of changing, learning, and making entirely new mistakes! "The Legend of the Great Tuber" reinvents the hero as a child facing the unknown.

## Telling Our Tales

I prefer telling stories to reading them. When we tell a story, we take on some of its life and share it in a direct way, looking at our audience, responding to them rather than to a book. Compare the feeling you get listening to a heads-up choir with one that is locked into its music. Watch new parents talk to their infant; they bring their faces up close, look directly into the baby's eyes, and mouth their sounds broadly, exaggerating their facial expression. The baby's face takes on a tentative smile, then a broad one; adult words become livelier, more emphatic. It isn't just a story; it's a love fest.

When we read a story, by contrast, we rarely improvise. We grant the book's author authority and privilege. Our voices slip into that singsong drone that says we are mouthing the words of others. Shoulders hunched down, eyes are locked in place—we are decoding, not experiencing. Even if we are captivated, our imagination visits the past; the recorded story is always history. When we tell a story, even the same story, we make it alive; it happens at the moment and is alive between audience and teller. Everyone, speaker and listeners alike, takes on the power of the tale.

One definition of art is that it draws our attention to the importance of something. Storytelling is a sacred art because it holds up those stories that deserve our whole attention, at least for the moment, and lets us connect ourselves to the experience of others. The reason one feels so naked standing in front of children without a picture book or script is that there is no disguising a failure to connect. We are at the mercy of our audience and our story. That's the way it should be.

This book is meant to be useful as well as entertaining. Those ready to try storytelling may use my story outlines or a version of them. Performance strategies accompanying each tale, supplemented at the back of the book, may be mixed and matched or applied to entirely different stories. Those interested in my sources and strategies for adaptation will find a few notes after each story. As further encouragement to story-making, a section entitled "From the Kids" provides five contemporary stories building upon ideas from children. I hope that their inventive exuberance leads to more such adult-child collaborations.

# CREATION AND OTHER BEGINNINGS

✳

# IN THE BEGINNING

✳

In the beginning, according to people we call Maya, there was water and sky, with darkness between. Water, sky, and silence—and beneath water lay the Makers.

What could the Makers have been like, the people wondered. Certainly the Makers contained in themselves a part of everything that existed: fire, water, feathers, and flesh. These Makers must have been able to swim like water snakes and fly like birds. Did the Makers have heads with big brains, eyes to see, ears, and large, capable hands? Certainly. And so the Maya imagined the Makers to be all things at once, male and female, containing all colors, all voices, all abilities—the Makers probably were feathered serpents who swam in the quiet deep. They were so much alike, this first Mother and Father, that the people spoke of them as being One, one Supreme God. Surely, the people thought, these wise serpents had a remarkable gift: When they agreed on the importance of something, that thing came into existence. From First Mother and First Father, we learn that when many minds agree, miracles can happen.

What was needed, these Makers agreed, was more life. They created Heart of Heaven, the great forces of the sky that make life possible. First was Huracan, the force of wind that is everywhere, like all the gods, then Lightning and Thunder, all streaming out of the mouths of the Makers. Together these storm gods conjured up a fourth, their sister Heart of Earth, source of growing things and rain. Later, when the work of creation was done, these powers of wind, thunder, lightning, and rain made their homes at the four corners of the earth, one to each direction. Yes, they were terrible, but there could be no new life without them, for who can live without rain?

New life! The Makers consulted and created wild things next—birds to haunt riverbank and thicket, birds to nest in trees and vines. They made deer to browse the meadows and sleep in ravines, then pumas to prowl the mountains by dark and jaguars to roam the jungle, and then fox, opossum, more serpents, iguanas, and the many crawling, buzzing, flying ones.

Now the Makers walked about and looked over their work. Birds twittered and pecked about, big cats called to each other, and deer cautiously, quietly sank their noses into grass. All was contentment. But as bird cried to bird, bee to bee, none of the creatures gave notice to the Makers among them. No one gave praise for the sun and the rain. None remembered what the Makers had done.

What was needed? Creatures more like the Makers. But for the first time they could not agree. And so Heart of Earth created humans by herself, out of her own clay. She called the other gods to watch as her humans began to explore their new world. Her clay people were slow and clumsy; when they stepped into water to bathe, they simply dissolved.

Evidently, humans needed to move quickly and easily

and needed to be made of more solid stuff. The next people were all action, chattery and excitable. So flighty were they that in the first big wind, they ran off to hide in the trees and became monkeys.

Now what? Lightning God decided that he would create solid, stable people with intelligence like his own. But he had no understanding of feeling, and so his humans were smart but stiff, inflexible, and cold, like figures carved of wood. They could speak, they could think and plan, but they were cruel. It was soon clear that these were not right either. Those creatures who were hurt by stick people rose up in anger, and the stick people were gone.

Rain God took over. She made people with pure emotion, all feeling. But her people were unable to think clearly, and when great floods attacked the land, most of these people floated away and became fish.

The gods recognized the source of their mistake. They talked. The world needs to be in balance, and humans must think, feel, all in harmony. Together, the gods created eight wise people, four pairs of humans with many qualities between them.

Now, to help this new life grow and to make use of the tremendous energy of the storm gods, the Makers created Quetzalcoatl, god of the dawn sun and evening star, bringer of food and heat. Quetzalcoatl brought another kind of light—he was the god of wisdom, which meant he loved songs and dance and art, which are the way to wisdom and happiness. With Quetzalcoatl as guide, the world would be good. Humans would rise at dawn and sing songs of praise; humans would play the pipes and dance. Humans could wear feather headdresses and snake skirts in honor of their Makers; humans could use the skills of Quetzalcoatl to create beautiful jewelry and pottery and buildings that celebrate the story of creation. Humans remember; they look far back and use what they know to look forward. Humans learn how to work together and use the gifts of the gods.

So it happened.

## COMMENTARY

The *Popul Vuh*, the collected wisdom of the Mayan people was originally recorded in pictorial form. Although all of the Mayan manuscripts were destroyed, the *Popul Vuh* was saved in Quiche, the language of a group of people related to the Maya. This too was later lost. We are left with Adrian Recinos's Spanish translation of a sixteenth-century Latin copy of the Quiche source. After passing through so many hands, how much of the original is left? One translator believes that the Quiche scribe used the story to document cultural conflicts faced by his people. The Maya favored their craftsman-god hero, Quetzalcoatl, bringer of architecture, writing, and music, to the military cult that took as its god Smoking Mirror, also known as Hurahpu the Hunter. Hurahpu later entered the pantheon of the violent, sacrifice-demanding sun god of the Aztec. With this in mind, I have emphasized the aspects of the earlier Mayan creator.

## STORY OUTLINE

- In the beginning are water and Makers who agree to create.
- Makers create Heart of Heaven: Huracan, Lightning, Thunder, Heart of Earth.
- Makers create birds, deer, puma, jaguar, fox, crawling things.
- Heart of Earth creates clay people.
- Lightning creates monkey people.
- Lightning creates stick people.
- Rain creates fish people.
- Gods work together to create humans and Quetzalcoatl.

## Performance Suggestions

A large curtain, drape, or blanket over a table establishes the staging area. The twin gods, in headdresses bearing both fish heads and feathers, sit behind the table. For each act of creation, they stand, consult in mime, and raise hands together. The new creations emerge from the two sides of the table and walk or crawl out front in character. Lesser gods (with their symbols on their headbands) create from the front; their creations can emerge from offstage (the sides of the room) representing the four directions controlled by the lesser gods. Clay, monkey, stick, and fish people can carry stick puppets and move in the manner of their stick puppets. A sound orchestra (or soundmakers in the free hand of all participants) sounds the cataclysms for each failed creation. Lesser gods move behind the table to join the Makers; all other participants drop previous character props to reenter the stage as humans. They mime the happy work of a village, then join hands to celebrate and remember the gods.

## ARES

When God created Ares, Ares was all alone. Ares looked around and saw only the mountains, so far away that they looked very small, and this made Ares feel very big. A little beetle went walking by, and Ares thought he might pick up a stick and play with that beetle, so he did.

God looked down and saw Ares turn the beetle upside down with his stick and thought this was not good. And so God created Snake, who was so big that when he crawled along, the ground shook. When Snake did this, Ares was frightened and pulled his shoulders in and dropped his stick, which made Snake laugh to himself as he twisted this way and that and came even closer.

God saw this was not good. And so God created Toad, who was so big that Snake could fit inside one of Toad's nostrils! When Snake saw Toad, he was so afraid that he crawled way off into the distance and wrapped himself around the mountains. Now Toad's eyes glittered with pleasure, and his body swelled up with pride, like this: Harumph, harumph.

God saw this was not good, and so he created River between Toad and Ares. River was so wide that Toad would have to swim all day to get across. But just in case River might get too proud, God sent down Angel, who was so big that when she sat in River to take a bath, all the water poured out, and there wasn't enough left to wash her face.

Ares looked up in the sky and saw a cloud float by, dropping rain. He called out to Angel, who stepped out of River and took Ares's hand. Angel and Ares walked over and stood underneath Cloud, who dropped rain so that Angel could wash her face.

As Cloud moved away, she called down to Angel and River and Toad and Snake and Ares: "Remember, even I am one of God's smallest creations!" And so it was that all the creatures came to live humbly together.

## COMMENTARY

My primary source is a story recorded by Charles Monteil, translated by Anne Twitty, in *Parabola*. Charles Monteil's version of this Sudanese story emphasizes God's efforts to control pride; mine looks at the events from the point of view of the amazed, innocent, and vulnerable child who was the first creation. It is now a parable on the possibility of cooperation between God's largest and smallest creations.

## STORY OUTLINE

- God creates Ares.
- Ares pokes beetle with a stick.
- God creates Snake; Snake frightens Ares.

- God creates Toad, who frightens Snake.
- God creates River and Angel.
- Angel sits in River for bath, spills out water.
- Ares points out Cloud; Cloud bathes everyone.

## Performance Suggestions

This story works well for large groups because children can portray mountains, gods, Ares/humans, beetles, snakes, toads, angels, and clouds. Mountain people enter first at back, join hands, and hold hands high to make peaks. Gods and angels enter together, turn to each other, point to Ares/humans. Ares/humans squat on the ground until gods point, then stand proud. Beetles crawl on all fours past humans, who poke at them with imaginary sticks; beetles scurry away. Gods point, Snake people (hands on each other's waists or holding hands) enter, and walk past humans; humans hunch shoulders in fear.

Gods point, and toads enter proudly, causing Snake people to move to surround mountains. River people form a chain in front of the toads. Angels and gods consult and step out. River people break apart as angels sit in the middle between two halves of River people. Cloud people walk past; Ares calls out and points to clouds. Angels and humans join hands, stand in front of clouds, and mime face washing. Some or all of the other creatures can join them. One of the clouds speaks: "Remember, we are still the smallest of God's creations!"

Other children can be the orchestra and shake shakers as each new creation steps out. A narrator can also tell the story as performed. With very large groups (it's been done with a hundred children), have each group perform its movement in place, then join hands to form circles at the end.

## THE CHICKEN STARS

✳

Far away, out beyond night and day, in a time before
stars, the god Indra lay on a cloud of sky-spirit. A great
distance lay between him and the land of humans. What
had happened to the people he created so long ago? He decided to step down through the heavens, down to earth,
and look for goodness. He wrapped himself in his sky-cloth
to make a disguise and walked through the deep dark. He
walked until he found the blue sky and green fields of
earth. He walked many weeks, many years, looking for kind
and loving souls. And so the sky-cloth grew dusty, and
Indra looked like a poor, hungry traveler when he walked
up to the small house of an old man and an old woman.

The old man was out beside his house, gathering bits of
rice that he and the old woman were to share with their
only possessions, a hen and her six chicks. "Please, I need
a place to rest," the monk whispered to the old man, who
nodded and led the monk inside. "It's a holy man," the old
man said to his wife. "He has been walking a long time
and needs a meal. What will we do?"

The old woman started a pot of water boiling on the fire as the old man went back outside looking for more food to put in the pot. But even looking as hard as they could, the old man and old woman could find only a few more greens to add to the rice. "Then I won't eat tonight," said the old woman. "Nor will I," said the old man.

Even with a guest to feed, the old man and old woman did not forget to feed their hen and her chicks. After the old woman tossed a few grains to the ground and went back into the house to prepare their thin soup, Mother Hen watched her chicks eagerly peck at the rice. Sadly Mother Hen sighed and said, "Dear little ones, I see what I must do. I must sacrifice myself for the holy visitor. Promise me you will be good and think well of me."

The chicks looked up with their bright eyes and watched as their mother ran through the cottage doorway and jumped up into the cooking pot. This was too terrible! As the old man and old woman and their visitor watched, the chicks ran after their mother and threw themselves into the fire, not willing to live without her.

At this, the monk threw off his sky-cloth, and the room was suddenly filled with light. He was not a poor wandering monk, but the god Indra himself! Indra pointed at the pot and fire, and out of the fireplace came seven brilliant balls of flame that rose up, up into the sky, where you can see them today: the Pleiades, as some people say, but others call them the Chicken Stars.

### COMMENTARY

The main elements of this story come from a tale from Thailand, recorded as "The Chicken Stars" by William I. Kaufman, in the *UNICEF Book of Children's Lessons.*

## Story Outline

- Indra on his sky-cloud descends to visit earth as a monk.
- The monk stops to visit an old man and woman, who make soup.
- A mother hen sacrifices herself by jumping into the pot.
- Her chicks in grief jump into the fire.
- Indra turns the hen and chicks into stars.

## Performance Suggestions

I told an elaborated version of Kaufman's story to my class; the children modified it and performed it as a dance/pantomime. This ceremonial dance/pantomime was performed to a recording of traditional music of India. Props were small wood bowls for the chicks; a two-yard piece of striped fabric for sky-cloth; a sheer curtain hung about two feet from the wall for sky (a sheet would do as well); small flashlights, one per chick, hung inconspicuously on a cord around their waists; a two-yard piece of gold-colored cloth for the sun. The girl who later played the role of Mother Hen acted as sun-dancer. We did not use a narrator, although this would work fine. The sun-dance was a ceremonial addition that placed the event in a magical yet important world, which elevated and transformed the story, making the story of sacrifice symbolic without saying as much. The bowls were not in the original story, but provided the chicks with a physical focus as a contrast to their previous play.

The set, as devised by the children: The sky-curtain hung at the farthest back part of the room designated as stage, leaving enough space for the chicks to stand behind it and flash their lights at the end. Indra's smaller sky-cloth was laid out in front of this; Indra positioned himself in a sleeping position on it. A red scarf with a big pot on top signified the fireplace. Three more small wood bowls sat beside the fire. A post (part of the room) marked the outdoors.

Staging: Hen and chicks offstage; man and woman sleep by the fire. Indra sleeps on his sky-cloth. The sun-dancer is behind the hanging sky-curtain. Music starts. The sun-dancer enters from behind the sky-curtain, wrapped in gold sun-cloth and moving ceremonially, turning and opening arms that hold the cloth, until in center stage the arms are fully extended, the cloth held open. The sun-dancer exits just as Indra awakens. He stands slowly, wraps himself in the sky-cloth (forming a hood over his head), and walks all around the stage twice.

As Indra walks, the chicks play, teasing each other and fluttering around. Mother Hen comes out, shakes a finger at them playfully. They continue to play as Indra is greeted at the "door" by the old man and old woman, who bow deeply and, with arms extended, point out the honored seat by the fire. They exit through the door and pantomime hunting and gathering for a few grains and stalks of greens. They place a few grains in each chicken's bowl, go in sadly, and pantomime putting ingredients into the soup. Mother Hen looks sad, gathers her chicks around her, puts her head down to "whisper" to them, and then runs and jumps onto the red fire-cloth. The old man and old woman throw their hands up and look horrified. The chicks jump onto the fire-cloth too. Indra stands, throws off the sky-cloth, and points to the hen and chicks, who stand and run behind the sky-curtain. The sun-dancer comes back from offstage to center stage in an open-arm pose, holding the cloth open behind her; the sun turns three times, slowly wrapping herself in the gold sun-cloth, leaving the stage on the same side she entered from. As the sun-dancer exits, the chickens, now stars, turn on their flashlights and shine them through the sky-curtain. The old man and old woman stand, look, and raise their arms to the sky in wonder.

# ETANA ASCENDS TO HEAVEN

✴

After the great flood in the land between two rivers,
all creatures had to decide how they should live together. The flood must have been a punishment. How
could they remember how to live together in a way that
would please Shamash, God of the Sun, and Ishtar, Queen
of Heaven? Would they remember to give prayers of
thanks? Would they stop quarreling so that the gods would
not be angry? This was the talk in the village and surrounding fields.

Meanwhile, miles away on the mountaintop, the
animals most beloved of the gods, Eagle (favored by
Shamash) and Snake (favored by Ishtar) made their own
agreement: Eagle would rule the upper world, and Snake
would command the lower. Eagle's fluffy young eaglet
could nestle without fear in his high nest, and Snake could
leave her eggs at the foot of the tree.

As Eagle flew high overhead, the people met and discussed how they would guarantee peace in their land. "We
need a king," the men agreed. But who would be wise

enough and brave enough to teach people how to work together? The floods had washed away the old kingdom, along with the priests who once guided them. Even the signs of the king, the crown and the shepherd's staff, had disappeared. The fields were covered with mud, and people would rather talk about who was to blame than make new tools and get back to work.

Only one person thought more about his sheep than his troubles, and that was the gentle shepherd, Etana. Here was someone who could help. But Etana was quiet and shy. He didn't give speeches or orders to others. Worst of all, he was young and did not have a son or even a wife. Etana listened to the men of the village talk and saw them look at him and nod. He wondered to himself, could he possibly be a king?

In this time of confusion, the people did not take good care of their land. Without grain in the field, even the rabbits and mice moved away, looking for better pickings, and Eagle grew hungry. He watched as Snake burrowed into the ground and found one last remaining rat. "Snake grows fat," said Eagle to his son when he came back to his nest with nothing in his talons. "We starve."

"Tomorrow will be better," the young eaglet said, but his parent did not answer. Instead, old Eagle flew down to the foot of the tree and came back with a speckled snake egg. "Alas, Papa, we will be sorry you broke your oath with Snake," cried Eagle's son, but Eagle only attacked the egg with his sharp beak.

"She has four eggs, and I have only one hungry child," cried Eagle.

That night Eagle did not sleep easy, despite his dinner. He waited for Snake to wind her way up the tree to complain about the loss of her egg. But Snake did not come, although Eagle could hear someone moving around at the bottom of the tree.

Next morning, Eagle circled the tree several times, watching Snake leave before he flew off to hunt. Then Eagle flew over the village and fields; he flew through the smoke of an offering and heard the shepherd Etana make a prayer to heaven. "Eagle, carry my prayer to the Queen of Heaven!" Etana called out. "Let me find a wife and have many sons. Give me the courage to talk to the village girls." Eagle only circled higher and higher, searching for prey, until sunset. Once more, tired and angry, Eagle returned with empty claws until he snatched up an egg from the nest of Snake and took it back to his son.

That night, Eagle did not sleep at all. He heard every sound of the night, including shuffling, rustling noises below him. Still, he did not see Snake. He warned his son to be on guard, then went off early, feeling Snake's eyes on him as he flew back to the fields of the villagers and shepherds. Again Eagle flew through the smoke of Etana the shepherd and ignored Etana's morning prayer. "Great Eagle," Etana cried up to the skies, "ask Shamash, God of the Sun, to grant me the plant of life so that I may make a name for myself, a name worthy to give my children. Tell me what I must do." Eagle flew away farther and farther in search of food, making sure that Snake didn't see him circle back to the nest at the bottom of the tree.

Again Eagle swooped down, his talons out. But as he reached for an egg, something happened. He was caught! He was caught in a vine that hung over Snake's nest. The harder he fought, the more he was tangled. Eagle was caught in Snake's trap.

Eagle lay all night in the twisted vines. He heard Snake quietly slip into her nest and curl around her remaining eggs. He could hear the pitiful cries of his young son, high in the tree, but he could do nothing, say nothing. He was bound tightly.

Next morning, as Snake left to hunt, Eagle could hear his son calling out, hoarse and weak. Then he heard no more.

Who knows how long Eagle lay in Snake's trap before he heard human footsteps. It was Etana who stood, trembling in front of him. "Great Eagle," said Etana. "I will set you free if you give me a ride to heaven. I must beg the gods for the gift of life."

And so it happened that Eagle carried Etana on his back, into the sky, high above the village and fields and mountains in the distance. Etana could see village dogs looking up in wonder as Eagle flew toward the clouds.

But not even Eagle could go higher. With one angry, sharp call, he circled back down and set Etana on the ground in front of the amazed villagers, and then flew away.

"I was flying to the throne of Ishtar," Etana said, his face flushed with excitement.

"What was it like, to see the home of the gods?" one of the pretty village girls asked, shyly.

"Oh, I wasn't as high as the gods," Etana said.

"Higher than any of us have ever gone," said the father of the village girl. "Surely that is a sign."

Now the records show that Etana the shepherd did become king of the land between rivers. We know he found a wife because the king lists say Etana's son ruled after him. The people learned to build canals for the river so that the land would be fertile and there would be grain to feed all creatures, including those that were hunted by Eagle and Snake.

## COMMENTARY

A Sumerian cylinder seal depicts a dog looking to the sky, intent upon a youth who rides toward the sun on the back of an eagle.

This was one of the most popular stories of its time, to judge by the number of times and places where the story is found. This version combines fragments described in Stephen Langdon's *Semitic*, volume five in the classic source *The Mythology of All Races*. Even though fragments of Babylonian and Assyrian texts suggest that Etana did not reach his goal of heaven, his name is found in king lists of the Sumerians, as shepherd and king. Perhaps the courage to seek the gods is what matters.

Stephen Langdon suggests that the early Hebrew people worshipped a sun god, El, a rain and thunder god, Yaw, and Astarte or Ishtar, who was identified as goddess of morning and evening star. Eagle was frequently pictured at the throne of the gods, while the Serpent is held in the hands of Ishtar and her priestesses in numerous statues and seals.

## STORY OUTLINE

- People after the flood consider Etana as future king.
- Eagle and Snake agree to respect each other's nests.
- Eagle can't find food while hunting, hears the prayers of Etana, and steals an egg from Snake.
- Unsuccessful again the next day, Eagle steals another egg.
- On the third night, Eagle is caught in Snake's trap.
- Etana rescues Eagle in exchange for a ride to heaven.
- Eagle fails and sets Etana back down.
- Etana becomes king; people and Snake and Eagle live in peace.

## PERFORMANCE SUGGESTIONS

Set up two main staging areas in the front—one for humans, one for Eagle and Snake. To the back and between them sits a chair on a table representing heaven. Eaglet stands on a chair seat to represent the nest in a tree. Snake has two cloths, one folded beneath the top one, which is formed into her nest. Paper cut in egg shapes works fine for Snake's eggs. Eagle and Snake make their agreement and move around the front stage area looking for food. Humans look around at the land after the flood, meet, and suggest Etana for leader. Etana moves away to pray; Eagle steals egg as people lie down to sleep. (This can be made more poignant by having Eaglet peep piteously in hunger before Eagle takes an egg.) People stand to signal a new day and pantomime hoeing and planting. Eagle and Snake circle around again; Eagle sneaks back for another egg. As Eagle and people lie down to sleep, Snake pulls the extra cloth out and places it next to the nest. To signal that Eagle is tangled in a trap, she throws the corners of the cloth over Eagle, who then waits until Etana approaches. Etana holds hands on Eagle's waist as they circle around "heaven" but do not climb up. Eagle brings Etana to the area of humans before flying back to the tree.

# THE MIRACULOUS BIRTH OF ABRAHAM

✴

The baby Abraham was born in a terrible time, the time of King Nimrod. Nimrod was a clever, powerful king who looked to the movement of the stars to tell his future. One night as he studied the sky, he saw a great catastrophe coming—an even greater king was coming! A male child, soon to be born to his Hebrew slaves, would lead and win a war against him. Nimrod called his advisors; they urged him to do a terrible and desperate thing: to murder all the boy children of his slaves.

Sly Nimrod had his workers make an enormous birthing building. Then he gathered together all the Hebrew women who were about to have babies. If a woman gave birth to a daughter, she was given gifts and honor. But if the new baby was a boy, the infant was immediately killed.

When Abraham's mother heard of this, something told her that she should walk away from the king's soldiers as quickly as she could. Without telling anyone, she left her home and family, crossed a valley, and climbed up into the hills until she came to a cave. Here, all alone, she had her child, a healthy baby boy. But at the moment of birth, her dark room of rock amazingly started to glow with light from an unseen source. It was just as she suspected: Her child had divine protection! Yet if she took her new son back with her, he would surely be killed.

"Alas," cried the mother, "it is better to leave you now than to have you torn from my breast by the king. I leave you in God's care." And sadly she wrapped him in her cloak before leaving him in the cave.

Truly, the baby Abraham did have divine protection. Yaw, the one great god, had sent his angel Gabriel to whisper in the ear of Abraham's mother and now sent Gabriel to help the infant. Gabriel touched Abraham's thumb, and milk flowed from the thumb whenever the infant stuck it in his mouth and sucked. This milk was so healthful that only ten days later, Abraham arose and walked out of the cave.

As the baby Abraham stepped outdoors for the first time, it was night and the stars shone. He had never seen such a sight, and he had no one to tell him what they were. He looked up and laughed and lifted his hands to touch them, thinking these wondrous sky lights must be the gods who saved him.

But as he walked, the morning sun dimmed the stars, and young Abraham saw that the sun was more powerful than the stars. Well, then he offered his praises to the great golden light of day.

As baby Abraham walked, it became evening again, and the setting sun dropped out of the sky and was replaced by the moon. The moon was much larger and brighter than the stars. Perhaps this was the greatest power!

When the moon set and another day began, Abraham thought to himself that neither stars nor sun nor moon could be the one god. There must be one who was not visible to him and yet was greater than all sun and moon and stars together. And this is how Abraham came to the knowledge he would one day give his people, knowledge that they were protected by the greatest god of all, a god who would lead them away from slavery to their own country.

## COMMENTARY

This story assimilates several miracle stories that can be found in abundance in the intertestamental literature of the Jewish people. Joseph Campbell and other scholars remind us that great prophets and leaders were expected to have a consistent set of remarkable abilities that allowed the completion of tests and trials (today we have graduate schools). Many of these oral traditions were edited out of the collection of books we call the Old Testament.

The Old Testament refers rather admiringly to an Assyrian ruler named Nimrod, who was "a mighty hunter before the Lord"; he is credited with starting many cities as well as constructing the famous tower of Babel. He is not listed in any of the king lists of Assyria or Mesopotamia, however, which suggests that he is a composite or quintessence of hunter/warrior kings of those times.

## STORY OUTLINE

- Nimrod learns of the coming birth of a Hebrew leader and orders his workers to make an enormous building for all Hebrew women to give birth in.
- Nimrod's advisors kill the Hebrew boy babies.
- Abraham's mother hides and gives birth in cave.
- Abraham, alone, is visited by the angel Gabriel, who touches his thumb. Abraham sucks his thumb for milk.

- Abraham walks out of the cave; sees the stars, sun, and moon; and worships each in turn.
- Abraham decides that one god is above the sun, moon, and stars.

## Performance Suggestions

Several children with soundmakers form a chorus surrounding Nimrod, who sits on one side of the staging area; several girls representing Hebrew mothers wait on the other side. A table at the back of the staging area, with cloth draped over the top, sides, and back, represents the cave. Abraham hides behind the cloth. A two-yard piece of cloth over the shoulders can be the cape of Abraham's mother. Another cloth draped over Nimrod's chair can establish the throne.

Nimrod consults the chorus, and the chorus approaches the Hebrew mothers (all but Abraham's mother) and escorts them to an area near Nimrod. The mothers lie down on the blanket that represents the birthing building, while Abraham's mother walks away and circles the cave twice before entering. She lies down inside the cave.

Soundmakers make a joyful noise. Abraham crawls into the cave and lies down. Abraham's mother awakens, lays her cloth over him, and leaves sadly. The angel Gabriel enters; soundmakers are shaken softly as he touches Abraham's thumb. Abraham takes a suck, crawls out, and walks away from the cave. Stars, sun, and moon can be children who played Hebrew mothers, wearing headbands with symbols or using dance ribbons. Abraham points to each by turn, then to the open sky as he joins his mother to loud and happy sounds.

## COYOTE CREATES

✳

At one time there was only water down here. There was water and a few ducks. Above the water, Maker of All Things talked about this with Coyote. He told Coyote to go down, make earth, and all things on earth. He let Coyote decide how to do this—quite an assignment. It's no trouble for Coyote, though. He found his own way down here, not the regular way either, and landed in the water. Coyote was swimming around, figuring what to do when he saw two ducks flying overhead.

"Hey you guys, come down, you can help," Coyote called out to the ducks. "You people are great for diving."

The ducks circled back and landed close to Coyote. Coyote said, "There's got to be something down under the water that can help us."

"We can help," the ducks said. And the first one, the female, dove down into the water. She was gone a long time; Coyote started to worry. But the other duck said, "She's all right. She has quite a bit of power." And so Coyote and the second duck waited some more.

After a while the first duck returned with a twig and a little bit of mud in her bill. "That's good," said Coyote. "We could use some more." The second duck dove down now while the first duck rested, and Coyote rolled the mud in his palms, making it more solid so that he would have a place to get out of the water and rest himself. He was tired of swimming.

Now the second duck came back with mud in his bill. Coyote rolled the mud and blew it to north and south, to east and west. Pretty soon he made land. Coyote jumped up on the land and started making the other animals. He kept making things while the ducks brought him mud. He made a man and a woman and blew life at them. This made the man and woman stand up and look around at the hills and grass that Coyote had already made.

"I think that's enough," said Coyote. He told the man and woman, "Be good to the earth and make many Crow children." Then he ran away.

## COMMENTARY

This version of creation comes from the Crow people of Montana. I heard it from Ben Pease, the first generation of his people to get a college education. Ben heard it from his grandmother, who never learned the white people's way of writing. How quickly did the Crow people, who acted as scouts to the newcomers, adjust? One of Ben's daughters is a college president and one son is a medical doctor; all take pride in maintaining their ties to the reservation.

Notice how the act of creation is a cooperative one, with no special emphasis given to any one part of creation. And Coyote does not use his magical abilities to maintain control of his creations. It's interesting to compare Ben's version of creation with that of the Blackfoot and related Plains tribes, which were filtered through white writers. Ben offers subtle humor and is quite respectful toward the ducks.

## STORY OUTLINE

- All is water in the beginning.
- Maker of All Things gives the assignment of creation to Coyote.
- Coyote gets help from two ducks.
- The ducks dive down into the water and bring back mud.
- Coyote rolls the mud and blows on it, making land and other animals.
- Coyote creates humans with the mud.
- Coyote instructs humans to be good to the earth and to make many Crow children.
- Coyote leaves.

## PERFORMANCE SUGGESTIONS

Start with a chair-table-chair setup in back, two blankets or equivalent (for example, two sets of sheer curtains sewn together) on the floor in front of the staging area. Coyote frisks about teasing audience members when Maker of All Things, standing on a chair behind the cloths, calls Coyote over and gives the assignment. Coyote clambers up and down and under tables and chairs before jumping onto the water-cloth. Coyote kicks around as two children "fly" past as ducks. Ducks crawl under the water-cloth and come back with imaginary mud (or use small sticks, even pencils, between their teeth). Coyote takes sticks to the ground-cloth and mimes forming animals. Two children representing human creations enter from the side near the ground-cloth and stand before Coyote, who blows on them. Now they come to life, moving limbs, and discovering each other. Coyote takes one hand of each, has them shake hands, then waves good-bye and runs off as they try to stop him. Humans return, shrug, and start folding up the ground-cloth to make the floor of their tent; they sit on their new floor.

## HOW THE DEVIL HELPED

✳

Before God created earth, there was nothing anywhere but water and more water. At first God had no idea what to do with it. It wasn't pure, clean water as we think of water now, but a mush of this and that, a goop that turned into things even as God squeezed it in his hand. Thinking of possibilities, but frankly without a plan, God went walking, swishing through the mush, wishing he had someone, maybe a brother, perhaps a friend, to help him.

Mucking around like this and irritated with himself, God clenched his fist and made a stick, something very like the kind of thought he was having at that moment. Ah! He threw the stick into the water. Instantly, a giant tree grew out of the stick and pushed its roots deep down, gathering sand as it went. The top of the tree rose up, pressing at the heavens, forming clouds. And on one of the stout branches sat a jaunty fellow, one we now know was the Devil himself, smiling and putting out his hand to God.

"Dear Little Brother," said the Devil, in a happy, chatty manner. "I am so glad you thought of me. Now we can create the world together."

The Devil hopped out of his tree and went walking along beside God, very purposeful and clever. They strolled through the universe for nine days, with the Devil suggesting this or that for God to create. But it didn't go well. God objected to creating a garden of golden fruit and a flock of angels waiting on the Devil, for instance. Finally the Devil said, "Dear Brother, it seems we cannot agree. Please start creating whatever you like so that we may each take what we prefer and go our own ways."

God scratched his head thoughtfully and tried to remember something he already knew. "All right, then. Dive deep into the water and bring me a handful of sand." The Devil did just that, diving down among the tree roots, bringing up a handful of sand to God.

"Good, go back for more," said God. But the Devil lingered.

"Don't you need something else? What can you make from ordinary sand?" the Devil asked, watching God carefully.

"This is enough," said God. "I know what to do." The Devil kept waiting for more information. "I will look at it, think of what I want to create—and say my name," said God.

"Ah!" said the Devil, and he dove down deep into the water again.

But this time when the Devil scooped up a handful of sand, he took care to come out of the water some distance behind God's back. The Devil lifted the handful of sand up to the heavens, thought about someplace warm and dry, and whispered his name, "the Devil!"

Instantly the sand turned hard—and red hot. The Devil dropped it as fast as he could. God heard something splash and said, "Friend Devil, do you have my sand yet?"

"I'm on my way," said the Devil, and he dove down again. This time the Devil found the rock he had dropped and came up even farther away from God. He lifted the rock far up into the air and said, louder, "The Devil, I say!" But this time the rock turned into molten lava and poured out of the Devil's hand, turning his whole body red, which is the color of the Devil to this day.

God looked over at the Devil. "I see that I have to teach you a lesson," said God. At that, a gigantic ox came running from behind the tree that was God's first creation. The ox charged, scooped up the Devil between its horns, and carried him off into the distance—which made the astonished Devil cry out, "My God! My God!" at the top of his lungs. The Devil shrieked so loud, in fact, that all the leaves fell off the tree! God saw this and laughed, and as the leaves dropped lightly to the ground, they turned into people.

That is how it happened that neither God nor the Devil knew exactly which one of them created people. Was it the Devil's cry for mercy or God's first laugh? We haven't been sure ever since.

## COMMENTARY

This version of creation follows the general outline of a common Hungarian Gypsy story told to Vladislav Kornel and recorded in Diane Tong's book, *Gypsy Folk Tales*. From their first home, in India, gypsy people bring stories wherever they visit—and take them. What Hungarian folklore collections call religious tales are impertinent, rather chatty inventions with a cast of Biblical characters. This Devil is friendly with a purpose, wearing out his welcome. From the Gypsy perspective, God is rather stolid and unimaginative; he needs the Devil's help to come up with good ideas. The Devil's motives may not be pure, but neither is the primeval muck, and the person who gets things going need not be that pure, either, do you think? A workable formula turns out to be a mixture of God's capacity with the Devil's fertile ideas and self-interest, a basic recipe for humans.

## Story Outline

- God throws a stick that turns into a tree with the Devil sitting in it.
- The Devil watches God and dives down for sand.
- The Devil copies the creative formula of God, but the sand turns into rocks that burn him.
- The Devil tries again, more emphatically, and gets burned worse.
- The Devil cries out, and God sees what happened.
- An ox comes out and carries away the Devil.
- The Devil cries out for God's help; God laughs.
- Leaves fall from the tree and turn into humans.

## Performance Suggestions

This story works well with masks and as a base for comic improvisation. Make masks for God, the Devil, and the ox (give God crepe-paper locks, the Devil horns, the ox floppy ears), or use headbands. Everyone else can be plants, trees, rocks, and animals created by God as the Devil watches, then surreptitiously tries to figure out how they work and what they are made of. The Devil can pluck at "leaves" or try to catch and hold a rabbit, for example. Children can wait curled up for God to touch them on the back, then take a form announced by God or take their own choice of form and begin growing. As the Devil starts to experiment with creation, all children (in a large class, this could be a separate group) form a tight circle, standing stiff and straight, backs together, and facing outward. When the Devil gets burned, one person in an ox mask emerges from behind the tree children and chases the Devil offstage. The Devil cries out to God; God laughs heartily. Children forming the tree step out one or two steps each (to provide more room) and fall, then stand up as people, surprised, begin talking to each other and looking around.

# MOTHER OF THE DARK

❋

How was it decided that men should rule over women when women are so much the wiser? It may not be this way tomorrow, but this is the way it has been for many yesterdays, and here is the reason, the way I heard from the mother of my mother, who heard it from hers.

Imagine it is the middle of the day, and a five-year-old girl of the rain forest does not understand why she must stay inside with her mother and grandmother.

"Why do all the men go to their secret house?" the child asks. "Why can't we follow?"

"They go to play the flute and dance," says her mother, sitting by the doorway. "Listen, you can hear."

"I want to see the dance," says the girl.

"We can't watch," says Grandmother.

Flute music comes out of the trees, across the flat place between houses. "It looks like this," says Grandmother, and she does a funny ducking, jiggling dance around the room that makes Mother giggle.

"How do you know if we can't watch?" the girl asks,

which makes Grandmother and Mother laugh so hard that Grandmother has to sit down.

"Why do they play, then, if nobody can see?" asks the child, and Grandmother says, "They forget," which makes Mother giggle again.

"They stole the flute from us," says Mother, and Grandmother nods from her hammock. The girl climbs into the hammock too, and Grandmother starts a story.

"The Great Snake who created the sun had two children, Jaguar and the One Who Is Our Mother. While Jaguar prowled about the new world, sniffing and coughing his dry cough, Our Mother climbed and swam, and all the world spoke to her—rock, water, mud, sand, trees, and the vine that winds through the forest.

Sun shone all the time, for there was no moon or night, yet Our First Mother did not grow tired—all the time she could climb higher and swim farther. She found nuts and seeds and fruit to eat, something on each tree. She was strong and happy.

Her brother Jaguar was not happy, though. He refused to eat the avocado and berries and nuts. Instead, he grew thinner and meaner. After a while he lost interest in exploring and slept most of the time.

When Our Mother spoke of this to her father, Great Snake gave her a magic flute so that she could create more animals. First she played a few slow, fat notes for fun. Ha! Thick-skinned Tapir appeared, blinking at the light. He went lumbering through the brush, bumping his long snout into tree roots as he walked. She laughed and played another song making fun of Tapir, and there was Sloth, grinning a stupid grin, pulling itself up a nearby tree where it ate leaves and moved so slowly, its fur turned mossy green. Jaguar woke up and watched.

And so Our Mother played and filled every branch, every leaf, every river and puddle and lake with birds, fish, lizards, and opossums, some creatures slow, some of them fast, some who ended their life as dinner for Jaguar. She played up so many creatures that trees and rocks and mud were too busy to talk. Now Our Mother wanted a friend, and so she sang up three Spider Monkeys, who climbed and played with her many long days.

After a long time, though, Our Mother decided that she should have a mate like the other animals, and her father Great Snake agreed. He gave her a husband. This young husband hardly noticed as his young wife stood among the trees playing her flute while butterflies fluttered around her head. What interested him was Jaguar. He watched the big cat pounce on a helpless little agouti, just as the ratlike animal dashed for its burrow in the tree roots. Without a word, Our Mother's husband picked up a spear, sharpened it against a rock, and followed Jaguar into the trees.

Our Mother's husband didn't come back until he was entirely exhausted, dragging bodies of deer and toucan and tapir and monkeys behind him. "All good to eat," he announced, and then he slumped to the ground. "I'm tired," he said. "Tell your father to stop the sun so I can sleep."

While her husband lay on the ground complaining, Our Mother called down her monkey friends with her flute. She sent them to her father, with orders to bring back the nut that holds night, and then she lay down beside her husband to wait.

The three monkeys did as they were told, at least until they raced back through the trees with the nut, using their tails and feet to swing from limb to vine. But as they swung, they could hear something rattling inside. They stopped for a little peek, knocking the nut against a tree trunk. The nut cracked, yes—and all night escaped, not little by little, the way Our Mother wanted, but at once, turning light to deepest dark. Howling and crying in the dark, the monkeys found their way back to Our Mother and handed her the broken nutshells.

Night couldn't be put back; it was everywhere. "Do something!" shouted her husband, as he shivered with fear. Our Mother picked up her flute and played a frog song and a cricket song to make us drowsy. She played another and made the giant potoo bird that goes "Boork!" and makes us laugh so that nobody would be afraid and so that we would hear something besides the quiet cough-cough of Jaguar in the dark.

Our Mother's husband listened as she played. "How do you do that?" he asked. "I do it," said Our Mother. "Now sleep."

Now that the husband could rest at night, he went out every day to hunt, bringing home more than they could eat. Our Mother's heart was sad, seeing so many dead animals on the ground. She could think of only one way to stop this. One afternoon she left her flute lying outside, where her husband would find it. When she looked again, her flute was gone.

"From that time to today," says Grandmother, "men only hunt enough to kill what is needed. The rest of the time they bring out the flute and try to play Our Mother's song."

"Didn't Our Mother miss her flute?" asks the little girl.

"She was carrying new life," says the girl's mother, stroking her daughter's hair.

Grandmother, Mother, and the girl listen; the flute music ends. "They aren't bad," says Grandmother.

"Pretty good," says Mother, and they tickle the girl until she laughs with them.

## COMMENTARY

According to the author of the Latin American volume of *The Mythology of All Races*, the Fuegian people of what is now Argentina had a story to explain why men rule. They say women invented government and gave it over to men because governing suited the male nature so well—and kept men out of the really important work, that of caring for home and children. I incorporated this notion into several other old legends and rumors, starting with the original story of the mother of the dark recorded by early Spanish explorers. Then there are legends, hints, really, of Amazonian goddess-warriors, also recorded very early. The story of the stolen magical flute was told to a German explorer in the late 1960s, recorded in a *National Geographic* story about Brazil. And in the same region of the Brazilian rain forest, an explorer photographed a carving on a rock—a dancing tapir or anteater. I looked at that carving, thought about a young Amazon with a flute, and said to myself, "I know this woman." Thus the blend of stories.

## STORY OUTLINE

- Men play the flute in secret; grandmother tells the story of daughter of Sun, our Mother.
- Our Mother is given the flute to create animals, while her brother, Jaguar, hunts.
- Our Mother asks for a husband; Sun creates one for her.
- Husband kills too much and wants night so he can rest.
- Our Mother sends monkeys to get the nut containing night.
- Curious monkeys let out the night.
- Our Mother uses the flute to create night animals to calm everyone. Her husband wants the flute.
- Our Mother sacrifices the flute to distract her husband from killing.

## Performance Suggestions

Although this can be performed indoors, it is interesting to stage outside, around playground equipment. Sun stands at the highest point, calls up daughter, and hands her a flute (or whistle). The girl goes down, plays on swings and ropes, pulling out the flute and playing it every few moments. Each sound on the flute brings out a playmate who joins her. Meanwhile, Jaguar (in mask or headband) prowls around the edges. After awhile the girl goes back up, and asks for a husband; a boy emerges from behind Sun and goes down with her; she has the flute stuck into the belt at her back. At the bottom of the stairs, the boy sees Jaguar and leaves her to follow him. The boy returns, pulling playmates, one by one; they flop into a heap as he drags them in. The girl beckons one playmate who is still alive to run for the nut. Sound-makers make a clashing noise, and everyone freezes and acts frightened to show that night has taken over. The girl picks up the flute and plays. Everyone else is happy and moves again, except the boy, who watches the flute. The girl sadly walks away, leaving the flute. The boy picks it up and runs off. The girl comes back, and playmates recover. They resume play.

# THE WISE AND HEROIC

✳

## BRAVE JOHN AND SHY MARIE

✳

Once there was an orphan boy who gained approval of the village toughs by showing no signs of fear. He could pass his hand through a candle flame, taunt a bully who beat him to the ground; in fact, he passed every test his friends could imagine. They were always looking for a new trick or challenge for John. John himself hoped that his demonstrations would win the approval, even the heart, of a young woman of the village who was known as Shy Marie.

One of the young men had heard of a large estate with a great ruin of a house that was said to present the ultimate test of courage. A baron, a giant of a man known for his miserliness and terrible temper, had died, and his buildings and lands were now deserted. Rumor had it that the stone mansion was inhabited by the giant's ghost and that anyone who tried to find the treasure—(certain to be inside) would pay with his life.

John's companions did not tell him the complete story. They told him only that this would be the greatest test he would ever face. Indeed, if he would spend one night in the mansion, he would be not only famous, but rich. John could see Shy Marie standing in the back of the group, listening as they talked. They didn't mention anything about a murderous ghost.

John agreed to the test. The group congratulated him on his daring and walked with him as far as the edge of the giant's estate. Then they handed John a loaf of bread and a sausage for his dinner and walked away, laughing to each other. They would be back in the morning, they promised.

Up ahead, John could see the great wood doors of an enormous house hanging open, the entry overgrown with vines. The fields and orchards were choked with weeds. He stepped off the path to pick up a ripe apple and thought of all the waste here and all the nights he had gone to bed hungry. Inside, he stood in the great hall and glanced into the adjoining bare rooms. He saw an ancient tapestry hung high above on the stone wall, a suit of armor at the other end of the hall, and a long, heavy table and two chairs. A stocking and an old shoe lay about, as if dropped on the way out the door. The few furnishings to be seen were gray with dust.

John sat in one of the chairs. He took out his knife and cut the apple and sliced some of his sausage and bread. Then he heard something rustling above him, perhaps on the roof. Another rustle, and there was a soft plop on the fireplace hearth. It was a crumble of leaves. John took a bite of his apple.

Then he heard a voice calling down from the top of the fireplace. It was a huge voice, perhaps an angry one, saying, "Shall I throw it?"

"Throw it," said John, in the steadiest voice he could manage. Down came something onto the hearth. Even in the dust and ancient cinders, John could see that it was a very large human leg. The voice called out again.

"Shall I throw it?"

John jumped up, lifted the leg out of the hearth, and set it beside him on the floor. "Throw it," he said, and another leg fell to the hearth. This continued—two arms and the trunk of a man followed, each time with the question asked first, each time with John assembling the parts. At last an enormous head floated down, placed itself on the body, and the ghost stood up.

John lifted a crust of bread. "To your health!" he said.

As if accepting an invitation, the ghost sat down beside John. He looked down, way down, at John. "This is my house," the ghost said.

"I hope you don't mind my spending the night here," said John, carefully. "My friends dared me to do this as a test of my courage." And he moved a share of his bread, sausage, and apple toward the giant.

"Then follow me," said the giant, who stood and walked down the hall. He reached high on the wall for a flint and candle. John followed the giant through a large dining hall, past a kitchen and pantry, then down some stone stairs. The candle's small light flickered ahead, mostly blocked by the giant's bulk. Once down in the damp cellar, the giant opened a pair of heavy, groaning doors and strode forward without looking back at John. As John walked bravely on, he realized he was walking past several wood chests with their lids open. The chests were full of coins, gold and silver coins! John stood and waited as the giant opened a cupboard and removed two dusty bottles of wine. Then the giant opened another cupboard and brought out two metal plates and two glasses. He handed the glasses to John and again without looking to see if John was following, went back up the steps.

Back in the entry hall, John and the giant set their dishes and wine on the table. Then, without a word, the giant picked John up, turned him upside down as if he weighed no more than an apple, and holding him by the ankles, shook John several times. John was so poor, he had nothing at all in his pockets, not a farthing. Then just as suddenly, the giant sat John down on his feet and said, "You are the first who did not help himself to any coins along the way."

John and the giant sat at the table and talked most of the night. The giant said that after he died, his servants and field workers, who had once been so obedient, came directly from their former employer's grave to the main floor of the great house and helped themselves to everything they could carry. The giant's ghost stood guard at the foot of the stairs to keep them from his treasure. The ghost of this once proud and fierce giant stood night and day, so long that his limbs loosened up and fell off. Now he was reduced to a heap of bones sleeping on the roof, ready to scare any invaders—scare them to death.

With the first hint of morning light, the giant seemed to stretch apart again, his arms and legs flapping as if they had a life of their own. "Come back again tonight," the giant said and then floated back up the chimney the way he had come down, one part at a time.

John looked out the door. He heard noise at the edge of the estate and went out to wave at his friends. He was their hero! And best of all, Shy Marie, overcome with happiness at seeing him alive, walked all the way back to his simple little hovel holding his hand, her eyes moist with tears. The admiration of the rest of the group meant little by comparison.

John confounded everyone by walking back to the ruined estate later that day. He carried a hoe and began knocking down overgrown grasses. He gathered up apples strewn about the ground. Marie appeared beside him, a kerchief tied over her brown hair. That day and every day after, John worked on the estate grounds with Marie before bidding her good night and entering the castle for dinner. Winter passed in this way. John spent no more time with his old friends and when spring came, the village prepared to celebrate John's marriage to Marie.

John informed the giant that he must begin work on his own place, now that he was marrying Marie. "I wish to give my estate to you," said the giant. "All I ask in return is that I dine with you and your wife every evening." John did not know how this might affect Marie, but already she had spent many days beside him, working in the estate gardens. She spoke of how she loved this place and how she might fix up the old mansion house. When he told her they could move in to the estate together and that they would have a guest for dinner starting on their wedding night, she smiled and nodded a small nod of acceptance. She did not share her concerns or the tales she had heard in the village.

That evening, after the wedding ceremony, as John and Marie came into the great hall, John took down the candle and lit it for Marie. He had left extra dishes and a table-cloth at the foot of the stairs, and he asked her to get them while he called their guest. As soon as she was out of the room, John called up the chimney, "Throw it!" and the giant threw down a leg. "Hurry," said John, who could hear Marie moving timidly through the rooms, protecting her candle with one hand.

The giant was down, or at least his body was ready. His head was floating toward it when Marie came back to the great hall. Her candle had gone out, and she was about to say that she would need another light to bring up glasses when she saw John hold out the giant's chair. The giant's head then settled into place, and John helped him stand to his fully upright, really enormous size.

Then the giant and John saw Marie. She took a deep breath. "I knew you were brave, dear John," she said, "but I did not know how kind you could be, also." And she set three plates around the table.

From this time on, Marie worked inside to bring the mansion back to order. A few gold coins furnished two sleeping rooms; more coins fed the poor and bought a new robe for the village priest. Other coins paid helpers who soon had the fields and orchards ready to produce again. One summer night the giant looked out the door before he sat down to eat. He smiled the first smile John and Marie had seen. That night, after dinner, the giant's limbs stayed attached to his body, and he strolled out into his now green fields. He lay to rest in the gathering dark and was not seen again.

## COMMENTARY

Stories of revenants, spirits of the dead who temporarily return to their former homes, are found throughout the world. I've found the story of a brave young man who spends a night with a fearsome giant spirit in several collections. It is in Italo Calvino's lively collection of *Italian Folktales* and appears as "Fearless John" in a 1958 *Hi Neighbor*, published by the U.S. Committee for UNICEF. Often, after some great wrong has been righted, the spirit can truly rest. Southern European versions have fearsome, dangerous ghosts and comic heroes. After surviving his trials, John sometimes dies of fright after seeing his own shadow.

A different attitude toward the dead is captured by Mexican-American ghosts, who may reveal the sources of hidden treasure and be quite friendly to those who disperse such treasure fairly.

Some of these spirits offer a warning of coming dangers to those occupying their previous abode. And in the Mexican manner, revenants retain peculiarities from their previous life, such as pleasure in a good dinner or the company of a friendly woman, nearly always named Marie. This provided my opportunity to bring in Shy Marie as partner to John.

## STORY OUTLINE

- Orphan John is challenged to spend the night in a decaying mansion.
- As John eats his supper in the mansion, he is interrupted by the voice and bones of a giant ghost.
- The giant reassembles himself and leads John through the house to the cellar, going past open treasure chests. John saves his own life by not stealing any.
- John and the giant talk. In the morning, the giant's limbs come apart again and float up the chimney.
- The returning village boys, followed by Marie, hail John as a hero.
- John returns to care for the neglected estate; Marie works beside him.
- John and Marie marry and move into the old mansion. The ghost returns to dine with them each evening.
- After John and Marie share the treasure and rebuild the estate, the giant's ghost finally lies down to rest.

## PERFORMANCE SUGGESTIONS

Ghost stories provide an opportunity to explore fears and ways to overcome them. To prepare for John's response to the giant, try a guided visualization, taking the part of John walking through the dusty mansion, finding objects that tell something about the giant. Discover something from the giant's baby days, childhood, youth. Discover something the giant was once proud of; something hidden because it made the giant ashamed.

For exploring night fears, divide into groups of five or so after making a group list of nighttime frights and monsters. Then list what kinds of helpers could banish or subdue the monsters. Use a table (and cloth for blanket, if you have one), and have each group pick a person to be the Sleeper. Others divide into Monsters and Helpers. Monsters lurk in a space designated as the closet or cleverly disguise themselves as bedroom furniture. They can be armed with soundmakers and use their voices to vocalize dangerous sounds (but not words). Helpers also hide on the other side of the room. They are allowed to speak. Sleepers climb into the bed, awaken when hearing a scary sound. They say, "I sure hope no _____ are hiding in my room." Sleepers can climb out of bed and look around if they dare. Monsters agree ahead of time on when to emerge and how to move around the Sleeper. They come out, threateningly, and then the Helpers come out and battle in pantomime. Use the No Real Touching rule. Leave space between Helpers and Monsters, with exaggerated movements, rather ceremonious. Helpers come over to Sleeper, over comforting words and gestures, then melt back into the room. I've had classes where every child took a turn as Sleeper.

This story also works well interpreted as comedy. Have the children stand in a circle and take turns posing as the village toughs, Shy Marie, Brave John walking to the giant's estate, and the giant. Then perform the story cartoon style or as commedia, with lots of goofy movements for John's so-called friends in the village. The Sleeper exercise can also be done as clown routine. Have the Sleeper exaggerate her or his fear, look in all the wrong, ridiculous places, only just missing the Monsters waiting. Have the Helpers upset or frighten the Monsters in surprising ways; the Monsters may have some peculiar fears of their own, after all. Prepare for this by watching videos of old movie clowns like the Keystone Kops.

An exercise to explore the inner life of giants and other monstrous-appearing folk is a variant of an old folk tradition, the "brag." Use a formula starter and have children write a brag or develop one in teams or small groups. One formula: "My name is _____ I'm half _____ and half _____. I can _____." What could you do if you were half bear and half girl, half fish and half boy, able to transform in an instant? Look at the famous cave art image of a man in antlers and mask; read stories of Taliesin and Merlin for examples. Then invent stories that put Brave John and Marie into new situations. How do monsters make friends and show their kindly side? This could be a writing assignment leading to noncliched stories.

A guided pantomime is another good way to explore the life of the deformed and rejected. This suggestion comes from a workshop conducted by Umo, a Seattle-area company specializing in buffoon theater. Everyone puts a nylon stocking over their head to change their appearance, then transforms. They could wear ear headbands or tails or use a shirt or towel to make a lump in some part of their body (Punchinello, the Commedia clown, had a hunched back). Now each monster picks a place in the room to hide. When instructed, they awaken hungry, look for food, face disapproval and discouragement (reject each other!). They search and watch others eating before they find a small morsel. Then they go back to bed hungry.

Another way to perform Brave John is to create cardboard giant body parts that are controlled from the back with poles. One person speaks for the giant. Operating the giant as one person takes practice and coordination in moving without direction or conversation, always a good exercise. This experience could lead into a study of making giant parade puppets that can then be the center of additional stories.

# SEVEN MOST OBEDIENT SONS

＊

In a valley between two mountains, next to a fast-running stream, lived a hard-working woman whose only reward seemed to be one more tribulation piled upon the last. From the day after her husband's funeral, she found herself working even more than before. She did have the assistance of her seven dutiful sons.

Although they were young, the seven boys saw how many tasks were left by their father's absence. They took their new responsibilities most seriously and divided the work among them. The older boys cut wood in the mountains, carrying it down in large bundles on their strong backs. The middle sons fished and planted and harvested the fields as their father had taught them. The younger two boys worked with their mother in the garden. Together the sons put fresh thatch on the roof of their cottage to keep out the fall rains.

Out of respect for their mother, the boys gave up the joking, teasing times they once spent with their friends. They were proud of their sense of duty, of how even the youngest of them stopped playing games in the village and put all attention to accumulating food and fuel and clothing toward winter so that their mother need not suffer.

The seven sons spoke to each other of how weary their mother often looked, how even with their help she was slow to rise and begin work in the morning. They became more serious, more dedicated. One of the younger sons confided to the eldest an incident that had taken place while he was working with his mother. He was shocked to see the old sandal-maker across the stream calling out and gesturing at them as they dug out turnips, inviting them over to visit. "It was so thoughtless and frivolous of him," said the youngest son. "He should know that winter is coming. We have no time to waste. I frowned at him, and he went away."

Before the harvest was done, a goodly supply of wood was stacked high near the house. But even as one son brought his mother a cup of tea in the morning, the widow spoke of how cold she was. The eldest son noticed that the hem of her skirt was still wet from the previous day's labor. What if she were to become ill? What would become of all of them?

That evening and early the next morning, the eldest son built a small fire under the house to warm the floor. He asked his mother how she was feeling. "Still cold," she said. That night, although it seemed like a waste of fuel, he built another fire to warm his mother's bed.

Several hours later, after everyone had gone to sleep, the eldest son woke up. The floor was cold. Should he get up and rebuild the fire? Suddenly he realized that his mother was gone. He waited in the dark, wondering what to do, where to look for her. After what seemed like a very long time, he heard his mother quietly come back. He could see in the moonlight that the hem of her skirt was wet as she stepped out of her straw sandals and crept under her quilt, leaving wet footprints behind her.

The next night the eldest brother forced himself to stay awake when the family retired to their mats. After all was very quiet, he heard his mother stand and walk out of the cottage. This time he followed her. He saw her walk along the path to the stream, stopping across from the hut of the old man. He watched the old man come down to the stream and reach out as his mother hitched up her skirts and waded across. "So cold!" she said to the old man, and her voice had laughter in it.

The eldest brother waited a few minutes before he walked to where his mother had crossed the stream. Through the open door of the hut, he could see his mother and the old man seated on stools, playing a noisy game of checkers.

His mother sounded as happy as a child. The eldest brother hurried home and awakened his six brothers. Quietly, in the moonlight, the brothers gathered large flat stones and built a path across the stream. Then they went home and crawled into their beds. They agreed to say nothing of this to their mother.

By the time the woman came out of the sandal-maker's hut, a light snow had fallen. She saw a most amazing sight: a path of glistening stepping-stones that crossed her stream. Had they been there before and she hadn't noticed? She had prayed for some kind of bridge across the stream—she dared not bother her sons about this—and now here it was! The woman called out to the sky, "The good souls who built this pathway deserve a place in the Heavens!"

And so it was. After the old woman passed on, after her sons had families and grew old in their own time, as each of the old woman's seven good sons died, a spirit rose up into the west to become a guide to others. They are the stars known to us in the Western world as the Great Bear.

## Commentary

I found this in *Folk Tales from Korea*, reported by Zong In-sob and retold by Son Zin-Te. It's an interesting contrast to "The Chicken Stars." There's more than one form of sacrifice. Many Asian stories contain an earthiness we westernized prudes don't consider appropriate for children. In the original, the eldest son notices that the sandal-maker's bedclothes are rumpled, suggesting that his mother crossed the stream for more than a rousing game of checkers. In the name of reaching a general audience, I emphasized the seriousness of the sons, as a contrast to the game of checkers.

## Story Outline

- The seven sons of a widow work hard and seriously to support the family. They give up opportunities to play; the youngest is proud of discouraging a friendly neighbor.
- The mother appears to be overworked, the eldest son noticing that the bottom of her skirt is still damp when she gets up in the morning. The oldest brother looks after her more closely.
- The oldest boy realizes that his mother is leaving their house at night. He follows.
- The mother's skirt is wet from crossing the stream to laugh, drink tea, and play checkers with the neighbor. The eldest awakens his brothers; they secretly build their mother a bridge of stones.
- The mother asks heaven to reward the makers of her bridge. After they die, the spirits of the seven brothers rise into the sky to guide others.

## Performance Suggestions

This story is more fun to perform with a little preparation. Talk about what each boy gives up in order to work harder for the family. Do some research into toys and games of Korea, if you can. One boy could be studious, reading for the civil examinations; another might dream of being a soldier and may look for partners in mock sword games. One could have a gang of friends who adore practical jokes. Incorporate this backstory and the sacrifice into performance of the story. If someone in your group has a game of Go or Gobang, an Asian predecessor to Checkers, learn to play it and use it for the game in the sandal-maker's hut.

Carpet squares don't slip and make good stones to place in the stream. Some old outdoor games can be played with these carpet squares as well. Carpet squares on a larger fixed rug are safest. The game called Skip Stone is adapted from a thirteenth-century journal. (My source is Iris Vinton's *The Folkways Omnibus of Children's Games*). Place the squares an easy distance apart, about one foot to start. Form the group into a line. Then, to music or shakers or tambourines, have each one jump across the stones. Those who do this successfully may circle back around to start again. Adjust the distances between "stones" and change the rules each time: jump with both feet; skip alternate feet. Increase speed and spacing until you have a winner. With younger children, use the carpet square "stones" for a game we call musical chairs (once called "Going to Jerusalem").

# WHAT SUN WANTED

✸

Sun, as you know, is very powerful and can see a great distance. Watch the sky, and you will see that Sun is also very particular, moving the same way every day. Sun wants no surprises. In the beginning, Sun wanted someone strong, like, well—like the Sun—to be in charge after everything was made. That would be right, and that would be good. So Sun showed each animal and plant where to put their feet or roots and told them they were supposed to Stay Where They Were Put after Sun went back up into the sky to start another day.

Now Sun went to the water. Fish wanted to swim around, look for food, and find a hiding place in the rocks, but this isn't what Sun wanted. Sun marked out a place in the water, put the fish inside, and ordered two alligators to guard them. Alligators are very large compared with fish.

Now Sun called the birds together and gave each one a branch on a tree, and then sent a puma to watch by day and a jaguar to watch at night. It was getting late, time for Sun to leave. Sun ordered the chattering woodpecker to sit on the highest part of the tallest tree and to peck out a warning if anyone disobeyed orders. Good. Sun went back to work in the sky.

I don't have to tell you that the fish didn't like this at all. Neither did the birds. The birds squawked and argued with each other and couldn't enjoy the morning sun, while the fish swam this way and that way, bumping into each other, looking at all the fish food on the other side of the alligators. It wasn't long before a fine, fat, and hungry fish sneaked out of the pen. One quick-eyed alligator was right behind. But when this alligator caught up with the runaway fish, she got so excited that she forgot what she was doing and ate the fish instead of chasing it back. A fair punishment, don't you think, and who would miss one fish? The alligator's mate saw this and moved in closer to the other fish, in hopes that another one might need to be punished. Both alligators kept getting closer, closer. The fish circled around more and more desperately, looking for a chance to get away. By the time Sun reached the highest part of the sky, more fish broke out of their fish place, and just as quickly a few more were eaten. The birds quit squawking at each other and began jumping up and down on their branches, complaining loudly. "Fish moved! Alligators moved!"

Tat-a-tat! The woodpecker knocked a warning to Sun.

Sun looked down, not at all happy about this, and ordered fences to be built everywhere and more guards posted. Lizards and frogs and more alligators around the fish! Foxes and wild dogs and snakes around the birds! While Sun was talking, giving instructions, the alligators ate a few more stray fish.

Sun turned back into the sky to finish the day. But now all the animals were tired of sitting still. Alligators squeezed in so close that fish bumped fish shoulders. Suddenly, all the fish burst out of their pen; alligators and frogs and lizards chased and ate everything they could see. Birds flapped in every direction. Woodpecker rattled an alarm to Sun, and the animals scattered even farther as Sun stomped down from the sky.

Alligators were afraid as they felt the heat of the angry Sun getting closer to them. They couldn't get away fast enough—they had to slither into the mud to hide from Sun and protect themselves from the heat.

And Sun was angry. Who broke the rules first? Where were the alligators hiding? Sun marched back and forth, back and forth across the mud, over the backs of the alligators. Stomp, stomp, stomp. Ouch, ouch, ouch! Flashes of Sun's power flew in all directions, into sky and water and forest.

It was time for Sun to go down behind the trees. Sun left for the night, and the alligators crawled out of the mud very slowly, with bumps all over their backs, which you can see to this day. But all this had been so much trouble that Sun gave up on keeping things organized on earth. That is why the Orinoco people say you can find sacred spirits everywhere, and that is why the animals of the earth wander where they please.

## COMMENTARY

The Arawak people of the Bahamas, related to the Orinoco of Brazil, were the first natives of America seen by Christopher Columbus. He reported in his ship's log, October of 1492, that these people were friendly and gentle, and "They would make fine servants. . . . With fifty men we could subjugate them all and make them do whatever we want." The outline of this story in the Latin American volume of *The Mythology of All Races* seemed to capture the way the Arawak people might feel toward bossier neighboring tribes, who had a habit of enslaving the Arawak whenever they captured any. Their story after contact with white explorers is much more tragic; few of the gentle Arawak survived.

## Story Outline

- Sun puts everyone in their place—fish, birds, and alligators.
- The woodpecker is sent to guard.
- One fish gets away and is chased and eaten by an alligator.
- The birds complain; the woodpecker warns Sun.
- Sun builds fences, gets more guards.
- All the fish get loose; the alligators chase them; the birds fly off.
- Sun starts back down; the alligators hide in mud.
- Sun stomps on hiding alligators.
- Sun gives up and leaves. Animals spread out and find their own places.

## Performance Suggestions

This story makes a good cooperatively illustrated book. Each child selects one incident to illustrate. After drawing an outline for his or her illustration in dark pencil or pen, each person writes or dictates a description of the action depicted. This can be written under, around, or next to the illustration or on a separate sheet of paper. Allow the story to adjust to the pictures rather than the other way around. Create a cover, title, and author page for all to sign. Photocopy drawings so that each person has a complete copy to color and take home.

Act out the children's version (drawing it first encourages their imagination). Blankets and large sheer curtains work well as corral for fish and mud waiting for the alligators. Give the Sun a pencil or "sun ray" stick to touch the backs of the hiding alligators, who respond with loud "ouches." This can be performed by very young children, either with soundmakers and pantomime or with a minimum of improvised dialogue. Add as many additional animals as you have additional participants. Allow plenty of time for each animal to find its own secret hiding place in the room before the Sun comes stomping back.

# NA HA CALLS DOWN THE STORM

✳

Only a few people live at the frozen ends of the world, like the fishing people of Cape Horn. Standing on a great stony ledge, watching storms come up month after month, they tell a story of how their land came to be held in a grip of ice and wind. They say that the cold was brought by their ancestor hero, Na Ha, who brought it not to hurt them but to save them.

When people first came to the islands, the weather was warm and the fishing very good, but there were many times, days that never seemed to end, when the people were afraid to pick up their fishing nets and take their small boats into the waters. In those days the ocean was crowded with undersea people, great hairy, noseless ones who walked the sandy bottoms of the waterways, watching for the shadows of boats. With horrendous roars these undersea monsters would burst up on the surface, circle the canoes, and drag their victims down, down into the sea.

The people of the islands grew hungry, and finally the only one still willing to go fishing was Na Ha, the mighty one, strong as the wind. Na Ha was the one who untangled lines caught in ropes of kelp. He willingly went out to fish alone and shared his catch of fish with those who did not dare to touch water for fear of ocean monsters, even though he had a young wife from the north country and a child waiting for him at home.

The people grew tired of waiting on shore, doing nothing, and even with the fish brought in by the mighty Na Ha, they did not have enough to eat. Na Ha had to venture out farther and farther and stay longer and longer to bring back enough to feed them. One morning he told them he could wait no longer. He must fight the undersea monsters. Some wept, while Na Ha's wife stood without tears or words, watching him go.

Na Ha's canoe had barely left shore when the people on the land could see the noseless ones following. The water around Na Ha's canoe was whipped into foam; the air filled with shrieks. Heads of monsters, all teeth and bulging eyes, crowded around his boat, then closed in. The little canoe sank under the weight of the wild, hairy attackers. The water churned for half an hour after Na Ha and the monsters had sunk below the surface. Then all was quiet.

For minutes, then hours, the island people stood on rocks, straining their eyes into the dying light, hoping to see Na Ha swimming back to shore. As darkness crept over water and land, the people sadly turned away and went back to their home fires. Only Na Ha's wife, holding her child, could be seen at the shoreline.

All night the people wept and told stories about Na Ha. But with daylight and the screams of the seagulls, Na Ha's wife came running toward them, and behind her came Na Ha, walking out of the water. What had happened? He told his people of fighting until he nearly lost his strength, then swimming until he found a door on the undersea floor. He pulled open the door to find a huge cavern, which he entered. Seated on a rock, her hair flowing around her like giant seaweed, was the Mother of All Animals.

Na Ha recognized her at once. He told her of the trouble caused by the noseless ones. She listened, then told him there was only one way to end the terror. Na Ha must call down the white death to the land, the white death that would drive the noseless people into their proper place. She reached behind her and found an enormous seashell, which she lifted high over her head, and then she solemnly spoke. One who was strong enough, she said, could use this shell to summon the winds and ice that would freeze everything, every monster of the deep, in its path.

Na Ha reached out for the shell, but as he reached, she shook her head and put the shell in her lap. She spoke sadly. "You must send all your people away before you do this," said the Mother of All Animals. "Your wife must lead them north to the mountains, teach them to dress themselves in skins and to make hooks so that they can fish from the ice. They must wait for the storms to pass."

Then she put her hand on Na Ha's shoulder. "Often we must die before we know what good we do," she said. "You will not be able to save yourself from the ice that will save your people."

Na Ha listened. He understood. He left the cave and swam to the surface with the seashell.

When Na Ha finished his story, his wife spoke. "I am not brave like you," she said. "I may be too full of grief to find the path back to my old home in the mountains. Perhaps I have forgotten how to sew skins. Someone else can blow the shell and call down the storms."

Na Ha only held tightly to the shell. "This is the way," he said.

And so it happened the only way it could. The land people said their sad farewells to Na Ha, packed their few belongings, and followed Na Ha's wife north to her childhood home. They made skin jackets and pants and boots and waited. Each day Na Ha's wife stood at the highest point and listened until, in the distance, they all heard the ring of the seashell. They saw the storms sweep in, clouds piling on each other. Down below, at the ocean's edge, the water thickened and turned white. The noseless ones crouched, hugged their arms into their hairy sides, and shivered. Arms that had churned up water and sunk the canoes of the land people shriveled into flippers good only for swimming. The noseless ones turned into seals, and they are seals today.

The people hurried down from the mountains, down to the shore, hoping that some miracle had saved Na Ha. They found only a cliff of ice high above the ocean—a high point of land that withstood storms and dangers like the mighty Na Ha—which became a lookout that would serve them well in many future generations.

### COMMENTARY

I am indebted to the UNICEF *Hi Neighbors* collection of stories and traditions for the main storyline of Na Ha. This is one of many Native American stories of sea monsters and incorporates one of the oldest ideas about a single god-figure, one we call the "Keeper of All Animals." Sea hunters from the extremes of North and South America express their combined awe and gratitude toward the bounteous waters in these stories. My version incorporates interpretations by many of the children who have performed it.

## Story Outline

- People fish for food but are frightened back by noseless undersea monsters; Na Ha fishes alone and shares his catch with them.
- Na Ha goes to fight the monsters and disappears.
- Na Ha returns and tells of getting a shell from the Mother of All Animals, which he must blow to bring on icy storms.
- People follow Na Ha's wife into the mountains of the north, where they learn to sew skin clothes and wait for the storms.
- Na Ha finally blows the seashell and brings down the storms.
- The storms freeze the noseless monsters into seals.
- The people come down from the mountains and look for Na Ha.
- They find only a cliff of ice (Na Ha has frozen into a cliff).

## Performance Suggestions

This sad, noble tale works well as a ceremonial dance where performers blend the roles of the people, Na Ha, and the Mother of All Animals. For my dance version I invited a guest, a dancer who showed the children how she turned her feelings into movement. We talked to her about the story, and she suggested appropriate actions.

First, divide the central space into three areas—shoreline, water, and cave. Rehearse the movements, then perform in sequence together. A sand drum or other drum and shakers are appropriate. Bring a large seashell if available. The dance:

- Walk from shore to water as if afraid; turn back.
- Return to the water as Na Ha, head high, brave.
- Walk around in a small circle, then walk with arms "swimming" to the cave place; sit cross-legged in a circle.
- As the Mother of All Animals, reach behind with one hand, cup a hand to hold the shell (or pantomime as if holding a shell). Bring hands together, stand, hold the shell high over-

head. Bring it down in front of you, with hands still held around the shell; extend it in front of you as if handing it to Na Ha.

- As Na Ha, take the shell, carry it slowly back to the shoreline.
- Form a line along the shore; lift the shell to your lips as if to blow.
- Freeze in proud position, hands now flattened, elbows still extended and lifted up to form a high cliff.

This also lends itself to exercises of transformation, starting with turning monsters into seals and Na Ha into an ice cliff.

This story can also be acted out in a more typical fashion. Sheer curtains (whose sheerness eliminates accidents) or blankets represent the seawater where the monsters hide and where Na Ha disappears when pulled underwater. Have a smaller cloth off to the side with the Mother of All Animals seated there, waiting. One child often volunteers to be a kindly dolphin or fish who guides Na Ha to the cave. Dance ribbons and scarves are effective as storm effects. People walking to the north country climb up tables and ledges, or they may simply congregate in another section of the staging area with Na Ha's wife, watching for the storm by standing on a chair.

Don't feel constrained by the sex roles of a story, by the way. Make Na Ha a heroine, make the husband a sister, whatever fits your fancy or group.

# HOW WISDOM SCATTERED

✳

Before people had schoolteachers and classrooms, they had eyes and ears and learned from other animals. Every creature, no matter how small or humble or slow of movement, had something to teach. Consider Tortoise: awkward, not especially friendly, and yet Tortoise produced many young and lived to a great old age. "Tortoise is clever, isn't that true?" they said to each other, and they sang out praise on the talking drum, a praise that went something like this:

> Tortoise is truly a child of the wise god,
> one who digs in the earth to hide
> and finds a water fountain.

After all, what could be more important than being careful and in the process finding a water well? Tortoise was called by other praises too and was famous for wisdom, so famous, indeed, that he feared that others would try to steal some of his secrets. But where to hide them? After all, Tortoise was known for digging. Aha, then he had an idea!

Late one night, as his neighbors slept, Tortoise wrote down all his tricks and secrets on little bits of paper, stuffed them into a gourd, bit down hard on the narrow neck of the gourd, and started walking.

But he was not alone. Cat watched as Tortoise lumbered toward the forest. Tortoise tried to hurry by without paying attention to Cat. He was trying so hard not to see Cat that he tripped over tree roots and didn't notice that one of the papers fluttered out of his gourd.

"Here, Tortoise, here's something you dropped," said Cat, respectfully, as she caught up with Tortoise. "You couldn't see the tree roots because you have a gourd in your mouth."

"Hmph, yes," said Tortoise, stuffing the piece of paper back in the gourd. Tortoise hoped that Cat couldn't read very well in the dark.

"Excuse me, Aged One, but won't your paper be safer if you use bark to stop up your gourd?" she said most brightly.

"Hmph, yes," said Tortoise, plugging the mouth of his gourd and walking on, the gourd still bumping against the ground.

"And you could see better if you tied a vine on the gourd and hung it around your neck," Cat added.

"Certainly, that's why I go into the forest," Tortoise said grumpily and pulled a piece of vine from a nearby tree, twisting it about, testing its strength as he waited for Cat to leave.

As soon as Cat ran away, Tortoise started walking again. He kept walking until he found the tallest tree around, and he started clawing his way up the trunk. But he couldn't even get his back feet off the ground. His gourd clanked into his chest and kept him from getting a good grip on the trunk. Over and over, he reached and fell, reached and fell.

He managed to climb up a few feet before he fell, clunk, down to earth again—on his back.

Early the next morning, Tortoise was still lying with his feet in the air, rocking back and forth on his shell, trying to turn himself over, when Antelope came by looking for fresh grass for her children.

"A good morning, Mr. Tortoise," said Antelope, politely. "You work hard this early in the morning."

"Since you are so kind, Mother Antelope," said Tortoise, "I will tell you. I am tired of living down inside the earth. I plan to live where the air is fresh, high in this tree."

"I am not as wise as you, Ancient One, but I have a thought that may help," said Antelope modestly. "If you hang your gourd behind you rather than in front, you should have no more trouble."

"Hmph, yes," said Tortoise, "if you could turn me over." And so she did, gently nudging him with her nose until he was back on his feet again. Tortoise did as Antelope advised and soon clambered to the top of the tree. He found the perfect branch for his gourd of secrets, out of sight of any animal below.

Oh, but as he reached around his neck for the gourd, he had a terrible thought. He was missing three secrets—the secret of stopping up the gourd, the secret of tying a vine around the gourd and hanging it to his neck, and the secret of hanging the gourd behind his neck as he climbed. He must add these to his collection! But Tortoise's round body was not as good for climbing trees as it was for digging and hiding in the earth. Trying to uncork the gourd while propped between shaky branches, Tortoise slipped, and the gourd fell to the ground, breaking into a thousand pieces.

That is how wisdom happened to scatter around the universe, and if we keep looking, you and I may still pick up a bit here and about.

## COMMENTARY

My source for this story was the *UNICEF Book of Children's Legends*, compiled by William I. Kaufman. His transcription of the story from Nembe, Rivers State, Nigeria, was digested by several groups of children, who brought in rabbits and cats and other favorite creatures to offer advice to Tortoise. They also decided that Tortoise would not give up his secrets voluntarily. The language here responds to the cadence found in the libretto of an operatic version of *The Palmwine Drinkard*, by Kola Ogunmola.

## STORY OUTLINE

- Tortoise writes secrets on papers and stuffs them in a gourd.
- Tortoise carries the gourd in his mouth looking for a hiding place.
- Tortoise trips and a paper spills out of the gourd.
- Cat finds the paper and suggests using bark to plug the gourd and twine to carry the gourd around Tortoise's neck.
- Tortoise finds the tree, tries to climb it, and falls down onto his back.
- Antelope finds Tortoise, suggests hanging the gourd in back, and turns Tortoise over.
- Tortoise gets up the tree and tries to add new secrets to the gourd.
- The gourd falls, breaks, and all the secrets fall out and scatter.

## PERFORMANCE SUGGESTIONS

You can turn this story into a game. Give children colored pencils, scissors, and colored paper to cut into strips. They each write their own secrets about the world, any secret of something that is good to know, on one or more of the strips (very small children may dictate or draw a picture). When the secrets are ready, take turns hiding them in a designated spot—another room is best. Make sure every secret is hidden. At the word "Go!" everyone goes on a search for secrets. Share what you learned—maybe tell how you will be able to use this secret.

My favorite secret was dictated by a four year old: "Cutting is good to do instead of ripping." A fine metaphor for the values of civilization, I think.

# GLOOSCAP AND BABY

✷

The first people to live in the state of Maine, the Passamaquoddy, say that the first person on earth was
their ancestor, the strong and brave Glooscap. Glooscap
continued to live among them for many years, and that
was good because the land was surrounded by monsters.
Look out in the distance; do you see mounds of earth covered with trees? Those are the giant people who threat-
ened us once. That's what the Algonquin people say.
Glooscap caught those giants, tied them up, and ordered
them to sleep until he called for them. They have slept for
so long now that they are covered with grass and trees
grow out of their sides.

Snakes were another problem. You don't see any snakes
here in our village, do you? Listen, do you hear songs of
sorcerers in the air? No, because Glooscap captured the
sorcerers, those magicians who can sing people into
snakes. Glooscap gathered them up in strong arms and
didn't let go until the sorcerers told their secrets. Then
Glooscap used charmsongs to turn the sorcerers them-

selves into snakes. They were sent off into the mountains, into the trees and rivers of the sleeping giants.

This isn't all. Our people were still frightened by the stick people, who were the spirits of the night who walk in the dark. Glooscap used the spells learned from the magicians to stop the night spirits and make them talk to him. Those stick people were the night spirits of the dead looking for a resting place. Glooscap was not a cruel person, but one who wanted to help. After all, each night spirit had a secret—a power it had gained by living and dying. Sometimes our people need to know these things. And so Glooscap found a home for each of the stick people in the rocks and trees and fish, a home for each night spirit who promised to share its powers with any of our people who ask with a good heart.

The last spirit was the most difficult. Hunters came to Glooscap to complain about the rainbow spirit, whose long hair of every color hung down among the trees and meadows and made it hard for them to hunt. But rainbow spirit was hard to catch—she was a great cloud of a spirit who slipped away when Glooscap reached out to catch her.

Finally, Glooscap gathered up strands of the rainbow spirit's hair and tied them to the sky. When she cried and said she wanted to look at humans only because she liked them, Glooscap untied her hair and allowed her to look down on the people from a distance for a few minutes after every rain.

Glooscap made one last request of all the spirits that had been conquered. They must appear when Glooscap called them. The spirits promised they would do this, so Glooscap left them in peace.

Now, as you might expect, Glooscap was terribly proud after all these great deeds. The people of the village walked up respectfully and offered many thanks. After all, Glooscap was still available to fight any new monsters that might appear. Of course, with all this responsibility, the great hero had no time for an ordinary life, like marrying and having a family.

And so it happened that Glooscap met a woman of the village one fine morning and boasted that there were no dangers left in the world. The woman laughed and said, "Are you sure, Glooscap? I know a small monster who cannot be controlled by anyone."

Glooscap, much surprised, asked who this all-powerful spirit was and where it could be found. The woman pointed inside her home, to a baby sitting on the floor playing with a rattle. "She is called Wasis," said the woman. "But I don't recommend that you try to take control of her. I've given up, myself."

"You can't control this small creature?" cried Glooscap.

"I admit I am her servant," said the woman, smiling.

Glooscap puffed out a strong chest and called to the baby in a friendly voice. "Come here, pretty one." But Wasis paid no attention. Glooscap pulled out a flute and played a charming song. A snake crept up to the door, and then another. The baby only watched and sat.

Glooscap frowned and put away the flute; the snakes left. "Come here, I say," Glooscap commanded Wasis. The baby stared and dropped her rattle. Glooscap shouted a spell and a demon flew in the door and circled around her. Glooscap shouted to the demon and said to Wasis in a terrible voice, "See how the demon obeys me!" Now the baby let out a howl, and to impress her even more, Glooscap sang out a most dreadful song, a song to raise the spirits out of the ground and bring the dead out of the hills. In a moment the room was full of stick people and the shouts of Glooscap and the cries of the baby.

Glooscap ordered the spirits to stop and bow down. Suddenly the room was quiet, as the spirits, one by one, bowed down at the feet of Glooscap and then left the room. The baby, too, was quiet.

It was time for Glooscap to produce the greatest wonder. A song rang out, the voice of Glooscap higher and higher, until it rang out of the room, across the village, and along the hills into the mountains. Out of the sky, from behind the sun came the magnificent rainbow spirit, down, down the valley until her long, bright hair filled the village and the little room with every color imaginable. At this the baby Wasis laughed and clapped her hands. "Goo, goo," she called out happily, and she crawled up and pulled on rainbow spirit's hair.

Glooscap thought the baby was calling out the name of Glooscap to show that she was not afraid of any monsters and spirits, not even the most powerful of all. Baby had clearly won the battle between them. Poor Glooscap could not say a word. As the rainbow spirit drifted away, Glooscap bowed to baby Wasis.

"I give up, Baby, you are the strongest," said Glooscap, and quickly walked away.

That is how we know that when a baby gurgles and says "Goo, goo," it is a reminder that the great Glooscap is not the strongest creature after all.

### COMMENTARY

In many stories Glooscap or Gluscabi is a cross between a comic-strip superhero and a smug Coyote. That is, he makes mistakes, then learns from them. His power over monsters, combined with ignorance of ordinary life, leading to humiliating "defeat" at the hands of the baby, have been modified by many children. This is a transcription of a performance by a class of five-year-olds. References to Glooscap are meant to allow a male or female ancestor hero. The original story can be found in *American Indian Myths and Legends*, selected by Richard Erdoes and Alfonso Ortiz, who took it from Lewis Spence, who heard and recorded it around the turn of the century.

## Story Outline

- Glooscap tames the giant people into mountains.
- Glooscap gets the songs of magicians and turns the magicians into snakes.
- Glooscap finds homes for the stick people, who are the night spirits of the dead.
- Glooscap sends the rainbow spirit into the far sky.
- A mother says she knows someone Glooscap can't conquer—baby Wasis.
- Glooscap calls out snakes with a flute; baby Wasis stares.
- Glooscap calls out the stick people; baby Wasis howls.
- Glooscap calls the rainbow spirit; baby Wasis crawls up and pulls its hair and cries "Goo, goo."
- Glooscap thinks the baby is telling Glooscap that she is not afraid and admits that baby Wasis is stronger.

## Performance Suggestions

Before the performance prepare props: a mask or headband for Glooscap, shakers for sound effects, and headbands for monsters and spirit people. Headbands allow each participant to play more than one monster role. My four-, five- and six-year-old girls made all the props themselves, headbands with flowing, multicolored strips of crepe paper for the rainbow people, trimmed sticks for wands to represent the stick people (spirits of the dead in the original). They made paper-plate masks for the other monsters. Finally, each made a shaker to accompany all the entrances of monsters. We simplified dialogue and movement and rehearsed with many switches of roles; in their recital they performed the play twice so that they could take turns in the roles of Glooscap and baby Wasis.

The storyline was simplified and so was dialogue. Each group of monsters marched on stage toward Glooscap, who grandly raised an arm and said, "Go away!" They did, shaking shakers and looking grim. Then baby Wasis crawled out, and Glooscap said firmly, "Baby, come here!" Baby didn't. Glooscap glared at Baby and ordered the monsters back, one by one, until the rainbow spirits surrounded Baby and she pulled their beautiful hair, saying "Goo, goo!" At this, Glooscap said, "I give up. Baby, you're stronger than me," and retreated. Baby gave one more shake of the rattle and said, "Goo, goo!"

# WHAT WE LEARNED FROM THE DEVIL

✳

The old Devil looked around hell one day and noticed that things were getting a little run down. Fires were burning low—people walked over them without even noticing. The path between his condo and the main reception area didn't seem any more threatening than the desert highway across southern Idaho. What's worse, the slab that was supposed to be used to roast tortured souls had been swept off and was being used for a poker game.

Hell was positively pleasant. People were sitting around, smoking cigarettes, saying to each other, "This isn't so bad." It was time for serious action.

Trouble was, too many of his assistants were taking vacations. They were tucking their tails into a pair of Levis, pulling a sports cap over their horns, climbing out of hell the back way, and hitching a ride to Las Vegas where they would try their hand at craps and take in a show.

The Devil was desperate. He needed help. The problem was, most of the people who came down to his district didn't make such good workers. He decided to take a trip to heaven and kidnap a few angels who would take orders.

That's how he ended up flying over heaven, watching for crowds. There they were, hundreds of sweet, fluttering wings at a gospel rock concert.

The Devil edged up close. The singer was a pretty young angel in shimmering pink; she sang "Jump little children, jump! Jump up for your Lord!" and the audience jumped right off their clouds for joy. This was all the opportunity the Devil needed. He grabbed an armload and flew off.

Being the kind of fellow he is, the Devil took a few more angels than he could comfortably carry. He lost altitude and was flying low, looking for a place to land and catch his breath when he realized he was just over Las Vegas. He looked down and saw one of his missing demons in a shiny new cowboy shirt, pearl buttons flashing in the sun, hair all slicked back. The lucky demon must have won big. He hooted at the Devil, "Whoo-up!" and grinned and waved.

The Devil, forgetting himself, waved back. Of course, when the Devil lifted his arm, the angels broke loose and flew off in all directions. At this sight, the rascally demon on the ground laughed and laughed and then got on a tour bus behind a woman in a yellow pantsuit. The Devil, disgusted, turned around and flew right back to heaven for another try.

This time the Devil circled around until he saw a calmer group of angels. These were seated in neat rows of folding chairs on a flat cloud, listening to someone. Their speaker wore a tweed jacket over his robe, and talked about "facilitating praise." Most of the audience only glanced up now and then at the speaker; they sat with their heads down, taking notes. They were so involved that the Devil was able to make a low dive and scoop up a dozen at once.

The Devil was too tired, now, to carry the angels in one arm, so he loosened up his belt and tucked the angels into his waist. This wasn't too difficult. They didn't squirm or cry; all they did was talk in quiet, polite voices about "prioritizing means of escape." The Devil buttoned his coat over them and flew off for hell.

This load of angels was older and heavier than the last. Again the Devil dropped lower and lower, until he was barely skimming the tops of trees. He was passing over Vegas again, and this time he saw another one of his vacationing demons coming out of a pancake shop. The demon burped and looked up. He winked and said to the Devil, "Sagging a little there, ain't you, old man?"

Well, we know it was the angels tucked into the Devil's belt that made him look fat and fly low, but the vain old Devil, trying to look slimmer, pulled up his shoulders and sucked in his stomach as he flew by. When he did that, of course, the angels wiggled free and flew back to heaven, every one of them.

The Devil is not one to give up. He headed back to heaven, determined to succeed. But when he flew over the Pearly Gates, his tail drooping from all the exertion, the rock concert was over, and the conference administrator was taking down posters and stacking chairs. There wasn't a cluster of angels to be seen.

The Devil sat down and waited. Soon he heard some sounds. Whack! Whack! Whack! Small bits of cloud dust were puffing past him with each smacking sound. He looked up and saw a dozen young angels on skateboards, gowns tucked up above their knees, their wings trimmed for speed as they took jumps off the clouds overhead.

The Devil chuckled to himself. The young angels were landing almost in front of him. He moved forward just as he heard the whack of a skateboard bouncing off the cloud above, then reached out and—whup—grabbed an angel off the board.

This time the Devil was taking no chances. These were lusty little angels who kicked and struggled; he popped them in his mouth as he caught them. When he had a mouthful, he set off for hell.

Now it was evening over Las Vegas. The Devil saw one of his chief assistants standing in a long line outside of a casino, waiting for tickets for the Frank Sinatra show. Angel arms and feet and wing tips were poking out here and there between the Devil's lips when the demon looked up and said, "I see you got us a load of angels."

Without thinking the Devil grinned wickedly and said, "Yeahss." You know what happened. A grin was all it took for those wriggly angels to bust loose.

That's why, when the Devil goes looking for souls today, he's got a different style. He keeps his hands in his pockets and his belt snugged tight, with a big fat buckle on top. If you chance to meet him and ask if he's caught any angels lately, he'll just look at you sort of sideways, lift one eyebrow, and mumble, "Um hmmm."

That's how we learned to talk that way.


## COMMENTARY

This thoroughly Americanized African story reminds us of where we get our bad habits. Roger D. Abraham's Florida version in *Afro-American Folktales*, adapted from Zora Neale Hurston, legendary interpreter of African American story, establishes Miami as the featured sin city. A child of the West, I place hell and the devil in the land of the laconic cowboy and gambling. One of the Devil's faults is being more concerned with how he looks to his minions than he is with showing respect for ancestors and elders. Just a warning.

## Story Outline

- The Devil looks around hell and decides he needs help.
- The Devil flies to heaven and steals angels at a rock concert.
- Overloaded, flying over Vegas, the Devil waves back to a demon.
- The angels from the rock concert fly off when the Devil waves.
- The Devil returns to heaven and steals angels at a conference.
- The angels from the conference wriggle out when the Devil sucks in his tummy.
- The Devil returns to heaven and scoops up skateboarders.
- The skateboarding angels break free of his mouth when the Devil grins.
- The Devil today mumbles and won't look you in the eye, and that's what we learned from the Devil.

## Performance Suggestions

When performed by children, this story leads easily to ecstatic screams and uncontrolled running. You can make use of that by turning the story into a game with rules. Establish bases of heaven and hell, with earth (about double the size of heaven and hell) in between. In this game, unlike in the story, heaven is a sanctuary. Angels who enter earth are fair game, captured if the Devil (and demons, if you like) touches them in earth territory. Then angels must tag along by holding the waist of a demon or Devil until a free angel manages to touch them. Captured angels taken to hell before they are freed by free angels are held captive until the end of the game. Put on earth something the angels want (skateboards, maybe?) so that angels have a reason to venture out of safety.

For adults, talk about other habits we might have picked up from the Devil, then have groups of people rewrite the incidents in the story. Act out or take turns telling your revised versions.

# THE POWER OF THE QUESTION

✳

When we say that someone is as wise as Solomon, we are remembering the king who turned Jerusalem into a glorious city admired by people everywhere. King Solomon not only ruled well, he wrote songs and gathered the stories and sayings of his people. The greatest teachers and students of the world came to Solomon's court; he learned from them all. And he put his knowledge to work, building a temple so magnificent that stories afterward said mere human beings could not have done the work. It seemed as though King Solomon understood everything! He could settle arguments. He knew the habits of animals, including birds and reptiles and fish. He could name a thousand healing plants and describe the movement of the stars in the sky. Couldn't a man like this harness the demons who troubled ordinary folk? Perhaps he could. And if we listen to his stories very closely, we may learn how to gain some of his power for ourselves.

The great temple of the city of Jerusalem was built by the finest architects and craftspeople and workers to be found anywhere. The master builder was from an island famous for its magnificent stone palaces. He knew how to make things last. And to make certain the work was done properly, King Solomon himself walked regularly through the construction area, asking questions, giving suggestions, and keeping close watch over progress.

King Solomon's favorite worker, indeed the favorite of everyone, was not the tallest or strongest or most clever, but the son of the master builder, who worked each day beside his father. This boy was so charming and worked so eagerly that the other workers took pleasure watching him. In appreciation, the King had the boy paid like any other worker—in fact, the child was paid double the usual adult wages.

Yet Solomon observed that as time went on, this child seemed to grow thinner rather than fatter, sadder rather than happier. And this was despite the fact that the boy was receiving choice food, his own sleeping quarters, and the kindly attention of a great king. Each day, the king walked by and asked how the boy was doing—did he like having his own room, was his bread fresh, his window large enough, and his sleeping mat soft enough? Each day the boy would drop his head and murmur politely even as his face grew pale and his arms and legs wasted away to sticks.

Finally, Solomon went up to his altar to speak directly to God. In one hand the king held his sacred ivy, the plant that stays green all year round. In his other hand he held a jasper, a sacred healing stone whose surface seems to picture the earth in all its colors and mystery. Solomon stretched out his hands and called out, "God of gods and King of kings, reveal to me what it is that torments the boy." Servants and temple workers watched from a respectful distance as Solomon stood listening to his God for what seemed to be a long time.

King Solomon waited until his workers were finished for the day. Then, when dinner hour was over, the King sought out the child and took him to one of his own chambers for questioning. He sat down beside the boy and said, "Have I not loved you more than all the other artisans working in the Temple of God, and have I not been paying you double wages and provisions?" The child nodded, miserably. "Why then," asked the King firmly, "are you growing thinner every day?"

Finally, the boy confessed. "When the sun has set and I am resting, an evil spirit torments me. It howls and sucks my thumb, stealing the food I eat and spoiling my sleep."

The King listened quietly as the little boy from a distant country described his pesky demon. Slowly the king took off his magnificent ring and handed it to the boy. "This is my signet ring," said the king, solemnly. "Wear it when you go to bed tonight. If the demon bothers you, hold up the ring to his face, order him to tell you his name, and then come immediately to tell me. The demon will have to follow you."

The boy walked back to his quarters holding King Solomon's ring as all the other workers stared in amazement. That night, soon after he lay down on his mat and closed his eyes, he heard howling outside his window. Instantly the boy sat up on his mat, held out the ring and shouted, "Solomon commands you!" and started running to the king's chambers as fast as he could go.

"King Solomon, I brought the demon. You can hear him crying in a great voice outside the gates," said the child. The King listened, then took back his ring. "I will bind up your demon," said King Solomon. "I will order him to cut temple stones in the quarry. From now on the demon will be your helper, and you can sleep."

And so after the boy was moved back to his father's sleeping quarters and the demon was converted to stonecutter, the temple construction went even faster, and the building seemed more glorious than ever. When it was completed and it was time for the workers to return to their own countries, King Solomon assembled all the workers to pay them their last wages and wish them well.

As the king walked by, the son of the master builder dared to ask the question he had heard whispered by all his father's friends. "Is it true, King Solomon," he asked shyly, "that you know the names of all the demons, and now that the work is done, you have bound the demons inside seven water jars?"

"I have not trapped all the world's demons," said the king. "Yet you may sleep in peace. You can make your demons work for you, just as I have done."

"I don't have a magic ring," said the boy, sadly.

King Solomon smiled and gave the boy a coin that had been pressed by the seal on the royal ring. "Here," he said gently. "Don't forget to ask for the names of your demons. Talk to them. Demons can't run away from questions."

## COMMENTARY

This is a humanized version of a story told in the "Testament of Solomon," part of a large body of literature that scholars call pseudepigrapha, writings falsely attributed to particular authors. They are typically filled with magical events and powers that combine Egyptian, Zoroastrian, Greek, and other Mediterranean sources. The demons believed to haunt the temple grounds may not have been as real to Solomon as they were to the son of the master builder. It is enough to know that the king took the boy's demons seriously and offered a remedy with many life applications.

## Story Outline

- King Solomon, master of all knowledge, builds a temple.
- Solomon grants favors to the child of his master builder.
- The boy grows thin and sad but won't tell why.
- Solomon lends his magical ring to the boy to use to trap his demon.
- The boy returns to his father, and the temple work goes well.
- Temple is completed, and Solomon gives the boy a coin to take home; the coin gives him the power of the question.

## Performance Suggestions

After the story, hold a discussion that records each child's questions that haven't been answered. In multiple-age groups, after older children write their unanswered questions (each on a single card), they act as scribes for younger children. This activity is at least as satisfying for adults.

If time allows, have each person create a mask of a wise person and name their Wise One. Take turns seated behind the mask, answering the questions with all the wisdom that can be summoned.

As an alternative, read aloud the questions and ask children if they can help each other. Keep track of questions that don't get satisfactory answers; go over them later and decide where answers might be sought. Invite guest speakers to the class to address these tricky questions and cope with the demons. With one group, I invited Vickie Douglas, a woman with a collection of Navajo Yei Bei Chei masks, to speak about the ceremonials in which the ancestors came back and danced among the people, then took off their masks to reveal that it was parents and elders after all. Ms. Douglas allowed the children to try on her masks and look through the eyes of the ancestors before we spent the rest of the hour making our own sketches of the masks.

# THE QUARREL

✳

O nce there was a village far from the city and city ways. Few strangers came to visit, and nearly every-one here was related to someone else. The people were so poor that they had never seen a mirror; the only thing new each day was the morning's quarrels.

One young man of the village had the misfortune of los-ing both of his parents soon after he was married. This made him very sad, which did not please his new wife. When he had reason to do business in the distant town, he chose to make the long walk by himself, to get his mind off his sorrows. "Bring something back to show you are thinking of me," she said with a little pout.

After he finished his business, the young man remem-bered his wife's request. He would bring home something pretty. He was walking past a mirror shop, admiring the gleaming frames of what he thought were pictures, when to his amazement he saw a face he recognized. "It is a pic-ture of my father as a young man," he said, staring at his reflection. "Surely my wife will be pleased when I honor the memory of my father." And he ran into the shop and spent all he had left for the little mirror.

The young man hurried home to show his wife, but she was not as happy with his choice as he. "Let me see," she cried, and took the mirror. "This is not a picture of your father," she said, quite upset. "You've bought a picture of a pretty young woman to make me jealous. Yes, she is beautiful, but you can see that she is vain and selfish."

The young man protested loudly as he tried to take back the mirror. Their voices carried across the village, and soon all their relatives were gathered around them.

The young wife's older sister took the mirror and said, "It's clear to me that this is a portrait of a goddess, someone accustomed to making others do her will. This picture is meant to teach my sister to obey her proud and foolish husband. I predicted something like this."

Now the young man's uncle stepped in. "Indeed," he said, "This face is very like your father's, but firmer, more strong-willed. It is a face that will bring order to a family for those who listen." And he looked warningly at the young wife.

At this, the young woman's cousin bumped the uncle's arm and quickly took the mirror, saying, ""Hah, it is a trick! I see a sly face, pretending to be friendly but secretly full of evil."

Everyone was shouting, now, until the wise woman of the village hobbled up. The crowd stepped back respectfully as she approached and the mirror was handed to her.

The old woman looked long and thoughtfully at the mirror's face. She turned it one way, now another. Then she spoke. "This is indeed a marvel," she said. "This picture changes from moment to moment. See how it flashes? Now it gives us a kind old face, one that can bring an end to quarrels. Why not hang this light-catcher from the rafters of the house? It can bring down the spirit of heaven and shine back good luck to all of us."

And so it was that the first mirror of the village hung from the rafters of the young couple's house and brought peace and happiness to everyone, perhaps because that is what they expected.

## COMMENTARY

This is a popular Buddhist tale, found frequently in China as well as Japan. This version is an expansion of one reprinted in *Parabola*, taken from Keigo Seki's *Folktales of Japan*. The mirror is a powerful metaphor for our difficulty in recognizing ourselves, with interesting parallels in psychoanalytic theory. Dangling mirrors and other flashy bits have entered contemporary Western décor as an aspect of the Chinese practice of feng-shui. This keeps unfriendly influences confused even as it encourages us to look for the reflections of our wise ancestors in ourselves.

## STORY OUTLINE

- The story takes place in a village that has never seen a mirror.
- A young man marries; soon after, both his parents die.
- The young man promises to bring a gift home from town.
- The young man buys a mirror and thinks it is his father's picture.
- His wife looks in the mirror and sees a selfish young woman.
- His wife's older sister sees a proud goddess.
- His uncle sees someone who likes to give orders.
- His wife's cousin sees someone tricky.
- The wise old woman sees the light of heaven, possibility of change.
- The mirror is hung from the rafters to bring down peace.

## Performance Suggestions

This story converts easily into a classroom exercise. Your only prop is a mirror. Everyone selects a character for themselves and a dominant quality. The first two are the young man and his wife, the last one is the wise old woman. Pass the mirror around, give each person a chance to hold it and to complete the statement "I see . . ." before passing it to the next person. This is a good warm-up activity with low performance demand and little embarrassment for failure because the mirror keeps moving. The last person should step into the center of the circle, moving around to look at each person in the circle through their reflection in the mirror, giving them another chance to strike a pose. A better exercise might be to stay in character after looking in the mirror and respond in exaggerated fashion to each succeeding person. You may want to make verbal expression an option or to repeat it with improvised dialogue the second time.

With children of eight and older, the mirror can be a way of discovering new powers. When the tricky uncle shows the mirror around, each person sees one of their faults or weaknesses. When the old woman catches their reflection, each person sees one of their good qualities or positive powers. These can be fictional qualities or real ones. Do this as an exercise, then reenact the story.

# FINDING OUR PLACE

✳

# MOST PRECIOUS

✳

Marika was a happy child despite her worn dress, her one thin blanket, and the small meals she shared with her tender-hearted father. Her father worked long days in the fields of his wealthy brother. And each morning Marika untied Nanny's rope from the stake in front of their cottage door and walked her goat along the pathways and roadsides, looking for bits and weeds. Marika was always careful to keep Nanny's hungry lips away from her uncle's fields just next door. For this she earned her uncle's grudging respect, and Nanny provided enough milk and cheese to keep Marika and her father alive.

The way Marika kept up her spirits was to pay attention to the countryside and talk to Nanny. Marika told Nanny everything—where a tiny spring produced tender grass, and why they must not set foot in Uncle's fields even though luscious turnip tops could be found there. Nanny seemed to understand. Still, Marika was surprised on Christmas Eve the year she turned twelve. Marika gathered a handful of Nanny's favorite greens, and after her own dinner of bread and cheese, she took a treat out to her pretty goat. "I wish I could do more for you, dear Nanny," she said.

To Marika's surprise, Nanny answered. "Look ahead then, to your future," said Nanny. "Offer yourself to work for your uncle, who has no children to assist him. Ask him tonight, when he is in a holiday mood."

And this is how Marika came to work for her uncle as his goose girl, always tending her Nanny at the same time and stopping each evening to leave her father his bowl of milk. Her father's brother quickly saw an opportunity for himself and told Marika and her father that although he could not pay Marika in cash, he could give her father a goose a year to begin their own flock. Marika worked two years, and the flock did so well under her care that it grew rapidly and she had goose eggs and goslings as well.

But this did not please the greedy uncle and his wife. Although they liked the work of Marika, they saw Marika's gains as their loss. "Work for us another two years," said the uncle on the Christmas Eve that marked the end of her service. "I have a sickly calf without a mother—take care of it and you may have it." Marika went out to the animal shed to speak of this with Nanny. Uncle was not easy to work for, and she longed to live with her father again.

"Look again to your future," said Nanny. "Share your milk with the calf, and you will soon have something of value." And so Marika continued working for her uncle. Now, because the calf was considered so valuable a form of pay, Marika had household duties as well. Still she took care of the animals. At the end of this two years, with the sickly calf now a sturdy heifer, Marika asked her uncle to release her from service.

The uncle protested, saying he'd only meant for her to care for the calf, not keep it, and raised such a temper that

Marika tearfully left. But it was Christmas Eve again, the night the animals can speak, and Nanny urged Marika to go to the home of the procurator, the local agent of the government.

The procurator was a young man who had just inherited his appointment from his father. He meant to do well, yet he was not at all sure of himself. He listened to Marika but could not simply accept the word of a poor servant girl, and so he asked the uncle to appear also. After listening to both the uncle's and Marika's versions of the story, the procurator said he wasn't sure who to believe, and so he would settle the quarrel with a riddle. Whoever gave the best answer would get the heifer. Here is the riddle: What is the swiftest? What is the sweetest? What is of greatest value?

The uncle went home pondering this and told the riddle to his wife. "Simple," she said. "The swiftest is your horse, Midnight. The sweetest is our barrel of honey, aged and protected in oak, the best honey to be found. And our chest of gold pieces surely is the most valuable in the land." Marika's uncle readily agreed and went to sleep.

Marika walked back to her uncle's shed to say her sad goodbyes to her heifer. "Do not fret," said Nanny. "We can help you. First, the swiftest is the human eye, which can see even into the future."

"And what is of greatest value is the earth itself, which provides the crops that Uncle trades for gold coins," said the heifer.

"And the sweetest is sleep, which brings us hope every morning," said Marika, embracing her heifer and Nanny before giving them their Christmas treat and then going to sleep herself in fragrant hay.

The next morning the procurator heard the answers of Marika and her uncle. "The girl is right," he said immediately, and he offered Marika the job of head of his household. "You are indeed clever," said the procurator to Marika, "but you must follow one rule here. I am asked to judge many cases. It is important that I am the only one who offers advice. If you ever interfere, you must leave. If you follow my orders for two years, then I believe we may marry."

Now for two years Marika, in a linen dress provided by the procurator, directed a goose girl and a stable boy and a cook. She left Nanny and her heifer and her flock of geese with her father, who could no longer work in his brother's fields. All was well, except that the procurator, like those before him, was becoming impressed by the wealthy and less concerned about the needs of the poor.

One day nearly two years later, an argument was brought before the procurator that reminded Marika of her own situation. By chance rather than by design, a rich farmer's stallion fathered a colt from a poor man's mare. Such a fine colt it turned out to be that the rich man claimed it as his due. He slipped a little extra money to the procurator, and the procurator ruled in favor of the rich man.

Marika heard this and stopped the poor farmer on his way out the door. The procurator was about to go hunting on Skarman Hill with his rich friends, which was near the home of the farmer. She whispered some advice to the farmer, with his promise that he would not betray where he got his idea. The farmer nodded as she spoke and immediately ran down to the little village on the river.

This is how it happened that the procurator and his friends were walking over Skarman Hill when they found their feet caught up in fishnets. The procurator recognized the farmer who was spreading fishnets on the hillside and made a fuss in front of his friends, calling the farmer a fool. Why would he do such a thing, the procurator asked, tauntingly. The farmer spoke deliberately, as if he were reciting his answer. "If a stallion can have a colt, then fish can be caught on the hillside," he said, as Marika had instructed him. The procurator heard his friends laughing. "All right," he said, "the colt is yours. But I know you did not come up with this trick yourself. Who gave you this advice?"

The farmer tried to withhold the truth as long as he could, but the procurator was accustomed to getting secrets out of country people. He went home in a fury. All the beautiful decorations and the smells of the Christmas Eve dinner did not calm him, and Marika knew immediately what had happened.

"Marika, do you remember your orders?"

"I do," she said, "but I cannot stand injustice."

"You know what this means," said the procurator. "I cannot marry a woman who will interfere with my duties. And I am releasing you from service to me. However, except for this one mistake, you have worked for me faithfully, and because it is Christmas Eve, I will allow you to carry home the one thing most precious to you. You may keep the bridal clothes and gifts in your chest, in fact my servants can carry it for you."

"My agreement was to work for you until midnight tonight," Marika reminded him. "Let us eat our dinner." And in silence she and the procurator ate—Marika not looking at the evidence of wedding preparations, the procurator signaling to his servants to refill his wine glass. That night, as the procurator began to snore in his bed, Marika changed into the plain dress and apron she had worn the day she came to work two years before. She placed her good dress and the wedding gown she would never wear in her wood chest and then locked it, along with all the doors and cupboards. She walked to the barn to bid farewell to the animals she had tended so lovingly for the procurator. Anyone listening at that sacred hour might have wondered at the soft voices weeping at first, growing gradually more hopeful. It was nearly midnight when Marika quietly came back in to her master's house.

Marika walked into her employer's room and hung the locks in her care on the post of his bed. Then to everyone's surprise, she awoke the servants and ordered them to lift up the bed on their shoulders. She led the servants outside and down the path, carrying the sleeping procurator to her astonished father's door.

Next morning the procurator awoke to see the smiling Marika before him. "You are still here!" he said.

"And why not, in my own home?" said Marika. "Good Christmas morning to you!" and she served him his customary tea in her father's rustic cup.

"What am I doing here?" asked the procurator.

"You told me I could carry away that which is most precious to me. It is you, who have won my heart despite your recent lapse in judgment," said Marika sweetly.

Now Marika and the procurator were married, and the hill country came to have what is most swift, sweet, and valuable: for their judge, a woman who loved justice.

### COMMENTARY

This story is based upon "A Clever Woman from the Hills" in volume 1 of *Fairy Tales from Czechoslovakia*, recorded by Bozena Nemcová, in a limited and numbered edition that I found in a favorite secondhand bookstore. Bozena Nemcová, who lived from 1820 to 1862, was the first collector of native stories in Bohemia. In this part of the world, wise animals talk to certain humans (or wise humans still learn from their animals). I included this tradition for Christmas Eve, when many European traditions say that the humblest of creatures can speak.

Youngest children and orphans are often folk heroes and heroines whose essential goodness and honesty allow them to survive trials that others fail. Christmas and New Year traditions have ceremonially honored this notion of the worthiness of the poor. A Babylonian new year celebration reversed importance in wealthy households; servants sat at the head of the table and feasted, while their masters brought platters of food and ate leftovers. This tradition became a European favorite, so infamously rowdy in England that the Puritans founding this country forbade any holiday celebrations whatsoever. The Czech tale, like others throughout central and western Europe, honors a humble woman who rises to power, not just for a season, but permanently, by proving her worth.

## STORY OUTLINE

- Marika cares for her goat, Nanny, while her father works in the fields of his rich brother.
- Christmas Eve, when animals talk, Nanny encourages Marika to work as servant for her uncle.
- Marika works two years for geese and two years for a heifer. But her uncle refuses her wages.
- Nanny tells Marika to go to the procurator. He asks a riddle: What is swiftest? What is sweetest? What is of greatest value?
- With help of her goat and heifer, Marika wins her wages by answering the riddle (swiftest is the eye that sees the future; sweetest is sleep; of greatest value is earth itself). The procurator hires Marika, promises to marry her if she doesn't interfere in his judgments.
- In a case brought before the procurator, he wrongly sides with the rich man. Marika secretly helps the poor farmer. The procurator guesses that Marika helped the farmer.

- Because Marika has interfered in his judgments, the procurator sends her away on Christmas Eve, allowing her to keep only what is most precious to her.
- Marika has the sleeping procurator carried home to her father's house.
- They marry; the procurator makes Marika the judge, giving people what is most swift, sweet, and valuable, a judge who loves justice.

## Performance Suggestions

This story can be the entry point for several exploratory activities. Begin with an exercise of having familiar, favorite animals speak. Take turns playing the role of a family pet or a zoo animal speaking of its hopes and burdens. This is an excuse to make simple animal masks and related gear; see the storymaking section at the back of the book for ideas.

A more abstracted exercise is to have children walk silently through a familiar room. Each child selects something—a rug on the floor, floor boards, a chair, window glass, lights. Give a voice to that object, each one describing itself, saying where it came from, what work it does for humans, how it is treated, what its fate will be. This could be performed as a tableaux, with objects by turns stepping out and speaking. Another good place to perform this would be a school playground or park.

This game and the story "Most Precious" could be performed as a television news story, with a reporter describing what has happened and several performers pantomiming the action behind the reporter. The contrast between magical events and the reportorial style would be humorous for all participants: "News Alive at Five has word that Hill County has a new judge today. Judge Marika was just appointed to the bench by her husband, the county's leading procurator. Here's our reporter at the scene."

A game of shared imagination takes advantage of the willingness of children to draw when asked to. (It's based on the game

"Exquisite Corpse," popular among *avant-garde* artists and writers at the turn of the previous century.) The assignment is for each person to make a drawing of an object, any object, at the top of a sheet of paper, then to pass the paper to someone. On the very bottom of the received paper, each person writes a sentence of what magical change takes place for this object on Christmas Eve. Fold up that answer so that the next person writes on the new bottom of the sheet without reading what has already been written. Keep passing this around, then return the sheet to the one who drew the picture. The artist creates a story using whichever suggestions are most appealing.

This story also presents an opportunity to look at more folk customs related to Christmas and the new year. Divide a class into small groups, have them select a tradition to perform for each other. One of my favorites comes from Mrs. Kingsland's *Book of In and Outdoor Games*. At family festivities to honor the Norse Goddess Hertha, fir branches would be heaped on Hertha's stone, which we still call the hearthstone, and each family member would pose a question about the coming year. It was believed that Hertha herself would be attracted to the smoke and would direct the flames to provide answers to the questions.

Other "How" legends, historical or imaginary, could be set in story form. Mrs. Kingsland repeats the legend that the first Christmas stockings belonged to nuns who gave hospitality to Saint Nicholas one stormy night. A grateful Saint Nick filled their stockings with sugarplums.

The old parlor game Compliments is appropriate to the season when people look toward the future with hope. Each person takes a turn completing the sentence "I would like to be _____. Why, do you think?" The desired goal can be practical or improbable. No matter how unlikely it seems, the rest of the group responds by saying something complimentary. "Because you are so _____. Because you can _____." Answers can be comic, but must be flattering.

# LADY GREEN OF THE SPEAKING TREE

✴

L ittle Green lived in the lowest branch of one of the world's greatest wonders. She was part of the Speaking Tree, which was known to everyone as a tree of life and knowledge. The lonely, the frightened, the disappointed, the daring—anyone could come to the mighty tree and find help. Some said the tree had been in this valley between two mighty rivers since the beginning of time.

It was a tree like no other. At the foot, like little sucker roots, were clusters of fish. The trunk was wound tightly with snakes. Lizards clung to the smaller limbs. On every branch where blossoms would grow between leaves of an ordinary tree were the heads of birds, donkeys, dogs, cats, and sheep, mixed in among the heads of men and women and other children like Little Green. The tree beings, looking down, felt sympathy for creatures living on the earth, the wandering, disconnected souls subject to storm and cold and wind. The Speaking Tree remained a haven. Its leaves provided shelter; its deep roots gave nourishment to all who lived there. Creatures of the tree had no needs and so no reason for arguments or jealousies. The tree sustained them. And everyone spoke at once.

Those on the ground could hear the tree from a hillside away—chatter and murmurings and brayings and barks and coos. People on the ground respected the vision that came from high branches. "Oh Great Tree," they would begin, "I know that you can see far and that you have no need to harm any that walk and breathe. Please look to the future for me."

Gradually the many faces of the tree would turn down to the speaker and listen. Then each would murmur an answer, and the listener, hearing best the one answer that was most needed, would leave satisfied.

As the tree grew in size, however, it became harder and harder to get the attention of the tree. The various creatures of the tree were often speaking to each other. The older and wiser ones were now high above, almost out of sight. Little Green lived low enough to see and hear the petitioners who approached. She saw their worried looks, while at the same time, she admired their freedom to gather and polish pretty stones, to weave and wear beautiful shirts. She began to develop a natural capacity to shout and get attention at about the same time she discovered that those who came to the tree were willing to pay for her assistance. Little Green passed on the word that a special necklace, a fruit delicacy, a flower for her hair would be appreciated—in fact, not just appreciated, expected—and the gifts began to accumulate.

As Little Green gathered her gifts, she had to develop her voice and speak in a more commanding way. This she learned to do, and as she did, she pushed herself away from the tree so that she could be seen and heard and understood. She found herself growing hands to wave and wear bracelets and even feet on which to stand.

One day a great king came to hear the tree. When Little Green saw him approach, with all his attendants on horseback, sunlight reflecting from jewels and silver and gold, she could not contain her joy. Before she would speak, she said, she needed gifts, something for each question. She would take a question and presents one day, give an answer the next. At night, after the king had gone, she called up the tree for information and had her answer ready the next morning, as camels and donkeys arrived, their bags heavy with presents.

Little Green's branch groaned under the weight of the gifts. Seeing this, Little Green demanded that the king leave some servants to feed the roots of the tree so that it could be strong enough to hold her bounty. But even as the king's servants carried jars of water from the river, the branch that Little Green lived on, massive as it was, moaned and then cracked with a terrible sound and dumped Little Green onto the ground.

As she suspected, Little Green found herself capable of standing alone. She ran about gathering up coins and jewels that had fallen out of her bags, while other creatures, once attached to her branch, scattered about. There was a terrific squawking and more pounding to the ground, as her parents and sisters and brothers, frantic with concern for her, also pulled themselves out of the tree and leaped down to help.

"My poor darling! Are you all right?" shouted her mother. "Hold on! We'll carry you back up," her father cried. Her brothers and sisters, standing uncertainly on their own feet, crowded around.

Little Green looked about. Without her connection to the tree, she felt very brave and free. "I'm fine," she said, and ordered the king's helpers to tear off a few more branches and build her an artificial tree, her own shelter. The servants were afraid at first, but she had learned to give orders.

Now to everyone's amazement, as Little Green's family looked up into the remains of the tree that had always been their home, everything began to change. The fish detached from the roots and flopped into the nearby stream. Snakes turned and twisted their way downward. Branches bent. Birds flew off, dogs tumbled, cats clawed their way down. The tree not only emptied, it shriveled before their eyes. No one could go back.

Green was not concerned. She had her reputation. She announced that she was now to be addressed as Lady Green, voice of the Speaking Tree. The King's men replaced her temporary shelter with a new one—a vast storeroom on stilts, with one high window. The front of the building looked like the old Speaking Tree, with gold and silver worked into twisting branches and leaves. From her magnificent window she listened to petitioners and answered questions as her family had done before. Even as she grew weary of this, tired of being asked to solve problems that people should be able to solve for themselves, she gathered payments that filled her storeroom.

At night, after her questioners had left, Lady Green walked alone, holding bolts of silk cloth and carved jade and pearl-encrusted drinking bowls to the moonlight to admire them. One such evening, standing by her window, she heard sounds that tugged at her heart. It was singing. Voices flowed into each other like some sustaining liquid. She leaned out and noticed that her relatives had built small houses near each other. Some distance away, a little cluster of homes with pathways between made her think of the branches of the old Speaking Tree. She'd hardly paid attention to the village before. It was no competition for business, making no claims of authority. Now, hearing the soft drums and cymbals and harp strings like wind through branches, listening to the sighing voices of her relatives, Green felt as though she were connected by some invisible line to the village.

Just then a little girl, barefoot, in a rag of a dress, came running past Lady Green's window toward the village, with a bleating brown and white kid goat behind her. "Child, you down there," Lady Green called out in her most bossy voice. "Stop." The girl stopped, uncertain. Lady Green called again, a cruel edge in her voice. "Tell me, how can you be happy?"

As the child stood wiggling her toes in the dirt, the goat butted her. The girl laughed and started again toward the cluster of houses. "Nana wants to be home and so do I," she called out and ran again.

Next morning, Lady Green sent a message to the village. She had builders add a lower hall to her house, and she invited her relatives to come for dinner. Her mother, sisters, and cousins hurried over to help. Lady Green's feast was followed by others. Her dinners became famous, not just for the food, but also for the music, known everywhere as songs from the Speaking Tree.

## COMMENTARY

In notes for *The Book of the Thousand Nights and a Night*, Richard F. Burton observes that Mohammed got his idea for a tree of paradise, one that provides for all needs, from the Hebrews, who in turn got the notion from the Persians. One such tree, Huluppu-tree, is the center of the universe in the Sumerian story of Gilgamesh. My inspiration for this story was an illustration on the cover of a study of Indian culture called *The Speaking Tree*, by Richard Lannoy.

According to Norse legend, a great ash tree, Yggdrasill, stands at the center of the universe. It connects the land of the gods to earth, our everyday Midgard, as its roots reach down to a dark underworld where a serpent gnaws at the roots of the cosmos. Heroes killed in battle live in high branches in Valhalla; a falcon, Odin's goat, four enormous stags, and many other creatures live on this tree. In fact, we all do.

Hindu mystics refer to the human body as an inverted tree, with the kundalini, snake, in our loins, as we send our energies like thread-roots from the top of our heads to the heavens. Divine nourishment flows back, even as we vacillate between attention to the heavens and succumbing to the influence of the snake.

Coming a bit closer to my interpretation is an Arab tale, "The Maidens of the Tree of Raranj and Taranj," where a prince finds inside the fruits of a giant tree, beautiful maidens fit to be wife of a king. Even when transformed into a dove by an evil djinn, pearls and corals fall from the eyes of one such princess when she weeps. In Siberian traditions, shamans still climb a tree to receive inspiration. There's a reference to an army of trees in Shakespeare's MacBeth, which may have its source in Celtic poetry. The great leader Gwydion, needing an army, used a magical charm to turn trees into soldiers. I've used a secular event to disperse the tree's occupants.

## STORY OUTLINE

- Little Green speaks to petitioners as the voice of wisdom of Speaking Tree.
- When branches are overloaded with gifts, Speaking Tree breaks, disintegrates.
- Lady Green continues as the voice of the Tree, ignoring her tree relatives.
- Lady Green tires of her role as prophet; she recognizes what she has lost.

- Lady Green invites her family back; their celebrations become famous as songs from the Speaking Tree.

## PERFORMANCE SUGGESTIONS

This story is especially suited to being performed on playground climbing equipment. Begin with mask or headband costumes. Attach ears and suspend beaks so that they don't get in the way of the action. For costumes, prepare cloth or cardboard neckbands with stapled, taped, or sewn-on leaves. A green paper roll is dandy, but lacking that, newsprint, even old newspapers will suffice for a one-time enactment. Participants can design their own leaves with green tempera paint, cutting them out and attaching the leaves to a neckband. (Treat the leaves as a cloak, leaving the front of the body open for movement.)

Indoors, a combination of chairs and tables will work to establish a variety of levels for the tree. A platform of any height will work too. Use masking tape to mark out roots, trunk, and branches. Carpet squares connected by masking tape work well too.

It's interesting to form a kind of procession to start the performance. Have fish and snakes and lizards and then everyone else crawl silently into place, freeze as a curled-up bud, then open like a flower and gradually take the character role. Agree on some action that establishes the cooperative relationship between the creatures of the tree. They could share the coming of a storm, perhaps, and all draw back into buds until a shower passes. Have some student-constructed soundmakers, shakers and drums especially, as sounds to accompany the destruction of the tree. Everyone can shake in place. Practicing this is reason enough to perform the show. Remember that the creatures don't prey upon each other or compete for territory until they come off the tree. This is worth discussing and rehearsing before performance; who eats whom?

Preliminary exercises pantomiming animal behaviors will also provide more thoughtful performance choices. Because the tree is a metaphor for the cosmos, it's an opportunity for exercises personifying nature. Props help. Hand out pieces of corrugated cardboard to each participant. Each person selects some aspect of nature to speak for: cloud, wind, rainstorm, snow, river, lightning, thunder, as well as trees and mountain crags. Use a conventional starter such as the Invitation: "Come fly with me; I am a cumulus cloud rising and gathering moisture as I go."

Expand on the kinds of questions visitors bring to the tree and to Lady Green. Use fortune-telling games or practices for ideas. Organize this to suggest how Lady Green could grow tired of having others depend upon her for advice they could give themselves.

# GOOD FROM BAD

✳

Once not so long ago, two brothers lived on the edge of the desert with their mother in a cozy trailer home. Working all day every day, the mother didn't earn much money, and so she asked the boys to gather firewood for the stove when they came home from school each afternoon.

There isn't much firewood on the desert, as you probably know, and so this task took quite a bit of time. The older brother, Spitzer, would rather sit on the couch and watch afternoon cartoons, to tell the truth.He was also bossy (not to mention the fact that he held on to the channel-changer), so the younger brother, Fitzer, often put on a backpack and went out looking for sticks alone.

Late one afternoon, as the sun was starting to set, Fitzer sat on a large rock to rest before starting back. He hadn't had much luck. Leaning his head against the stone, he heard the oddest "knockety-knock." Was it the stomping of little feet? Was it coming out of the stone? When he looked around, he couldn't see anything except . . . a golden necklace creeping across the ground all by itself!

As it circled around and then came closer, Fitzer could see that it wasn't a necklace after all, but a line of golden ants, marching and singing a song in tiny voices.

Fitzer put his ear to the ground and listened. The ants were moving in a kind of slow dance, singing these words, over and over: "Monday, Tuesday, Monday, Tuesday, Monday, Tuesday, Wednesday." Then they paused, as if they were trying to remember something, and started the same words over.

Fitzer was a clever child as well as a helpful one, and so he couldn't help himself for what he did next. He started to sing, softly, "Thursday, Friday, Thursday, Friday, Saturday, and Sunday!"

The ants were very excited about this, as you can imagine. They started talking at once, milling around in a close circle. Then one of the ants spoke to Fitzer. "Kind sir, you know the words to the song we have forgotten. Will you do us the honor of coming into our house and teaching us?"

The moment Fitzer agreed, the rock he had been sitting upon cracked wide open to reveal a cave inside. Fitzer walked with the ants through the rock doorway into a big hall. Now, mysteriously, the ants were larger. Fitzer and the ants formed a big circle and danced and sang the whole song together. If you think you know it, you can sing it with me. Ready? Monday, Tuesday, Monday, Tuesday, Monday, Tuesday, Wednesday! Thursday, Friday, Thursday, Friday, Saturday, and Sunday!

As they sang the song, their feet moved faster and faster until Fitzer said it was time for him to go home because he still had to find more firewood. No sooner had he spoken these words than he found himself back on the surface of the earth, next to the big rock, wearing his backpack. Only now, his backpack was heavy. In fact, it was very heavy.

Fitzer walked back to the trailer home as fast as he could and took off his backpack. "The ants gave me firewood," he announced to his astonished brother, and he emptied out his pack, only to find not firewood at all but piles and piles of golden coins.

"Where did you get that?" demanded Spitzer, not a bit pleased by his brother's good fortune.

"I got it from the ants inside the sitting rock," said Fitzer, and he started to explain, but before he could tell it all, his brother ran out the door with a flashlight and his own backpack.

Spitzer ran up to the rock and shined his light all around, impatiently. He saw nothing special at all. Irritated, Spitzer picked up a stick and pounded on the rock, shouting, "Come out, ants, wherever you are."

And out of the rocks, like a gently bouncing golden necklace, came the ants, in a straight line, singing happily, "Monday, Tuesday. . . ."

Before they could finish their song, Spitzer interrupted them, saying, "Put money in my pack, or I'll step on your back!" Before you could say "swat," the ants disappeared, and Spitzer's backpack was very heavy. Spitzer rushed home, poured out the contents on the living room floor, and what do you suppose he found? Firewood.

### COMMENTARY

This is a variation of "The Two Hunchbacks," an Irish tale retold in *Parabola* by Paul Jordan-Smith. I placed this story, found in variants all over the world, on the edge of a city much like my own. I also softened the fate of the selfish brother, turning what is an enormous hump in the Irish version into a backpack. Rather than bending him down so low his nose becomes a plow, as the

Irish do, I gave him something useful to donate to the fire. And in honor of young audiences, I added a song they can sing with the storyteller.

## STORY OUTLINE

- Spitzer watches television, while Fitzer hunts for firewood.
- Fitzer rests, hears ants, and finishes the song of the days of the week.
- Fitzer teaches the song in the magic cave and is rewarded with coins.
- Fitzer shows the coins to his brother, who looks for the ants.
- Spitzer demands money from the ants, but doesn't offer anything.
- Spitzer gets—firewood.

## PERFORMANCE SUGGESTIONS

This is a favorite to act out. Sometimes the ants are elves and the related activity is making elf hats as well as cutting gold "coins" and locating a pile of sticks. Squares of cloth tied to a stick make a good backpack substitute. A standard conference table makes a good cave for the ants/elves, particularly with a cloth thrown over it. A pillow on the floor takes the place of the resting rock. The dance should be done out in the open, of course! Adjustments like this pass without mention when your performers are too young to be literal minded. When it's time to put the surprise in the packs, have two or more ants/elves take it from Fitzer or Spitzer, go out of sight, and load it up. This causes great anticipation and delight among four-year-olds—the act of filling the pack is pleasurable for this age too. Don't worry about quality control. It's more important that the coins have been manufactured by participants, and paper sticks cut by five-year-olds are just right. For elf hats, let the children design their own or start with a circle cut from paper, decorate it freely, slash it to the center, and overlap the cut edges to make a conical shape to fit. Add yarn ties to keep it on and a feather for panache.

## BETTER RUDE THAN SORRY

✳

That's what my grandmother says, "Better rude than sorry," and she has a story to prove it. It's a pity Grandmother isn't here to tell it, for she is another Slovak with snapping eyes, and it could almost be her story, except the Rude she means is a girl who lived a time ago, a girl called Rude the Orphan and also Rude the Wolf Child.

If you saw Rude standing in front of you, clad all in sheepskin, you would wonder why she wasn't called Rude the Sheep. Well, look closer. A wolf is carved into her belt buckle, and another wolf is carved on her walking stick. She carved them herself, her back to the wind while she kept an eye on the sheep. But I'm getting ahead of my story.

I'll start with two sisters and one handsome, careless man they both loved. Only a few weeks after the quiet older sister married the young man, she disappeared. Oh, and that left some suspicion on the shoulders of the younger sister everyone called Katz, born Katrina, who was rumored, only rumored, I'm telling you, to have the powers of a witch. Could Katz turn herself into a cat when it suited her? Hmm, you'll have to decide for yourself.

Well, that young groom grieved when his wife couldn't be found, but what could people say when he went ahead and married the younger sister, gave up his former reckless ways, and settled down? The new pair looked happy enough. All that was left to bother the young husband as he watched over his little flock of sheep was a wolf.

It was not an ordinary wolf, either. It was a big-eyed female, sleek and quick, who seemed more determined to get his attention than to attack the sheep. Everywhere he went, that wolf was beside him, trotting along with a curious, inquiring look. It made Katz nervous for her husband's safety, and she got herself a gun.

One winter morning there was a knock on the door, which the husband answered. Imagine his surprise to see, at his feet, a newborn baby, naked and bawling—and only a few feet away, the wolf! He called out to Katz, and then had an awful thought just as Katz picked up her gun. "No, no!" was all he said before Katz fired her weapon. He fell silent; silent, I'm sorry to report, for the rest of his life. He looked at Katz hauling off the wolf carcass; he picked up the babe, and he never spoke another word.

I don't know if this child ever had a regular name because as far back as anyone could remember, she spoke her mind, plainly and loudly, and so everyone called her Rude. The husband looked after her, what looking she got. You can probably picture how well this ungrateful orphan got along with Katz.

It isn't too surprising that in a few short years, Katz pushed the child out and set her guarding sheep, even sleeping in the sheep shed at night. "No room in the house," said Katz sharply, and true enough Katz had two small sons sleeping in the corner. The husband added a few boards to the shed, and Rude chinked up the cracks with straw herself and seemed to get along.

Rude had a way about her, a fearless way that made sheep feel safe. Neither wolves howling in the distant fields, nor a whining, moaning wind that always wound around the sheep shed seemed to bother her. "I'd rather have a wolf in front of me than a cat behind me," said Rude, sharp-tongued as always. She spun her own yarn on a spindle as she walked, she stitched up caps and boots of sheepskin, and she kept a stout stick beside her to ward off wild animals and such.

Katz might have booted her down the road except for one peculiarity. No matter how hard everyone in this family worked—and everyone worked—only the sheep seemed to thrive. Once, only once, after a particularly bad set-to, Katz sent Rude to board with a neighbor. And wouldn't you know it, the family sheep came down with something, the few lambs born that spring were sickly, and the wolves got the rest of Katz's yearlings. Katz's boys complained about the cold. All along, the neighbor's animals watched over by Rude looked fat and healthy. Katz called her back.

But it didn't last. Katz's husband, the one person who looked kindly on Rude, died of a fever. "Meaned to death," said Rude, which didn't help. One dark night soon after, with only a sliver of moon for light, Katz sent one of her sons to the sheep shed for Rude. Katz handed her a pail and a candle and said, "The well is dry. Go to the lake for water."

The lake, as everyone knew, was guarded at night by water nymphs, and who knows how many demons and spirits of the dead lingered in the forest on the way! Some children would take a beating instead, but Rude took the pail and set off, even leaving the stub of a candle behind. While she was still in sight of the house, she did take one precaution. She picked a straw from her clothes and dropped it into the pail as a friendly sign for any spirits who wanted a drink.

Rude knew this country better than anyone, at least in the daylight, and so it isn't surprising that she found the lake and filled her pail without trouble—taking care, I'll remind you, to save the straw that is necessary in order for dead souls to drink from a pail. It was on her way back, in the darkest part of the forest, that she saw a flickering light. She was so distracted by the light that she lost the path and, what's worse, found herself walking right up to the keeper of the light—a tall, pale woman in a long, white gown, simply standing there in the forest.

I said pale. Not just pale. This woman was almost transparent. With the light of the candle she was holding, you'd swear you could see through her.

"May I have a drink?" the woman inquired politely. "Have some," said Rude, for once in her life turning her eyes so that she wouldn't have to see if the woman used the straw. "You're very kind," said the woman, handing back the pail.

"I'm not," said the girl, taking the pail. "Everyone calls me Rude."

"A hard name," said the woman.

"I'm not likable," said Rude. "Even my mother left me to be eaten by a wolf."

"That wolf was your mother," said the woman mildly. "Your mother was under an enchantment."

"And my father?" Rude said, trying to absorb this information.

"Your father was the silent one, the one who left you bread and soup in the sheep shed."

"And Katz?"

"She cast the spell. And she had to kill the wolf before her husband spoke out in pity and turned the poor creature back into her sister."

"Thank you for these terrible words," said Rude, and she

walked back to the house. She handed Katz the pail of water without a word, first pouring a bit in a dish, setting the dish and the stick of straw on the windowsill to feed any wandering souls seeking satisfaction. Then she walked back to the sheep shed.

Nobody could explain what happened next. Certainly Katz would not touch the dish with the water and straw, and people swore that a wolf of a wind moved from sheep shed to house and set up a dreadful racket every night, so disturbing that it wasn't long before Katz herself was sick and died of the same fever that took her husband.

Even before Rude and the boys buried Katz, Rude moved herself into the house. As the boys watched, Rude tore off a plank from the roof to let out Katz's restless soul. Then she began cleaning, cleaning everything and everywhere. She scrubbed the house, floor to ceiling, and swept the thrashing floor and the animal stalls. She cooked peas and barley, millet porridge, and flour cakes and honey, all the foods needed to honor the dead and prepare their souls for the long journey to rest. She set the food aside.

Rude led the procession to bury Katz, then heated water for the tub and ordered everyone to bathe, herself included. While the boys took turns in the wood tub, Rude set out their best clothes. Quietly, the boys assembled at the dinner table, around the feast set before them. Rude took a small portion of each dish and placed it on a saucer that she set on the windowsill. She looked out the window. "Katz, go get your reward," she said, and went back to the table.

Rude replaced the saucer with a new one and lit a candle. She held it by the window. "Come, restless Spirit," she called out, and blew out the candle.

Rude and the boys sat in the dark, listening to the groaning wind. Finally Rude lit the candle again, and they ate. When they had eaten all they could, Rude stood up and lifted her hands.

"Mother," she cried out, "I never knew you. I don't know if you were a good person or a bad one. You gave me a sturdy body and a stout tongue. May your soul now fly to heaven in peace."

The wind had died down. The boys helped Rude take the leftovers to the cemetery, where they set the food in the family plot for wandering souls and beggars. On the way back home, one of the boys started crying. "It's all right," said Rude, glancing at him, handing off her kerchief. "Cry. Better to howl while you are alive."

## COMMENTARY

For this story, several of the beliefs of the Slovakian people were brought together (taken primarily from *Celtic / Slavic,* by John A. MacCulloch, volume three of *The Mythology of All Races*). When I showed this story to a Croatian friend of mine, she said the events were "within my Grandmother's realm of the possible. She told us stories of maidens who responded to spirits and were never seen again." In this culture, water nymphs were children or young women who died without Christian burials; Rude's attendance to proprieties saved Katz's soul, as well as her mother's. Inside the story I explain events and spirits no more than they would have been explained to Rude herself; other storytellers may prefer to add interpretations.

This story was written at a time of great conflict in Serbia and Croatia, the land of people who still fear (and continue) the revenge of the dead. I wanted to suggest the possibility of forgiveness and healing.

## Story Outline

- Two sisters love one man; the older one marries him.
- Soon after marrying, the older sister disappears.
- The younger sister, Katz, then marries the man; they seem happy.
- A wolf follows as the man tends his sheep.
- A baby is left at their door; Katz kills the nearby wolf; the husband stops speaking.
- Katz and her husband look after the baby and call her Rude.
- Katz sends the young Rude to watch the sheep and live in the sheep shed.
- The husband dies; Rude is sent to a lake to fetch water at night.
- Rude gives a drink to a pale woman in the forest and learns her mother's story.
- Rude leaves food and drink for her mother's spirit; Katz dies.
- Rude buries Katz with respect and holds a ritual to release her mother's soul.

## Performance Suggestions

This story has as much background as foreground and divides neatly between spirit worlds, acted out in dance/pantomime and narrated interaction. Pantomime the two sisters flirting with the young man, his choosing the eldest and walking off with her, her disappearance, his search for her, then finding the younger sister, walking off, and gradually cheering up. Then he walks off with his shepherd staff as the wolf lurks. Finish this with Katz shooting the wolf and the man lifting up the baby.

Perform the rest with dialogue, using spirits (expanding the number if you like) to continuously move through the action unseen until the ritual dinner. A budding choreographer could turn the entire story into a dance.

A good exercise to accompany this story is to assign partners, one saying the things we say to be polite, the other acting out true feelings. Pair up partners into sets of four people, have them come up with a conflict situation in which the speakers are polite but the spirits express honest feelings.

# WATER OF LIFE

✳

Once upon a time, when wishes still came true, three orphans had to make their way in the world. They hadn't a nickel or a crumb of bread or a pallet to sleep on in the beginning, but they had something else. Each one of them had a gift. The oldest, Ben, was as strong as Samson and could work all day without growing tired. The next oldest, Tim, was more clever than you can imagine. Why, he could look at a thing—a clock even—turn it over in his hands, say "Mmm," and figure out how to make it. The youngest, their sister Claire, had such tender and caring ways that she could melt a heart or make carrots grow out of a rock.

You won't be surprised to learn, then, that the three orphans managed to feed and clothe themselves by working for neighbors. In fact, they weren't much older than you are when they bought their own farm and built one of the finest stone houses in the countryside. Everyone who had helped them along the way now came to congratulate them and offer suggestions to the orphans.

"Handsome building. Kinda bare out here, though," said one. "Made my shoes muddy." Right after he left, Claire began planting shrubs and flowers and trees, while her brothers built pathways and a fountain.

Now more people came to admire the garden, and Claire took them on a tour of the stone house. "It feels cold in here," remarked one woman. "Probably all those empty walls. You need hangings, paintings, swords and armor, handsome stuff like that." The orphans looked at each other and nodded. No sooner had the visitors gone than Tim was out looking at metalwork in town. Back home he started hammering and forging whatnots, while Claire set up a loom and learned to weave.

While the orphans worked, more people gathered to watch, strangers as well as friends. One looked at the fancy tin and silverwork coming out of Tim's workshop and said, "I'd put up a fence if I were you. A high, strong fence with points at the top." Tim agreed, and started to think about ironwork for the gate. Ben grumbled and complained, but he hauled in load after load of stone for the wall.

"I know what you really need," said a peddler passing through, looking beyond the gate of the new fence to the fountain, "What you really need is the water of life."

The water of life! More precious than jewels or castles or gold! When the orphans asked around, they learned that many people had heard of it, but nobody had actually found it. Rumors were that it could be found at the very top of a distant mountain. Many were said to have gone in search of it there, but none had returned.

Ben could think of nothing else. He packed a rucksack, took a sack of food from Claire, and started up the path to the mountain.

The path became narrower and more difficult the higher he went. Pebbles were replaced by stones that waited without warning on the many twists and turns. But Ben was strong and proud of it. He rehearsed the warnings he'd heard. "You'll think you're hearing voices," the peddler had said. "Don't turn around, whatever you do. Don't look back."

After many hours Ben was high above the tree line. All he could see beside and ahead of him were boulders the size of a man, with a little stream trickling through. He picked up a smaller stone to defend himself and kept his eyes on the path. Then his foot hit a stone and a voice cried out, "Watch it, Clumsy!"

Where did the voice come from? He couldn't look! Ben kept walking, staring straight ahead, hands clenched on rocks, and he stumbled again. "Can't you be careful, Stupid?" said someone loudly. And then he heard another voice, and still another, a whole chorus of voices around him, so many that he spun around ready to throw something—and he turned to stone himself.

Days passed with no word from Ben. Tim could wait no longer. He packed a bit of food and a pitcher he'd made of hammered copper, and he started up the path his brother had taken. At first he ran, then trotted, then walked more and more slowly as trees thinned out and all he could see was stone, stone everywhere. He was tired, and he'd eaten all his food. What he wanted more than anything was to find his brother and leave this place. He no longer cared if he found the water of life. That's what he was thinking when he thought he heard a voice.

"He's quitting, he's quitting," it said. Tim shuddered, then muttered to himself, "If Ben were here, . . . "

"He's here! He's here!" a chorus of voices rose out of the rocks.

"He is not!" Tim shouted without turning his head. "He is, he is," mocked the voices in the rocks.

"Don't listen!" cried out one voice that sounded familiar. Tim forgot everything he'd been warned about. "Ben?" he called out, turning to the last voice—and he too turned to stone.

Claire had never been this alone in her life. Even after her parents died, she had had her brothers for comfort and help. She waited, and then she waited a few more days before she put on her warmest cloak, put a cork in a silver bottle Tim had made for her, and started toward the path. Then she remembered the warnings they had been given. She had always relied upon her brothers before this. "I don't know if I'm strong enough to resist," she thought, and she went back to stuff her ears with cotton wool.

The voices started as soon as Claire reached the stones. She heard someone laughing and saying something that sounded like "Alone, alone, poor thing, alone!" She kept walking. At the very top of the mountain, she found a tiny spring and filled her bottle with water.

On the way back down, Claire hurried to get away from the voices. A few drops of water clinging to her bottle fell on one of the stones at her feet, and before she could step over it, the stone turned into one of the villagers who had disappeared many years before. He jumped up, nodded to her, picked up a rusty pail, and disappeared up the path. Claire carefully poured a drop on another rock, and it too came to life. Now she walked down the path putting droplets on rocks and hoping to find her brothers until her last two drops of precious water brought Tim and Ben to their feet.

The three orphans started joyfully up the path for more water, only to be met by the people Claire had brought back to life. "It's gone, all gone," the last few people were crying out angrily. "The water is all gone."

But Claire and Tim and Ben were ready to go back to their farm and the house they had built themselves. Each evening for many years after, they sat down by their fountain, talked about the next day's work, gave thanks for the gifts they had, and had a drink of the ordinary water of life.

## COMMENTARY

This widely told story has vengeful older siblings contesting for the water of life in some versions, working together in others. Sometimes the water is the fountain of youth; in others its magical properties are never explained. The living stones come out of a workshop conducted by the great storyteller/teacher Dorothy Heathcote. She had a group of handicapped children who called themselves the Talking Stones. My stones are more psychological, people paralyzed by fear and envy, set free by the innocent goodness of Claire. I've also added a message for children about their right to follow their own inclinations and find happiness without seeking someone else's idea of a magical potion.

I first wrote this as a one-act play and later adapted it as a tale to tell.

## STORY OUTLINE

- Three orphans work for their neighbors and build their own stone house.
- The orphans follow everyone's advice for gardens, the house, and the wall.
- Ben sets out to find the water of life.
- Ben hears voices calling him stupid, turns, and becomes stone.
- Tim sets out when Ben doesn't return.
- Tim hears voices reminding him he's scared; he turns when he hears Ben's voice and turns to stone.

- Claire stuffs her ears with cotton and gets all the way to the top.
- Claire brings one stone to life by accident, then frees other stones.
- While Claire seeks her brothers, others take the water of life.
- Claire finds and releases Ben and Tim.
- The orphans return to appreciate their home, their own advice, and ordinary water.

## PERFORMANCE SUGGESTIONS

The simplest performance of this story requires a small bowl or another way to mark the spring of water on one side of the staging area (a drawing of mountains in the distance makes a good backdrop), with a bench plus chair for the stone house of the orphans on the other side. Expand the struggles of the children to suit the improvising skills of your participants; those who are visitors later can first be neighbors who hire the labor of the children.

You can add a ceremonial aspect by having each visitor or group of visitors who leaves the stone house start toward the spring, then silently crouch down and turn to stone, thus forming the path with their bodies. The chanting of the stones can be eery and powerful—extend it for extra drama.

# SHAYDOOLA

✳

Once there was a kind young man who loved his wife and son but was tired of working in the fields all day. How much nicer it would be to sit in the shade! He thought, "If Allah our God would make us rich, I could play with my son and eat fine food without all this effort." He announced to his wife, "Good news! I am going in search of God to ask him to make our lives easier."

And that is why Shaydoola's wife rose very early the next morning to pack food for her husband's journey before she and her son went out in the field to work.

The first creature Shaydoola met on the path to God was a gray, bony, heap of a wolf by the side of the road. As Shaydoola passed by, she lifted her shaggy head and cried out hoarsely, "Where are you going?"

"I go to ask God to make me rich," said Shaydoola.

"Please," said the wolf, "tell Allah about this great pain in my stomach. Ask him why my stomach hurts and why I am so weak. Tell him my children will die if I cannot hunt."

"I will, and may God take pity," Shaydoola said, and he continued on his way.

Next Shaydoola passed under a big apple tree. When he stopped to look for apples, the tree called to him. "Where are you going, traveler?"

"I go to speak to God, to ask him to make me rich," said Shaydoola.

"Please speak to Allah for me also," said the tree. "For years now, I have borne no apples. I yearn to make the fruit that I believe God intended me to produce for travelers like yourself."

"I will do that," said Shaydoola. "I would have liked an apple." And he passed on.

Now Shaydoola came to a large river. As he was swimming across, the water turned to giant waves and then the waves parted as a huge fish swam up. Shaydoola was more than a little afraid until the fish began speaking. It coughed as it spoke, saying, "Please ask Allah what is stuck in my throat and choking me. I can no longer guide travelers across."

"Poor fish! Indeed I will," said Shaydoola as he swam away as fast as he could.

At last Shaydoola climbed out of the river and began walking again. He walked and walked until his clothes were dry. In the distance he could see a light against the sky and an enormous walled garden—the garden he had heard about. Inside the garden, as he approached cautiously, Shaydoola could see flames leaping up to the heavens. He had found the garden of God! Inside, surrounded by the most beautiful roses, he saw a bush in flame with a fierce orange fire. He had never been so afraid in his life and fell to his knees.

A voice came out of the flame. "Shaydoola! What do you wish?"

Shaydoola was so frightened that he gave the requests of the others first. "Oh please, great Allah, the wolf wishes to know why she is weak and has a great pain in her stomach, the tree wishes to know why she cannot bear apples, and the great fish in the river wishes to know why he is choking—and I would like to be rich, oh Great God."

The voice spoke again. "The fish has a precious stone stuck in his throat. Whoever reaches in and removes the stone will cure the cough. The tree has a treasure chest entangled in her roots. When the chest is dug out, the tree will again bear fruit. The wolf need only eat a stupid, lazy man."

"Bu-but what about me, oh, Great Allah?" asked Shaydoola piteously.

"Go home, Shaydoola, and all will be as it should be," said the voice in the flames.

With joy in his heart, Shaydoola started for home. He swam eagerly through the river and was not even afraid when the enormous fish swam up. "What did Allah say for me?" it coughed. "You only need somebody to reach way down, ugh, in there, to pull out the precious stone stuck in your throat. Then you will be fine," said Shaydoola as he swam hurriedly by.

Next Shaydoola skipped happily past the apple tree. Without pausing, he looked up to the tree and called out, "All you need to do is find somebody to dig down through all this dirt to remove the treasure chest stuck in your roots. Then you will grow apples aplenty again."

Finally, Shaydoola came to the miserable wolf at the side of the road. The wolf lifted its head, and Shaydoola called out, "Oh wolf, Allah gave me your cure. You only need to eat a lazy, stupid person, and your pain will end."

At that, the wolf leaped with her last remaining strength and devoured Shaydoola. And then, as Allah had said, all was as it should be.

## Commentary

Eastern European tales can reflect a stern sense of justice, which I've tried to honor while maintaining Shaydoola's basic likability. My source is an Azerbaijani tale found in *Eurasian Folk and Fairy Tales*, translated by I. F. Bulatkin.

## Story Outline

- Shaydoola is tired of working.
- Shaydoola leaves his wife and son to do the work and journeys to ask God to make him rich.
- Shaydoola meets a wolf with stomach pain and promises to ask God about it.
- Shaydoola meets a tree that doesn't produce apples and promises to ask God.
- Shaydoola crosses a river, meets a fish with something in its throat, and promises to ask God.
- Shaydoola finds Allah and gets the answers: the fish has a jewel in its throat, the tree has treasure in its roots, and the wolf needs to eat a foolish, lazy man.
- Shaydoola heads back for home, passes the fish, tree, and wolf, but doesn't help them; the wolf eats him.

## Performance Suggestions

This is a good story for puppet theater. Puppets turn the story into farce without diminishing the moral or forcing any young actor to be theatrically consumed by a wolf. (After age seven, of course, this is great fun.) If you can find examples of jointed Turkish puppets in your library, they will make excellent models or displays, since this part of the world has saved the medieval tradition of puppetry most purely. Another approach is to have the children each draw a character, then cut them apart and add extensions to arms and legs at the shoulder and hip (use models of jointed paper puppets to guide you). Photocopy the puppet parts, color the photocopies, cut out and mount them on heavy paper, and join the limbs with paper fasteners.

As an alternative, you could use children's drawings as they are, turning each into an upside-down pocket by cutting them out, leaving a margin around the edge, cutting a facing piece of paper for the back, then gluing up the margins on three sides. Pencils or tongue depressors can be inserted to maneuver the puppets; a change of characters can be achieved by mounting the new character on the same tongue depressor. If you have an abundance of tongue depressors or similar sticks, glue the reinforced cutouts directly to the stick.

For other ideas, see pages 244–247.

## OF COURSE

✳

The Han people of China tell of a landowner with a temper so hot that the people who worked on his land called him Pepper-Peel. Everyone hired by Pepper-Peel worked from early morning until dark, lifting, carrying, and digging as they planted and harvested the crops that made the old Pepper-Peel rich.

Only one person brought them any happiness. This was Zhao Da, a gentle man who lived in a hut on the banks of a river far from the large house of Pepper-Peel. Despite his own labors and advancing age, Zhao Da had a kind word for everyone as he passed them carrying a load of straw on his bent old back.

What was most remarkable about Zhao Da, though, was his gift with clay. At night, by the light of a single candle as he sat in conversation with his neighbors, Zhao Da could turn a ball of clay into a whistle. Not an ordinary whistle, either, but a whistle that looked exactly like the bird whose song it mimicked. These whistles he did not save or sell in the village markets, but gave freely to the children who worked on Pepper-Peel's estate, and so you could hear happy whistlers in every direction when you passed one of Pepper-Peel's fields.

Pepper-Peel looked darkly on this frivolity and was always ready to seize the whistle of a child who seemed to be playing instead of working at a task. There was no time on these lands for a song after dinner or even such comforts as a cleared path between fields and barn.

It isn't surprising, then, that one day as Zhao Da was carrying an especially large load of straw across a littered path, the old man stumbled and fell. He arose in pain, and it was clear he would not be able to work for some time.

Pepper-Peel fell into a rage and ordered Zhao Da off the estate, even though there was no other use for Zhao Da's little hut or the clay bank of the river. Sadly, leaning on a stick for a crutch, Zhao Da struggled into a nearby village to find a place to live and a kindly soul to feed him until he was well enough to work.

That evening the people gathered and agreed they must work together to teach Pepper-Peel a lesson. For a year, Zhao Da lived quietly in the village. One woman shared her allowance of rice; another brought vegetables from a small garden. Always, someone carried home a pocketful of clay from the riverbank. With leisure at last, Zhao Da helped care for the family garden plots and spent many hours making the most beautiful whistles anyone had ever seen.

On market day, the neighbors of Zhao Da included these whistles in the baskets of food they sold in a nearby town. With the money from selling the whistles, they bought articles that were part of their plan. Zhao Da was walking a little better each day. It was time to teach old Pepper-Peel a lesson! The people bought a set of fine silk clothes for Zhao Da and a magnificent parrot, which they had time to teach to say only one thing: "Of course!"

One year to the day after Zhao Da's accident, a group of the workers sneaked back to Pepper-Peel's estates late at night. They hid a packet of something under a rock on a hillside and dropped something else in a shallow part of the fish pond. Finally they lowered a small pot into the well.

Early next morning Zhao Da put on his silk pants and jacket, set the parrot on his shoulder, and walked out to the country home of Pepper-Peel. All the workers knew what would happen next. They were watching, covering their mouths to keep from laughing, as Zhao Da knocked on Pepper-Peel's door.

"Good morning, kind landlord," Zhao Da began when Pepper-Peel answered his knock. "I came by to say that I hold no hard feelings about leaving your farms. In fact, this was the beginning of my good luck. I thank you." Zhao Da bowed as if to go, but Pepper-Peel, always looking for new ways to get rich, stopped him.

"Where have you been all this time? Whose clothes are you wearing?" Pepper-Peel demanded. Little by little, as if he were reluctant to brag of his good fortune, Zhao Da told the story he had hatched up with his friends.

"I am doing wonderfully well thanks to the goddess and my parrot," Zhao Da said. He told Pepper-Peel that he had made a clay whistle in the shape of a parrot, which so pleased a goddess that she brought the parrot to life. "It is a magic parrot," said Zhao Da, proudly. "My Pretty Polly finds treasure for me."

Pepper-Peel scoffed at the story, as everyone expected. "I don't mind proving it to you," said Zhao Da modestly. With Pepper-Peel and a goodly crowd following behind him, Zhao Da walked over to the hillside and pointed to a particular rock.

"Pretty Polly, is there a string of cash under that rock?"

"Of course!" said Polly. Pepper-Peel pushed away the rock and there, to his surprise, was a string of brass coins. Zhao Da smiled happily and made no effort to retrieve the coins. Instead he strolled a little farther to the pond.

"Pretty Polly, is there silver in this pond?"

"Of course!" said Polly. Pepper-Peel thrust his hand into the place where Zhao had pointed, and amid the mud he pulled up a silver coin.

Zhao did not look at all surprised. He walked on, and by now all the farm workers were following as Zhao reached the well.

"Pretty Polly, is there gold in this well?"

"Of course!" said Polly. No sooner had the words been uttered than Pepper-Peel, unable to control himself, climbed down the sides of the well and came up triumphantly with a small pot of golden coins. If he hadn't been so excited, he probably would have bit into the coin and discovered that the gold paint was very thin indeed, but instead he shoved the pot into his sash and said, rather grandly, that he would be happy to honor Zhao with a banquet that evening.

Word spread quickly and all Pepper-Peel's family and important friends assembled for the big meal. This was what Pepper-Peel wanted; he wanted plenty of witnesses for the moment when he had filled Zhao with food and strong drink. The silly peasant would not be able to resist when Pepper-Peel offered to buy the parrot.

The banquet was a great success. Even the estate workers were invited. After many toasts and courses of good food, Pepper-Peel lifted his glass and called for quiet. "I am willing to buy Zhao's parrot for a very good price. After all, Zhao, if one of your whistles pleased the gods, surely you can make another and the gods will bless you again."

Zhao agreed. "I am honored, my former master, by your offer. All I ask is to own the hut and garden and clay bank that was my home so many years." Pepper-Peel quickly called for paper and brush and both signed the agreement. Delighted, Pepper-Peel put Polly on his shoulder and went outside. By torchlight, Pepper-Peel led his family and friends to the hillside.

"Pretty Polly, is there more treasure under these rocks?"

"Of course!" said Polly. The dinner guests in their finest silk clothes set to digging with their bare hands. After an hour of rock moving, though, they found nothing.

Glowering, Pepper-Peel moved to the pond.

"Pretty Polly, is there more silver in this pond?"

"Of course!" said Polly. Pepper-Peel ordered the pond drained, and before the water was all gone, he waded out and thrashed around in the muck, tossing handfuls of mud this way and that. Not a coin.

Now Pepper-Peel was in a frenzy. He stomped to the well.

"Pretty Polly, is there gold in this well?"

"Of course!" said Polly.

Pepper-Peel jumped in and the water became filthy with his mud. Even the town mayor tried to help him. But no pot of golden coins was found because none was planted.

Polly flew off Pepper-Peel's shoulder and landed in a tree.

"Polly, you have lied to me!"

"Of course!"

"Polly, you tricked me!"

"Of course!"

Pepper-Peel dragged himself out of the well. "Nobody will ever let me forget this," he said disgustedly.

"Of course!" said Polly, and she flew off toward the river where old Zhao Da sat on the bank with a property deed in his lap and making clay whistles.

## COMMENTARY

In China native lore was first collected in *The Book of Odes* by the citizen-philosopher we call Confucius. Around the turn of this century, there was a renewal of interest in stories, songs, and the languages of the many different Chinese people as part of what became the Chinese revolution. In his foreword to *Folktales of China,* folklorist Richard Dorson suggests that the Communists wanted to discard their old image as bandits and did so by associating themselves with the hardworking peasants who were frequently exploited by the landowning class.

The source for this story is John Minford's translation of *Favourite Folktales of China,* a highly digested volume of tales produced by the People's Republic of China. The People's Republic has revised this large body of lore by single-mindedly editing out fanciful characters and magical events associated with courtly life and literature. I have kept their emphasis on the ingenuity of the peasants and the hope for justice without attributing evil motives that justify bloody reversals of fortune.

## STORY OUTLINE

- Landlord Pepper-Peel works his people hard.
- Old Zhao Da makes clay whistles for the children.
- When he trips and falls and is unable to work, Zhao Da is ordered off Pepper-Peel's land.
- The villagers plan revenge and help Zhao Da by selling his whistles.
- The villagers buy Zhao Da fancy clothes and a parrot. The parrot is taught to say, "Of course!"
- One year later, the workers plant coins on Pepper-Peel's estate.
- Zhao Da returns to Pepper-Peel and uses Polly to "find" the coins.

- Pepper-Peel holds a banquet, buys Polly, and sells Zhao Da the hut and land that was his old home.
- Pepper-Peel gets what he deserves.

### Performance Suggestions

The storyteller should tell the children that they must help with the story. When they hear you ask "Pretty Polly, . . ." they must be ready to help Polly say, "Of course!"

This is also fun to perform. One child can act the part of Polly; one group of villagers can go off to the mountains and catch her while others buy her for Zhao Da. One class of experienced story performers spent two happy hours improvising the village life around the story before bringing about Pepper-Peel's comeuppance.

# THE LESSON

✳

When Man and Woman first came to live in his neighborhood, Jackal thought it was good. The people moved around, and sometimes they would leave a little something behind when they moved, or a small animal would straggle out of their reach and turn into Jackal's dinner. When the people settled in houses and planted gardens, Jackal thought this was better, because he knew where to look for his dinner. They kept a yard full of chickens, and chickens are fine and fat and slow.

Unfortunately, people have great powers. For instance, they place some kind of spell around their chickens, a weaving of vine so thin you can look through it and yet so strong that when you jump at the rooster, your claws and paws and nose hit something hard and you are knocked to the ground.

Jackal was discouraged, but he did not give up. He crouched in the trees and watched as the chickens scratched and strutted and clucked and crowed and kept one nervous eye on him.

Jackal moved farther back into the trees and waited. Sure enough, one day a fine fat hen decided that the scratchings were better farther away from the other chickens. With a great fluttering of wings, she flew up and over the mysterious magic of the humans, and WHOMP! into the paws and jaws of the waiting Jackal.

Jackal took a good grip on Hen and trotted happily to his den. When he reached his burrow in the roots of a tree, he dropped Hen and sat up to look at her as she lay in a crumple under one of his paws.

"Is this it?" said Hen, meekly, barely raising her head. Jackal just looked at her and laughed, thinking of what a good meal she would make.

"I suppose you'll put me in your pot and set me in your fireplace to make a delicious stew," said Hen, quietly, looking around at the empty burrow.

Jackal said nothing.

"That's how the woman gives strength to the man," said Hen.

Jackal licked his lips and said nothing.

"You'll need a fire, at least," said Hen, more alarmed. "That's how the woman prepares to speak to the god who gives the food she cooks for herself and her mate and all of us. Fire carries the smell of food to the heavens. Fire is what makes her god so generous."

"Quiet, Hen!" said the Jackal. "I'm going to eat you raw, and I'm going to eat you now!"

"If you want the man's magic, you have to pray first," said Hen very softly. Then she was silent.

Jackal thought. He thought of the magical fence and the overflowing granary and the smell of chicken stew. "You could tell how the man prays," he said gruffly.

"Bow your head," said Hen.

Slowly, Jackal lowered his head, keeping his eyes on Hen.

"Fold your hands," said Hen.

Slowly, Jackal brought his front paws together, still keeping his eyes on Hen.

"Close your eyes," said Hen.

Jackal's head jerked up at this, and he stared hard at Hen.

"Just while you say your prayer," said Hen. "It can be very short."

Jackal had heard prayer words coming out of the small shelter of the humans. So that was their secret! Very slowly he lowered his head, brought his paws together, closed his eyes and said as quickly as he could, "Thank God for dinner, Amen."

But even as he said his amen, he heard a desperate rustle of wings and looked up to see his dinner sitting on a tree branch just out of reach.

And so it happened that Jackal watched helplessly as Hen fluttered and hopped her way through the trees back to the woman's yard. That's when Jackal gave up on the people's magic.

## COMMENTARY

I found the seed of this story as a passing reference in Joel Chandler Harris's introduction to the original *Nights with Uncle Remus*, published in 1883. As a child, Harris heard many versions of the stories he later attributed to Uncle Remus. He suggests that Africans "cook" a story to suit circumstances whenever it pleases them. His example is a Hottentot story of Brother Rabbit escaping from Brother Fox by teaching him how to pray.

I assembled my own farmyard cast of characters and circumstances. The moral of the story is mostly unchanged—don't imitate what you don't understand—while Rabbit, the trickster, has been swapped off for Hen, whose behavior bears similarities with female coping strategies over many cultures and generations.

## Story Outline

- Jackal watches people walk by and catches what food he can.
- Jackal finds the farmyard, jumps at the chicken fence, falls, and waits.
- Hen flies over the fence, and Jackal captures her.
- Jackal takes Hen to his dugout.
- Hen plays for time, trying to talk Jackal into making a fire.
- Hen teaches Jackal to pray and escapes when he closes his eyes.

## Performance Suggestions

The dialogue of this story can be easily simplified for children's improvisation, and incidents can be blended so that they follow one right after the other rather than occur over a period of time, as suggested in the verbal form. The Story Outline works as a guide to action. A cloth on the floor sets up the hen yard. (Make sure it doesn't slip when Hen jumps out.) Play up Jackal's prowling around the hen yard. Have Jackal make as many practice jumps into the "fence" as time and energy and desire for nonsense allow. Modify the capture of the hen so that Jackal throws a rope or holds Hen on an imaginary rope, and you will have a satisfying escape. (It's a good idea to establish a No Real Touching rule.) Simplify the conversation according to the ages of children. Little ones can just have Hen teach Jackal to pray by demonstrating.

This also makes a good puppet story. For finger puppets, use a shoebox with the center of the back side cut out for a hen yard.

# Familiar Tales and Characters

✳

## I'LL NEVER BE OLD

✳

Once there was a pretty girl, so lively and smart that she was a joy to all who knew her. Hers was a life of happiness, with everyone doting on her. The only unpleasant part of her day was walking great-grandmother to church every morning. Great-grandmother was slow and wrinkled and grouchy, always complaining about her crippled-up hands and a pain here and another there. She leaned on the pretty girl and took little, shuffling steps all the way to church, three long streets and back.

One day, the pretty girl was turning cartwheels in the front yard as she waited impatiently for great-grandmother to put on her coat and hat and gloves and scarf. As great-grandmother buttoned her coat, she said rather meanly, "Just wait, you'll be old like me some day."

The pretty girl thought of these words as she leaned against the cold brick wall, waiting for great-grandmother to come out of church. She could stand it no longer. "Not me, I'll never be old," thought the pretty girl, and she started walking.

Soon she met a group of teenaged girls dancing down the market street, laughing and talking to each other as they watched sideways to see who was looking at them. The pretty girl joined them and said, "Hello. Will you ever be old?"

"Who cares," the older girls said. "We play soccer and sunbathe in the park and talk to boys—we're going to have lots of fun before we get old."

"Not me," said the pretty girl. "I'll *never* be old." And she walked away.

Next the pretty girl passed an outdoor cafe where a young woman studied a book without pictures while sipping on a cold drink. "Hi! I was wondering, will you ever be getting old?" the pretty girl asked.

The young woman watched the teenagers go by and said, "I'm going to study and become a manager so that I can buy good medical coverage and marry an executive and travel to interesting places. I'll be ready when I get old."

The pretty girl shook her head. "Not me, I'll *never* be old," she said, and she walked away.

Now the pretty girl was out of the main part of town. She saw a woman working in a yard with two children and a dog beside her. One of the children was complaining, and the dog started barking when the pretty girl walked up. "Quiet, Bitsy," said the woman, as she leaned over and wiped the little boy's nose.

"Are you ever getting . . . older?" the pretty girl asked the woman, who stood up and brushed the dirt from her pants.

"Some days I look forward to it," the woman said as she again tugged a handkerchief out of her pants pocket and aimed again for the nose of the boy who now stood with his hands wrapped around her knees.

"Not me. I'll *never* be old," said the pretty girl, and kept walking. Now nothing looked familiar. The road was dark, the trees bent in close, and the pretty girl was getting hungry. After a very long time, she came to a house that stood all by itself, with beautiful music rolling over the fence and across the lawn. When she looked up, the pretty girl saw a strange sight—a woman both old and young at the same time, with long, flowing white hair and smooth skin, who sat on a chair smoking some kind of pipe. The pretty girl had never seen a woman smoking a pipe. A servant held a tray full of wonderful-looking food for the white-haired woman, and the pretty girl remembered how hungry she was.

The woman leaned over her balcony and beckoned to the pretty girl. "Come on up," she said.

"First let me ask you a question," said the pretty girl. "Are you ever going to get old?"

"Never!" laughed the woman.

And so the pretty girl came to live with the woman who knew how to live forever. They played cards and roller-skated in the courtyard and swam in the pool, and someone brought food whenever they were hungry. The pretty girl forgot about what day it was and how old she was for weeks and months and years, until early one morning, when she was eating breakfast on the balcony. The wind was from the direction of town and she heard church bells in the distance.

"I'd like to visit my family," said the pretty girl.

"But you can't," said the white-haired woman. "If you go back, you'll grow old like everyone else."

The pretty girl was no longer content. She wondered what happened to the woman with the two children, and the student, and the teenagers. And her great-grandmother. She suddenly remembered that she had not said good-bye to her family.

"I'd like to tell my family that I'm okay," she told the white-haired woman.

"Your great-grandmother has been dead for years. Your mother and father and brothers and sisters are gone," said the woman. "Nobody remembers you."

The pretty girl was quiet for a long time. Finally she said to the white-haired woman, "I want to go back anyway, to see the place where I once lived."

"You can go back only one way. I'll take you in my limousine. But don't forget. If you step out, even for an instant, you'll start to grow old."

And so the pretty girl and her companion drove away from the house, down the road in the white limousine. Just as the white-haired woman had predicted, nothing was the same. The pretty girl had trouble finding the right street and house, and when she did, another family seemed to be living there.

An old woman with a bag of groceries and a cane was hobbling by. The pretty girl rolled down her window. "Excuse me, do you remember the people who used to live at this house?"

The old woman turned slowly and looked at the house. "Oh, yes, those were the people who lost their pretty girl," the old woman said. Just then the grocery bag slipped in the old woman's arm and oranges scattered all over the ground.

The pretty girl opened her car door and jumped out. As soon as she touched the street, her feet felt heavy and slow and it wasn't as easy to bend and pick up the oranges as she thought it would be. She heard the limousine drive quietly away as the old woman put her hand on her arm.

"Thank you, dear," said the old woman. "Isn't it a nuisance growing old?"

## COMMENTARY

The traditional stories of Powerful Ones who live alone frequently attribute a kind of malignancy to the solitary genius— the Russian grandmother Baba Yaga, who eats strangers, and Koschei the Deathless, a god in pre-Christian eastern Europe, who will do a favor when flattered but is otherwise perversely evil. One exception is the old woman of the north in the Finnish *Kalevala*—she has remarkable powers that she will share with heroes who are deserving. I drew on James Branch Cabell's version of Koschei from *Jurgen* to create my white-haired woman of powers, who is essentially amoral. This was to focus on the choices made by the pretty girl, who eventually learns that there is a price to any bargain, as she accepts the cost of being human.

## STORY OUTLINE

- The pretty girl leaves her old great-grandmother at the church.
- The pretty girl leaves her family, the teens, the young student, and the mother.
- The pretty girl finds the white-haired woman and stays many years.
- The pretty girl wants to go back, but learns that her family is gone.
- The white-haired young/old woman takes the pretty girl back after warning her that to get out of the limousine is to get old.
- The pretty girl jumps out of car to help the old woman who remembers her family and grows old as the limousine drives away without her.

## PERFORMANCE SUGGESTIONS

This story can be acted out as it is or could be the basis of some theatrical explorations. Each child could talk about responsibilities or problems they would like to leave behind. They could meet at the home of the white-haired woman and set up an ideal society. This could lead to conflict when some people decide to go back. For an elaborated version of this premise, see "Back to Reality," a performance that started in such a manner, on pages 216–224.

# WRITTEN IN GOLD

✳

White Lotus lived with her stepmother, Madame Bawang, and her stepsister, Rose. After the death of her father, White Lotus understood that there would be no plump bed mat for her, no fine new clothes. She was expected to be at the fish market early each morning and to look after the house when she returned from market with the day's provisions. She ground and roasted the day's spices, then prepared the evening rice, vegetables, and fish. Finally, she would sit to wait as Madame lifted out one side of the fish for herself, the other side for Rose, and passed the platter with only the head and bones remaining for White Lotus. Often, Lotus would be too tired to eat.

One evening Lotus left the table and sat in the doorway, looking out at the bright moon as she picked bits of meat from the bones. Rose taunted her. Wasn't she skinny as a fish and moon-pale? How could she sit so dreamy when her evening chores were undone? Madame agreed. Moon watching cleaned no pots, earned no coins for the chest. The moon had stolen her brain if she couldn't remember which of her tasks sat undone. Lotus found her sorrow to be larger than her hunger. She carried the bones into the backyard and buried them.

After this Lotus found a small comfort in burying the evening's fish bones. She looked up to the moon and stars, composing her thoughts, as she performed this simple ceremony. "If I have no ancestor trunk, if I have no silk-embroidered dress for my wedding day, if I have no necklace or rings from my mother," she thought, "then the moon will be my silver, the stars will be my jewels."

In the evening's cool light, she thought she saw something growing from the place where she first dug in her bones. It was a shoot of silvery gray-green unlike any she had seen before.

In the days that followed, the delicate shoot grew into a little silver tree with golden leaves. White Lotus plucked off one of the leaves and, with a bamboo pen, impressed her thoughts on it. Then she lifted it high to catch the breeze and watched her little poem lift to the heavens. Her heart lifted with her words, night after night, and she wrote of how beauty was a comfort, how she looked beyond her home and the life she had known for hope in the future. She spoke of how the little tree, cheerful in dark as well as daylight, comforted her lonely heart. Although Madame and Rose did not seem to notice, Lotus found her heart grow lighter as she performed each day's duties, composing her evening poem as she swept and walked to the market.

Unknown to White Lotus and her family, the king of their realm, a strong and confident man, died suddenly. His son, still grieving the loss of his father, found himself dressed in fine robes and directed to the throne. The new king, who had been ignored as a mere youth only days before, was now expected to solve every problem in the kingdom. He felt inadequate and alone. To gather his thoughts, as soon as his courtiers retired for the night, the young king stepped into his walled garden.

One night, as he looked up at the distant stars, a beautiful gold leaf dropped into his hand. It had writing on it. Here were wise thoughts, just as he needed them! From this night on, the king looked forward to his time alone in the garden, reading the poetic thoughts of someone so like himself. He showed one leaf to his advisor, who said he had never seen anything like it. It seemed to be the thoughts of a young woman, the advisor said.

The young king realized that he needed to marry soon, and he had no idea how to choose a wife. It was expected that his father would do this for him. He looked at his collection of leaves. Whoever wrote these seemed to understand life's cruelties. Yet she remained tender and caring. And didn't the wind, coming from his father's home in the heavens, carry these messages to him? Perhaps she was the woman his father would have selected for him. The king announced that he would search his country until he found the woman who spoke with the spirit of the heavens.

None of his advisors had heard of a tree with gold leaves, and so the king set out to visit every home with a garden. At the Bawang house, Madame insisted she had never seen such tree. But then Rose came running in, breathless, with a plain gold leaf identical to those the king had seen. "I have the tree, it's in my mother's garden. And I could be a poet," said Rose.

"That is good. Compose a poem for me, then," said the king.

"Ahh . . . My name is Rose . . . this leaf is yellow. Gosh, you are a handsome fellow!" gushed Rose, clearly impressed by the king.

The king saw Lotus peeking around the corner. As Madame frowned and motioned for Lotus to leave, the king began to speak. "Only wind and cloud will know . . ." he started.

"What heart inspires leaf to show," Lotus finished.

"My dear wife," said the king, holding out his hands to White Lotus.

And so gentle White Lotus became queen of the realm. And by her orders, a fine, fresh fish, the best from the daily market, was carried to the home of Madame Bawang and Rose on a golden leaf-shaped platter every morning.

## COMMENTARY

The story of the sweet stepdaughter we call Cinderella traveled back and forth along the old silk road, on ships across distant waters, and in the memories of Christian crusaders. I've provided the prince with the recent loss of his father to help explain why such a desirable young man would be single in a culture that takes care of such important matters. This Asian version of the Cinderella theme makes use of a metaphor found in other stories of India, that of a tree of gold and silver that grows out of a grave. Here, it grows from the fish bones, from sadness given back to the earth when it has no other form of expression. The metaphor: Grief and loss can be the seed for something remarkable. This is true, at least, for those with a naturally noble soul, which here is revealed in poetry. (The story also contains a parable about gaining wisdom and good cheer by practice, an understanding at the core of Eastern religions.) And what a wise young prince, who must be surrounded by lovely, eager maidens, to seek out a poet! Quite superior to putting confidence in a small foot and a glass slipper.

## STORY OUTLINE

- White Lotus serves fish to her stepmother and step-sister, but gets only the leftover bones for herself. She buries the bones.
- A silver tree with gold leaves grows from the bones. Lotus writes a poem on each leaf; the wind carries them away.
- The old king dies, and the new young king is lonely. The wind brings him the gold leaves; their poetry comforts him.
- The new king searches the kingdom for the poet who has written in gold.
- At the Bawang household, Rose tries to win king's heart by flattery but fails.
- The king and White Lotus compose a poem together; he proposes.
- After they marry, White Lotus has one fish sent every day to Bawang house.

## PERFORMANCE SUGGESTIONS

This story lends itself to variations of puppet shows. Puppetry helps those who don't want to be on stage or prefer not to learn lines.

Start with a simple, flexible puppet-show stage. Mine is based upon a good-sized cardboard box, painted and trimmed with wallpaper leftovers, with little curtains and ruffles tacked around the cutout that frames the 'stage.' The box is easily carried and stored. For performances it can be set on a table with a cloth skirt. Agree on who has what lines; make cue cards, which have a couple of words from the previous character and then one's own words. These are easier to handle than a full script in the compressed space behind a puppet stage.

Children's drawings, mounted on thin cardboard and then fixed to tongue depressors, make satisfying puppets. Use one stick for the tree and one for a leaf so that the leaf can fly away and circle in the sky, waiting for White Lotus to exit and the Prince to enter from the other side of the stage.

Try a performance variation suggested in Roberta Nobleman's outstanding book for teachers, *Mime and Masks*. Use a puppet theater to tell the story of White Lotus with actor's hands. Have everyone stand in a circle to practice the many ways our hands reveal our feelings and personalities. How would Madame Bawang divide up the fish each evening? How would she serve the evening's rice and vegetables? How would hands express Rose talking at the table or White Lotus waiting? Practice the old king's hands on his deathbed, suddenly weak, and the son's hands as he is called to the bed. Another way to practice this is to have one person say the words and another person behind the stage make the hand movements. Go beyond the story to act out little scenes of each character alone, two characters together, giving everyone in the group a chance to express each character before putting it together into a single performance.

This is an opportunity to do some background reading on Thailand and southern Asia. How would the Cinderella story arrive here? Look up and compare a French version, for instance. Find examples of fabrics and illustrations of costumes; use these to create paper puppets. Even if the story will be performed by puppets, look at a map of Bangkok. Where would a palace sit? An old-fashioned home with garden for the Bawangs? How far would White Lotus walk to the fish market? What vegetables would she carry home and how? Mime how she might walk through the market, filling her eyes and imagination with objects she cannot expect to own.

# WITLING'S TREASURE

✳

Once there was a boy named Witling who was as young, awkward, and impatient as his parents were old and kind. As Witling grew larger and stronger, he became bolder. He insulted the hired man, laughing as he chased the chickens until they squawked and fluttered around him. The day he tied a chicken to the tail of the family's faithful donkey, Pearl, just to watch it flap, his father called him into the house. Witling's mother put down her sewing and nodded sadly as his father said, "Witling, I am growing old, and I fear that you are not ready to inherit what I have always wished to give you. I want you to take a journey, learn what you can from the world, and then return."

"All by myself?" cried Witling loudly. "Do you want me to get lost?"

"You can take Pearl," said Witling's mother. "Pearl is never lost."

"When you return," said his father, "I will give you this silver box, which contains all that I have of value."

"Tell me what I'm going to get," said Witling, reaching for the box.

"I can't," said his father sadly, setting the box back on its high shelf. Witling's mother touched him gently on the shoulder—pat, pat—and handed him a bag containing three loaves of bread for his journey.

Witling didn't like this. What kind of adventure could he take with an elderly donkey and a bag of bread? He said, a little cruelly, "What if somebody steals the box while I'm gone? What if Pearl slows me down so badly that you are dead when I get back? Maybe I should take your wagon and horses so that I can get back faster."

"Your treasure can't be stolen," said his mother sweetly, "and you will know it when you see it. You'll know it by a certain gentle glow."

And so without understanding where he was going or why, Witling left. He traveled what seemed like forever—several days—and ate most of his bread, as Pearl patiently carried him mile after mile. But Witling had little money and no desire to work and soon spent all he had. Before long, Witling had turned around and started back to his parent's house.

Which way to go? Witling hadn't been paying much attention to road signs and directions. Luckily, he was with Pearl, and the old donkey knew her way home. Witling grew impatient when he started to recognize the neighborhood; he cut a switch and swatted the back of Pearl's legs to hurry her along the path to his home.

But it was gone, without a trace. No house, no silver treasure box, no yard where he once chased chickens, no barn where Pearl once rested. And no parents. Angry and confused, stopping only to give Pearl a short drink at the well, Witling started down the road again.

Soon Witling met up with a knight in white armor riding a fine horse. The knight asked where he was going. Witling told him what had happened. "The Black Knight is to blame. It's he who has killed your parents, burned down their house, and stolen your treasure," shouted the White Knight.

"Did you see him?" Witling asked.

"No, of course not," said the White Knight. "Otherwise, would I still be looking for him?"

Witling could not answer that. "Swear to the cause, and I can help you," said the White Knight, turning his sword over and over in his hands.

Still feeling very empty and strange with the loss of his family, Witling agreed, and after saying "Yea" to many long oaths, he was handed spurs, a long, shining sword, and a helmet to protect himself.

And so he rode on, with poor Pearl panting from the extra weight of the helmet and the sword, when Witling saw something black lurking up ahead at the side of the road. Surely it was the Black Knight hiding in the grass! Witling kicked Pearl with the spurs, and she lumbered ahead. But then Pearl stopped short, just as Witling swung his sword. The sword's blade came down harmlessly in the grass. Before Witling could say anything to Pearl, there was a loud *yowl*, and a black cat ran off through the bushes. Witling took off his helmet to see better and saw that the cat was skinny and hungry. Feeling much embarrassed, Witling turned over his helmet, put his last crust of his bread inside, and left it for the cat.

Witling and Pearl soon caught up with a long line of pilgrims who walked along the side of the road, singing to each other. Witling watched in amazement as they walked, one by one, each careful to step only on the line that marked the edge of the paved roadway. "Join us, stranger, and you can share in our treasure," they said to Witling. They gave Witling one of their great cloaks of comfort and said he was welcome to travel with them as long as he stayed on the line. They told him of their great king, who waited to give them each a share of his kingdom. But they warned him that they were strict, and if he stepped off the line he would be judged unworthy. Witling thought of how his own treasure was lost and so he joined them, watching his feet so he would not step off the line.

Suddenly an old woman behind Witling started screaming, and Witling looked up to see Pearl in the ditch at the side of the road, eating grass. "Get her out of there, or we will have to leave you behind," the woman warned him.

"She's hungry. I forgot to feed her this morning," Witling said sadly.

"Get her back in line this minute!" scolded the woman.

But Witling was hungry and thirsty too. He stopped to wait for Pearl, and the pilgrims went on without him.

Witling led Pearl down to a nearby stream for a drink. While he waited, he saw a strange sight in the field nearby. A man and woman and several children were pushing a huge crystal ball along a rut in the meadow. "Help us, won't you?" called the man. "We're searching for our lost treasure." The man shared food out of his knapsack with Witling as he explained that, according to their book of secrets, the crystal would help them see into the ground where their treasure lay hidden. Witling obligingly hooked Pearl up to a harness, and he and Pearl pulled while the family pushed the enormous round crystal along its path. The ball moved ever so slowly, and everyone put their heads down and shoved and sweated and moaned.

Pearl pulled her best for mile after mile, but as the sun started to set, so did Pearl. When Witling tried to get her to stand, she shook her head and gazed off into the distance. Now Witling looked around and said, "We're traveling in a circle!"

"This is the path set out for us," said the man. "Besides, the crystal is too heavy to lift out of the rut."

Witling looked at Pearl, who had stood up again but was limping sadly. "I'm sorry," he said, "I'll have to give up my share of the reward."

Witling walked beside Pearl, trying to encourage her as she stumbled along. Storm clouds were moving toward them. Now Witling was ready to stop under the nearest tree, but Pearl kept walking, somehow, until they reached an outcropping of rock, where at last they were able to rest in safety. Witling spread his cloak as far as it would go over Pearl's back and his own, and they slept through the thunder and lightning.

Next morning, the sky was clear, but Pearl did not get up. Witling covered her carefully with his cloak and walked out to gather fresh grass and fill his cup with water for her. When he came back, Pearl was lying stiff and still where she had slept the night before.

In grief, Witling buried his faithful donkey and built a shrine with his cloak, his harness, and his sword. When travelers came by, he told them he was honoring his great and wise friend, his Pearl. Soon word went around of a devout young man who was guarding a shrine to honor a dead saint, and those who sought wisdom came to see. One by one, without a word to disturb him, they sat down beside Witling and joined in his grief. Hour after hour the number grew, until Witling at long last looked up and saw love and concern glowing in the eyes of his silent companions. Suddenly, Witling knew he had found the treasure his parents had promised him.

## Commentary

This is a coming-of-age story, traditional style, wholly invented to inspire more such efforts from my listeners. The people Witling meets on the path are my metaphors for distractions on the spiritual journey. Although it was meant to describe one person's personal odyssey, it has been universalized. Its sentimental tone is an antidote to the anti-odyssey of Shaydoola.

## Story Outline

- Witling is a pest who insults the hired man, chases the chickens, and bothers the old donkey, Pearl.
- Witling's parents send him into the world to seek wisdom before returning for his inheritance.
- Witling returns home without learning anything.
- Witling finds everything gone, no house, no parents; he starts out again.
- The White Knight says the Black Knight is the cause; Witling finds only a black cat. He feeds it and goes on.
- He meets pilgrims walking a narrow path, but they are too strict for Pearl; Witling leaves them.
- He meets people pushing a huge crystal, but they are in a rut; Witling leaves.
- Pearl dies; as Witling honors her, he finds his treasure in the love and respect of others.

## Performance Suggestions

This can be performed in a modified Greek chorus style, with members of the chorus stepping out, narrating the action that is mostly mimed by Witling and Pearl (in mask or headband with nose and ears). Pearl and Witling merely walk together, not trying to simulate Witling riding Pearl. Chorus members, standing in a line across the staging area, can use soundmakers as Witling and Pearl move back and forth in front of them. Witling and Pearl will then join the chorus line for encounters with the People of the Narrow Path and the People of the Crystal. Finally, the chorus forms a protective half-circle as they sit, one by one, beside the grieving Witling. One person can narrate, or members of the chorus can take turns narrating an incident each.

This would be a good time to talk to a class about the beginnings of Greek drama in religious, ritual dance.

# LEGEND OF THE GREAT TUBER

✳

The reason most people believe in the story of the Great
Tuber is not because they heard it from the biggest
story stretcher in town, Boots Adams, but because they
heard it from Jerry the Gem, the most sincere, the most
polite, the most honest seven-year-old south of Rexburg,
Idaho.

Jeremey E. Mallovey, Jerry the Gem, always caught the
school bus on time and wore his socks only once before he
put them in the hamper, and he said "yes ma'am," and
"yes sir" without being reminded and didn't believe ridiculous stories because somebody else told him to. That's why
Jerry felt mighty silly walking across a potato field with
Boots Adams one September day after school. Boots told
everyone in the second grade that she had the *Guinness
Book of Records* record-breaking potato plant growing in
her parents' field right outside of town. It was a mutant
potato that was growing arms and legs as well as eyes and
would someday rise to be the friend of humankind. All
they had to do was come to her farm and see it.

Everybody told her they wouldn't believe it unless Jerry saw it too. And so Jerry rode home with Boots and her mother instead of catching the school bus, and now they were walking through the weeds at the side of the road, sharing Boots's potato chips left over from lunch.

"Go ahead, you eat the rest of them," Boots said. "It's right over this way, on the other side of the canal—where I used to play when I was little. I used to talk to the potatoes and play in the mud, and that's how I found out it loves socks. Because when you fill your socks full of dirt, they look like potatoes. Watch your step. This potato plant is so tall, my dad parks the pickup under it for shade."

"Maybe we can walk on the same road the pickup uses," said Jerry, picking the stickers out of his pants.

"This is the shortcut," said Boots. "Anyway, I mean my dad could park under it if he wanted to. It's right around the other side of these trees. Be sure to talk nice to it as we get close. I think it's ready to hatch out the greatest tuber ever seen."

But when they walked around to the other side of the trees, they saw, not a giant potato plant, not a small potato plant, but plain dirt in clods and rows, all that was left of a field that once grew potatoes.

Boots threw her arms up to the sky. "He's gone!" she said. "The Great Tuber has risen out of the field and is gone."

"Maybe your dad knows something about this," Jerry offered, but Boots only said, "My dad is a farmer, not a believer." She sat down, and Jerry thought she was going to cry.

"We need a plan," she said. "We need to lure back the Great Tuber so the other kids will believe me." But Jerry had to hurry home for supper and couldn't help with the plan until the next day.

*Familiar Tales and Characters* 167

Jerry's mother always called him Jerry the Gem. "What would I do without you," she said as she picked up the socks of Patsy, his older sister. "You're so dependable," she said as she went out to the car and drove back to school to find Missy, Jerry's youngest sister, who wouldn't get on the bus because Boots Adams told her a rattlesnake lived under the seat.

"Boots saw it—this fat. She's gonna catch it and feed it to the Great Tuber," said Missy when Mom brought her home.

But Jerry only shook his head and wondered what a rattlesnake would eat on the bus, and Patsy said, "Boots Adams is the town liar. What's for dinner, Mom?" as they sat down to supper.

Jerry had only one problem. He loved potatoes. Now that's not a problem in most families in Idaho, but for Jerry it was. That's because he was the only potato lover in his family. He tried to be sensible. "Potatoes don't have many calories," he said hopefully, but Mother said, "They do the way I eat them," and then Jerry said, "It's all a matter of how you fix them," and then Mother said, "I don't have time to cook."

Patsy said, "I want canned spaghetti," and Missy said, "Spaghetti turns into snakes when you sleep; Boots told me that," and Patsy said, "Boots Adams can't tell a snake from a shoelace," and Jerry thought about potatoes while Mother said, "All right then, if you can't agree," and reached into the freezer for a frozen pizza.

Jerry didn't get mad at Boots Adams for scaring his little sister. He was too nice for that. He liked Boots because she told stories as good as the ones in books and because she shared her potatoes. Every day Boots brought potato something. She had potato chips, potato puffs, potato salad, and potato curls. Some days she walked over to the fast-food counter down the street and bought milk and french fries.

"Here, help yourself to some more fries," she said the next day. "I have a plan. Today after school we will go down to the field and plant some more socks for the Great Tuber."

"The Great Tuber, hah! Boots, you are such a liar," said Patsy, who was listening. "I'm going to tell the principal about your scaring Missy with your rattlesnake story."

"It could have been a snake," Jerry said. "Maybe a garter snake somebody brought for show and tell."

"Garter snakes don't sound like this," said Boots, and she made a very loud hissing sound like this [make sound]. But Patsy had already left.

All their plans went astray. Jerry got a message from Mother saying she wanted him to ride home on the school bus and sit next to Missy and be sure to look under the seat first, just in case. Then as the school bus drove up, the principal, Mr. Fount, came out and sternly asked to speak to Boots Adams, and all the kids waiting in line for the bus stared and snickered when Boots and Mr. Fount went back into the school.

That evening, while Jerry and his sisters ate macaroni and cheese and drank lemonade, Jerry made up his mind that he would go back to the potato field by himself. After he excused himself from the table, he went out to the garage, where his mother kept her gardening supplies. He sat down on the grass and took off his socks, but put his shoes back on when Missy saw him and asked where he was going. "I'm going to fill my socks with fertilizer and help Boots grow the biggest potato plant in the world," said Jerry.

"Wait," said Missy, and she ran into the house and came back out with her little flashlight, the one she always took camping. Jerry thanked her and was in the garage carefully scooping fertilizer from the bag into his socks when Patsy found him.

"Where do you think you're going," Patsy asked gruffly, but when Jerry explained where he was going, she said, "Wait," and came back with an old broom. "You better take this," she said, "to mark the spot so you can find it again—and in case of snakes."

Jerry thought he remembered how to get to the Adams place, but it wasn't the same walking by himself or starting from his house instead of from school. The streets were strange, it was getting darker, and by the time Jerry got to the gravel road, he was squinting into the dark looking for the patch of trees that marked the beginning of the potato field.

He tried to find the place where he and Boots walked in the weeds the day before, but Missy's little flashlight wasn't much help. He swung the broom handle back and forth to scare away snakes for a while, but when he did that, he had to hold both socks in one hand and the fertilizer turned out to be heavier than he expected.

All of a sudden he found himself slipping—he was falling down the bank toward the canal! Jerry caught a handful of weeds and scrambled up the side of the ditch, but as he did, he dropped his broom handle and heard it drop into the water. Now he walked very carefully, putting one foot in front of the other and testing the ground until he saw a big concrete culvert, and he slowly pulled himself across it to the other side of the canal.

Jerry thought he could see the outline of something large against the sky. He walked cautiously, crouching a little like this [crouch], trying not to think about his shoes getting muddy, shooting his little flashlight at the big shape, and hoping it was trees and not giant tubers. Then right in front of him he saw something glimmer in the moonlight, a thin, shiny line on the ground. Jerry turned to run, tripped on something hard, and fell. When he stood up, he saw two huge, bright eyes staring at him. Before he could think the words "Giant Tuber," the eyes blinked, and he realized they were pickup truck lights signaling him from the road.

As fast as he could, Jerry stumbled and ran toward the lights. He didn't remember that he'd dropped his socks until he opened the pickup door.

"What are you doing out there?" asked the man in the pickup.

"I was trying to help a friend of mine grow a great . . . a great, big tuber," Jerry told the man.

And the man said, "Sounds like your friend might be Boots Adams." Then he started up the pickup and asked Jerry for his address.

"The Great Tuber is one of Boots's best stories," said Jerry, putting Missy's flashlight back in his pocket. "He's a friend of humankind. I wish it were true. I'd like to get some potatoes at my house." And Jerry told the man about the pasta and the pizza and the cooking problem.

Jerry had already put on his pajamas when he remembered the muddy shoes he'd left on the front porch. He walked past the bedrooms where his sisters were already asleep, past his mother's bedroom where he could hear the TV behind the closed door. He walked through the dark living room and opened the front door just in time to see two bright lights, like the eyes of a Great Tuber, or a pickup truck, backing quietly out of his driveway.

He looked down beside his shoes, and there was a cardboard box full of potatoes, with a note and a small booklet. The booklet was "101 Easy Ways with Potatoes," and the note said, "To Jerry from the Great Tuber." Jerry's mother came out to the porch in her housecoat, turned on the light, and read the note and said, "I give up." Jerry offered to read the recipes and cook fried potatoes for breakfast himself. He told everyone afterwards that a Great Tuber was out there, after all.

## COMMENTARY

In the season of television specials for Halloween, an Idaho radio announcer whose name is lost to legend made a joke about a great tuber. That was the start of my invented legend. The relationship between town and farm reflects my youth as an adolescent riding the school bus from county road to city school in Great Falls, Montana. Long bus rides seem to stimulate the imagination.

## STORY OUTLINE

- Boots talks her friend Jerry into coming to see the Great Tuber.
- The Great Tuber has been harvested. Jerry and Boots make a plan to plant socks full of fertilizer to bring it back.
- The plan is stymied when Boots is held after school.
- Later, Jerry goes alone with socks full of fertilizer.
- Jerry gets lost in the dark.
- Boots's father finds Jerry and gives him a ride home.
- Late that night, a box of potatoes is left for Jerry on his porch. Jerry uses this evidence to support the story of Great Tuber.

## PERFORMANCE SUGGESTIONS

This story can be a starting point for inventive dramatic play. After telling the story, talk about other legendary persons—Santa and the elves and the tooth fairy, among others. What would happen if a child on a quest happened into the country where all of these magical helpers could be found? Have each child take a role, make a personal space in the classroom or staging area, and send in the child who needs help. Each child picks a role, either as a child or children in need or as a living legend. They act out the possibilities in character, then talk about what they did, how it felt, and how their free-form play could be organized into a genuine play. Take incidents out of their spontaneous play and shape them into scenes with a beginning, middle, and end. Script out key lines and rehearse this finished form. That is how the story "Back to Reality" in the section "From the Kids" evolved.

# NO STRANGER AT THE DOOR

✳

When Doctor Albert Schweitzer built his hospital in Africa in 1913, he made it as comforting as possible for those who had never seen a brick building or a white doctor. Other medical workers later built hospitals with tile floors and gleaming, intricate machines. Dr. Schweitzer, however, created an African village with many beds and rooms for patients, doctors, and nurses. He hated gadgets, he said, and so while fancy anesthesia machines and electrocardiographs turned to rust in other hospitals, neither time nor moist jungle air discouraged the good doctor.

And so the people came. Word went out into the forest that nobody was turned away from Dr. Schweitzer's door for lack of money. From hundreds of miles away, upstream and downstream, patients came carried on the backs of their relatives and in the bottoms of pirogues and motorboats. Many times a family would come with all their remaining wealth, a few chickens, a pitiful clutch of clothing, and a scruffy, bad-tempered dog. They would look in the buildings constructed especially for visitors, marvel at the wood floors and say, "A good hut, Doctor! A good hut!"

The 350 beds were never empty, and the leper colony was filled. Because nobody, not man or woman or child or beast, was ever sent away, Dr. Schweitzer's village accumulated animals too—a small herd of dogs, cats, and friendly goats who waited by the dining-room door for scraps each night, and ducks, chickens, two rude pigs, pelicans, sheep, monkeys, and parrots. Only six beloved antelope were kept within a fence for their own protection; the rest of the animals wandered around watching for a handout from the doctor, who always had a small sack of rice in his pocket.

Dr. Schweitzer's concern for his fellow beings made him a legend and a curiosity. Visiting dignitaries were treated as respectfully as goats and chickens and were also fed out of the doctor's generous pockets. Frederick Franck, one of the hospital's assistants thirty years ago, remembers the day the boats brought not one or two, but thirty women from a cruise ship who came to see Africa's famous Dr. Schweitzer. A nurse had to be excused from her duties to escort the women around the hospital grounds.

"Dirt paths!" said one, looking down at her dusty shoes.

"Where is your equipment?" asked another.

"Excuse me, Miss, but a huge pig is blocking the door," said someone else.

"Are there powder rooms in our quarters?" a plump woman asked, and the nurse shook her head as she led them to the village latrines.

And so while the hospital's workers quietly gave up their beds and their chairs at the dining room table to the thirty visitors, the women wandered through the village, shaking their heads at dirty children, snapping pictures of the lepers, who tried to hide their sores. When the boats returned the next morning and every woman had her picture taken with Dr. Schweitzer as proof for friends back home, someone asked the doctor why he allowed these interruptions.

"One never knows," said Dr. Schweitzer, "exactly which person is in real need of help."

## COMMENTARY

This lovely reminiscence, originating in Frederick Franck's memoir *Days with Albert Schweitzer,* captures the love of humanity and service that was at the core of Dr. Schweitzer's work. As Franck observed, when he was working at the hospital, there was no one too humble—or too proud—to be neglected.

## STORY OUTLINE

- After it became famous, people came to Dr. Schweitzer's modest hospital in Africa.
- The hospital gave the kind of help needed, including tending to families that came together.
- Money was spent on nurses instead of equipment.
- Animals, then visitors, got in the way.
- Dr. Schweitzer is polite to guests who cause inconvenience because "one never knows exactly which person is in real need of help."

## PERFORMANCE SUGGESTIONS

The telling of this story leads into talk about people we admire and the reasons we admire them. It makes a good start for a workshop on family folklore and local legends. Participants take turns, in small groups, telling about someone they admire, then find one incident that captures the essence of the subject of their admiration. Shape this reminiscence into a story, doing additional interviews or research as needed. (For other ideas, see pages 276–289.) Write, rehearse, then perform the stories for each other. While people are going through the writing process, introduce other well-told hero and heroine stories from varied sources. Participants can take turns modifying written stories and delivering them in oral fashion.

# THE SECOND SHEPHERD'S PLAY

It was a night full of ordinary troubles when the shepherds came together cold and grumbling so long ago. Coll, the first shepherd, is worrying about crops and taxes as he stands shivering in his old wrap. Gib, the second shepherd, complains about the weather and his wife. Now Daw, the young one, wanders in late. He's lost his cloak somewhere and is thinking that he'd rather sit and play with his juggling balls than chase after sheep in the dark.

"Sir and Master, both of you I greet! A drink I would like and something to eat!" says Daw.

Coll answers, "You are a lazy cheat!"

And Gib adds, "Nay, you must wait for your meat until we've made it."

"The pay comes late," Daw complains, looking most forlorn.

"Where are the sheep?" Gib wants to know.

Daw tells him: "In the corn."

Just then, the three shepherds notice someone trying to slip past them—a man wrapped up in a cloak, hiding his face. This someone looks suspiciously like the rascal Mak, who makes his living by helping himself.

Mak puts on a funny accent and pretends not to know the shepherds. "Ich be a yeoman of the king. A Lord who's rich and everything. Fie on you, get thee from my presence," says Mak most grandly. "Get thee hence!"

But no one is fooled. Daw recognizes the cloak as his own and snatches it from Mak's back. Coll and Gib are also suspicious. Still, the night is bitter and the men's hearts are kind, so Mak is invited to share their small fire.

"Father, lead our sheep," the shepherds pray.

"Into my hands," says Mak, and down he lay.

As soon as the shepherds are asleep, Mak slips away and picks a plump lamb for himself, throws it over his shoulder, and hurries home to where his wife, Gill, tends the fire and finishes a beer. The door is locked.

Mak knocks at his door. "Gill, art thou in?"

She lets him in grumbling, "I was set for to spin."

Mak shows Gill the lamb, but she isn't pleased. She expects the shepherds to discover their loss.

"You'll hang for this," warns Gill, "without a trick. Pretend the lamb's our baby and I'm sick."

And surely enough, the lamb has only just been wrapped in a cloth and stuffed into the cradle when Mak hears a knock at the door.

"Ooh, ooh, I'm sick," bawls Gill.

"Lullaby, go to sleep, you lousy little baby," growls Mak.

"Will ye hear Gill and Mak," says Daw. "How they croon!"

And Coll, "Never a voice so clear out of tune."

Mak reluctantly invites the shepherds in and explains that he hurried home because his wife was sick and they had a new baby. He tells a convincing story as Gill moans.

"I shall make you a fire, if you would sit. A nurse I would

hire; can you think of one yet?" And Mak offers the shepherds a crust of bread on a plate and the dregs of beer from the bottom of Gill's bottle.

In the cold room, despite Gill's groans, the shepherds look about sharply and explain their visit. The men are suspicious: Mak is most mild.

Gill cries, "If I offend you, God, I'll eat this child!"

The shepherds are full of sympathy for Gill and decide to leave. But just as they walk out the door, Coll remembers that they forgot to give a gift to the newborn babe. "Not while he sleeps," Mak protests, but then the lamb wakes up and gives a bleat.

"He's awake!" says Daw, and pulls back the blanket to give the baby a kiss, only to be startled by a long snout.

Gill recovers quickly. "At midnight," she says, "He was took by an elf. He's been cursed with this muzzle. I saw it myself."

"And gave him my earmark?" says Coll, pulling back the blanket a little further.

Gib is furious, and Daw is all for punishment, but Coll looks up into the sky, which is filled with light from a new star, and says, "For this trespass, we will not fight."

And the shepherds walk into miraculous night.

## COMMENTARY

The oldest known form of "The Second Shepherd's Play" is the thirteenth-century Wakefield cycle of English miracle plays. These were created by worker guilds, performed as part of holiday church services. This story form was written for a Christmas Eve church service and translated from old to contemporary English by Homer Watt, in the textbook *The Literature of England*.

## STORY OUTLINE

- Shepherds Coll, Gib, and Daw stand on a hillside one cold, dark night, complaining of cold and hunger.
- Mak the thief tries to disguise himself and chase them off.
- Daw recognizes his lost cloak on Mak; Mak himself is recognized.
- Mak is invited to share the fire.
- When the shepherds fall asleep, Mak steals a lamb and goes home with it.
- Mak's wife Gill comes up with a plan for hiding the sheep in the cradle, pretending she's just had a baby.
- Suspicious shepherds, missing Mak and a lamb, knock on the door, and are invited in.
- Mak is hospitable and Gill gives a convincing performance as a woman who has just had a baby.
- The shepherds try to kiss the baby before they leave and discover their lost lamb.
- Coll urges the others to forgive Mak; shepherds walk out into the light of the star of Bethlehem.

## PERFORMANCE SUGGESTIONS

Given the difficulty of memorizing the dialogue, most performers will use a script and perform this as a staged reading. It works well with a narrator plus individual parts. Try performing this in front of a Christmas crèche scene or next to a Christmas tree with a star or an angel at the top. The kind of trickery and implied behaviors of Mak and Gill aren't suitable for performance by children. It should be done in a spirit of prelude to the wonder and joy of the birth of Jesus, which has actually taken place at the same time and which will change the lives of the shepherds (and perhaps reform Mak and Gill) in only an hour or two.

## MIGHTY RED RIDING HOOD

✳

Red was her color from birth. This girl was a red, squalling baby who grew up to be a puzzle to her gentle mother and a challenge to the neighbors. Where Red toddled, more children followed. In a few years you could tell by the sound of the ball hitting the side of the house who was batting and who was throwing. "High color, hot temper. Nothing like her mother," people would say to each other.

All around town parents shook their heads and muttered about wild animals when Red asked for a red wool traveling cloak so that she could go all the way through the woods to her grandmother's place. "Too far," her uncle said. "Your mother tried it once and came back crying."

"I never cry, almost never. Anyway, when I am twelve, I'm getting a horse," the child announced, and after that, as she dashed around town in her bright wool cape, everyone called her Red Riding Hood.

One day the word came from a traveler that Red Riding Hood's grandmother was ill. Despite terrible predictions, her mother's gloomy face, and gory stories from other children, Red packed a basket of goodies and threw on her cloak. She pestered her uncle for directions and, rehearsing them all the way home, kissed her mother good-bye. She patted her unhappy mother on the shoulder. "Look, Ma, muscles," she said, displaying a sturdy, downy brown arm. With that, she walked confidently into the shadows.

Along the path, Red met a tall wolf in a black leather jacket, who immediately switched directions and walked along beside her. He had a shock of bright red, uncombed hair and gray eyes that didn't seem to blink. She didn't like him at all, not at all, but he didn't appear to notice. "Red, Red, lemme think. I believe I knew your mother once," the wolf said, smiling as if he had an unpleasant secret.

"You don't know me," said Red.

"Well, well, I guess I don't," said the wolf. "Where you goin', if you don't mind my asking."

"To grandmother's house. I know the way," said Red, marching and looking straight ahead.

"Please yourself," said the wolf, and he disappeared behind a tree.

When Red arrived at Grandmother's house two days later, she noticed that the flowers hadn't been watered and that the cat was stalking around the front door, mewing hungrily. "Come in," said a hoarse voice when Red knocked.

Red was shocked. The kitchen was a mess of unwashed dishes. What was even more suspicious, piles of beer bottles and crumpled clothing lay all around Grandmother's bed. Could it really be Grandmother lying in that huddle of blankets, wearing the hideous old bonnet she usually wore outdoors for long trips and for gardening?

Whoever it was in that bed wouldn't turn to look at Red—and yet somehow knew her. "Dear Red, come and kiss your poor sick granny," said the voice in the bedclothes.

Red's stomach flip-flopped. Grandmother didn't talk like that—or smell like that. The person in the bed faced away from Red, who reached over by the fireplace and picked up Grandmother's ax, slowly and carefully, and held it to her side.

"I've brought you a surprise, Grandmother," she said.

The person in the bonnet turned and reached for Red, lunged in fact. "What big eyes you have," said Red, swinging the ax as hard as she could. She sheered the tip off one hairy ear and permanently ruined Grandmother's bonnet as the wolf bounced out of bed and ran out the door.

Red washed clothes, fed the cat, watered the petunias, and was packing empty beer bottles into her grandmother's garbage when a man in a plaid shirt and pants with suspenders walked up the path.

"You must be the granddaughter," he said when he saw Red. "I've come by to pick up a change of clothes for your grandmother. She's finally getting out of the hospital."

"Thanks," said Red. "The laundry should be about dry. Would you like a muffin before you go? I brought plenty."

## COMMENTARY

This variant on a familiar tale contrasts a bold Red with a mother who stays behind as an attempt to find a parable for the modern girl, who must find her place in circumstances quite different from those of the previous generation. For adults, I've added the interesting issue of the other half of Red's parentage. What do we get when we combine the characteristics of predator and prey? Mine is a rather optimistic conclusion, but that's what fairy tales are for.

## Story Outline

- Red Riding Hood hears that her grandmother is sick and decides to visit.
- Red is discouraged by everyone, but prepares a basket and puts on her traveling cloak anyway.
- Red prepares herself with directions from her uncle.
- Red meets a wolf and keeps going; the wolf leaves.
- Red is suspicious when Grandmother's house is unkempt.
- Red attacks the wolf with an ax and chases him off.
- A man comes by to say that Grandmother is coming home from the hospital.

## Performance Suggestions

Favorite stories like Red Riding Hood are a good place to start storytelling and performance and provide an opportunity to give the familiar a new twist. After telling a story, talk about how the female character responds to a crisis. Look at a book like R. Munsch's *The Paper Bag Princess* for examples of a bold princess and a priggish prince. Try swapping the sex of characters from other well-known stories or give characters entirely new qualities. Assign roles and act out a scene. How might the story of Cinderella be different, for instance, if the stepsisters were adorable, slender, and homely while Cinderella was plump as well as beautiful? If all three were vain and competitive? If the Prince adored Cinderella but she had other career plans and only went to the ball on a lark?

## MOSHE'S MIRACULOUS SHIRT

✳

So miraculously wise was the Rabbi Abu that his synagogue was regularly crowded with people of all ages
and conditions. The rich and content sat in front, nodding
to each other as they listened to the Rabbi speak. They
gratefully brought gifts to their Baba Abu and spoke of
how their generosity had been repaid many times.

At the same time, the unfortunate and unhappy ones,
like poor, bedraggled Moshe, sat in the back of the synagogue and silently sent up their prayers and dreams for
better times. So many people came to listen, and from
such distance, that eventually the Rabbi found himself
tired from the attention, the chatter, even the great pile of
presents that filled his small room.

One day after he finished speaking, watching the merchant's wife drop off another neat pile of shirts he would
never wear, watching poor Moshe stumble out the door in
his tattered rags, the Rabbi took pity. He called out, "Wait,
Moshe, I have something for you," and then handed Moshe
a beautiful white silk shirt too fine for his own taste.

"For me, Baba?" asked Moshe, overcome with happiness.

"For you, Moshe. Wear it and stop playing the fool," said Rabbi Abu fondly.

Moshe immediately tore off his patched and faded shirt, and put on the shimmering shirt of Baba Abu. He puffed out his chest and smoothed down his hair with his hand.

The Rabbi nodded his approval. "Good, Moshe, now you are a *mensch*," he said and watched as Moshe walked out of the synagogue a changed man.

With this deed done, the Rabbi decided to give himself a rest. Why not slip away for a few days? He could walk to the home of his sister several towns away, he told himself. There, certainly, he could lead the quiet life he desired.

As Baba Abu picked up one favorite text and left town by one direction, Moshe took the opposite path and strutted into the community tavern to celebrate his good luck.

Moshe's friends quickly gathered around. "You look so good, Moshe! A miracle!" exclaimed his friend Yisral.

"It's the shirt of Baba Abu, he gave it to me," declared Moshe, as the eyes of his friends grew wide in wonder.

"I'll buy—a hundred drinks!" said Yisral, clapping Moshe on the back.

"No, no, I'll buy. For a year's worth of drinks," cried someone else, and all the men in the tavern cheered.

While Moshe considered this with his mouth hanging open, the bartender looked at the men pushing their way into his tavern and said, "Free drinks, free drinks to the man in the wonderful shirt of Baba Abu."

Now everywhere Moshe went he was the center of attention. He was invited to tea at this house, to dinner at that one. He was escorted to sit at the head of each table; no door in town was closed to him. The merchant's wife nodded as if she knew him when they passed on the street.

As he walked along from one invitation to the next, children followed and danced ahead of him, asking, "Is it true that the shirt you wear is blessed?"

The merchant himself approached Moshe respectfully and inquired, "Tell us, Moshe, where now is our Rabbi Abu? Has the Rabbi simply disappeared?"

Someone else ventured, "Has Baba Abu gone to his rest, as the rumors say, leaving only his miraculous shirt . . ." and Moshe's friend Yisral finished the sentence, "left the shirt with the one he has chosen to replace him—Moshe!"

You won't blame Moshe, then, for standing in the middle of the bazaar shouting, "Blessings, blessings, two coins and your wish will be granted! Travel in safety! Drink without getting sick! Stand tall and be a *mensch*! Two coins to touch the hem of the shirt of Baba Abu!"

That's what Moshe was proclaiming on the third day of the shirt when he turned around and saw standing quietly behind him the Rabbi himself. Moshe took a fast, deep breath, then seized the Rabbi by the sleeve and pulled him around the corner, out of sight of the others.

"Here, Baba Abu, take these coins, as many as you want. I can pay you now, for your shirt," said Moshe, emptying out his pockets.

The Rabbi smiled sadly. "No, no, Moshe," he said. "I believe I'll go back to the home of my sister. You keep the money. The story is worth more than the shirt."

## COMMENTARY

The opening incident of this little morality tale comes from Diane Wolkstein's "The Seer of Lublin's Shirt" in *Parabola*. I updated it with a news report in the *New York Times* on February 14, 1993, wherein reporter Joel Greenberg describes miracles taking place at the tomb of a saintly man in Israel. I increased contrasts between rich and poor and the subtlety of the Rabbi against the more commercial message of Moshe to make another point. The poor have so much respect for the Rabbi that they hardly dare approach; Moshe brings comfort for only two coins. Perhaps the Rabbi suspects that with time, Moshe is capable of becoming a worthy vessel of sacred history. Truth moves in mysterious ways, and the Rabbi needs a rest. How often does a wise man get the chance to retire?

## STORY OUTLINE

- Rabbi Abu, affectionately called Baba Abu, preaches to rich and poor.
- The rich give Baba Abu many gifts; Baba watches the poor, like Moshe, continue to stumble around.
- Baba Abu gives a new silk shirt to Moshe—"Be a *mensch*," he tells Moshe.
- Baba Abu leaves to visit his sister.
- Moshe is a changed man; he gets respect; people believe he wears a magical shirt.
- Moshe is selling a touch of his shirt for two coins when the Rabbi returns.
- Moshe tries to pay for his shirt, but the Rabbi refuses.
- Rabbi Abu decides to go back to his sister's house and not interfere with Moshe's new position or business. "The story is worth more than the shirt."

## PERFORMANCE SUGGESTIONS

Moshe is a natural clown character, allowing for the introduction of clown theater to this performance. Clowns are holy fools in many traditions, from the Buddhist processional clowns to Hopi performance clowns. The clown familiar to Westerners, out of the European circus, is a degenerate laugh-puller who tries to be funny; true clowns are funny because they reveal common human folly. If you have someone with special gymnastic or musical talent, use the role of Moshe to show it off. Moshe could be extended to be a family of performers or a traveling troupe that drops in to hear the Rabbi, puts on a quick show for him, and earns a new set of clothes. They could be flashy performers in the marketplace, singing, dancing, doing cartwheels, and juggling like the performers who created the early Greek medicine shows and became roving theater troupes in medieval Europe.

Children adore wearing clown makeup. Check out a video or invite a guest specialist in theatrical makeup and give every performer the chance to design and wear a new face for this story. Or make half-masks like those used in commedia dell'arte.

For young people ready to explore alternative performance styles, this story could be done in Chinese theater style or as Kabuki, with stylized, exaggerated movement, sing-song voices, and, of course, face paint.

# FROM THE KIDS

*

# HOW BLONDES CAME
# TO BE KNOWN AS AIRHEADS

✳

In the beginning, things were a lot more equal. People looked more alike than they do now, and one person was about as smart and good-looking as another. Life was peaceful. Two boys, George and Sam, started the trouble. They acted as though being alike was bad. One day they were particularly obnoxious, making fun of three girls who were walking home from school together. After a while, the girls were tired of this. As soon as they could get to a telephone, the girls called the Devil over to help.

Instantly the Devil strolled in the back door, carrying an enormous black pot. He filled the pot with water, set it on the stove, and asked the girls what they wanted.

While the girls were thinking about this, they could hear a serious commotion outside. George and Sam, not knowing the Devil was in the house with the girls, stood on the front porch, banging on the door.

Sam called out, "Girls are stupid!"

"We want to be smart," said one of the girls.

"Sure 'nuff," said the Devil, pulling a paperback dictionary out of his pocket and throwing it into the pot.

"Ugly, ugly," George called out, getting the idea.

"We want to be pretty, definitely," said the second girl.

"Adorable," said the third.

"No problem," said the Devil, stirring a stuffed toy kitten into the boiling pot.

"Beady eye, beady eye," crowed the boys outside.

"Blue eyes, *big* blue eyes," said the first girl.

"Blonde too?" asked the Devil, holding a photograph of Marilyn Monroe over the pot.

"Why not," said the other two girls, and so the Devil dropped it in.

"Body like a yam," sang the boys. "Boop, boop, boop, boop!" They were doing some kind of waddling dance on the porch.

"A body to kill for, if you please," said the first girl, sweetly. The Devil winked, pulled an hourglass out of his back pocket and flipped it into the pot.

"Croak like a frog," screeched George.

"Stringy hair, stringy hair," croaked Sam.

"A voice like honey," said the second girl.

"And long, fluffy hair, big hair, really big hair," said the third.

"Don't know why I didn't think of this before," said the Devil, grabbing a Barbie doll from a shelf, aiming it at the pot. The doll sank like a stone, the pot boiled up in every color of the rainbow, and the Devil grandly passed around a cup.

Just as the girls finished drinking the Devil's potion, George and Sam pushed in the front door. Instantly the Devil disappeared in a burst of crystalline rainbow sparks. When the sparks cleared away, all Sam and George could see were the smartest, most beautiful blondes in creation, girls with round blue eyes, baby doll voices, bodies to kill for, and fabulous big-Big-BIG hair. Sam and George were speechless as the girls sashayed out the door.

The trouble is, the Devil did his work too well. Nowadays blondes are so pretty, hardly anyone notices how smart they are, and the only thing some males notice is what is on the head, not what is inside. That's how blondes got to be called airheads.


## COMMENTARY

This story is based on an idea developed by workshop participants. The students heard the Gypsy creation story, "How the Devil Helped," on pages 29–32. They were part of a large drama class that broke into groups, each group inventing its own tale with occasional suggestions from their roving guest teacher. All the girls needed was a "What if " kind of suggestion. What if the Devil helped? I've added some details and literary niggles.


## STORY OUTLINE

- In the beginning, people were pretty much alike.
- George and Sam cause trouble by making fun of girls.
- The girls ask the Devil to help them change.
- Girls ask for and get brains, beauty, blue eyes, curvaceous bodies, honeyed voices, fluffy, big blonde hair.
- The boys burst in, the Devil disappears, and the boys are so struck by the beauty of the girls, they don't notice the brains part.


## PERFORMANCE SUGGESTIONS

This is simple and satisfying to stage. Vary the Devil's gifts according to prevailing taste and available props, if you like. The girls can run offstage or behind a screen, come back with a scarf, a wig, or a headband with yellow crepe hair. A big finale is to have life-sized drawings of really boffo female bodies, colored and cut out, mounted on cardboard, a hole for each face, waiting behind the screens. Keep other prop changes simple until you get to this one. If you can manage to have some fireworks come out of the pot (I leave this to you and your fire code), all the better. Dance ribbons accompanied by cymbals will work.

The Devil can be any authority figure the group selects in horns and forked tail—your choice, male or female. The satirical possibilities are endless.

## OUR HEROINE EVA KNEVA

✳

Eva was part human, part tarantula, the oldest child of the god Spider Man and a human mother. It's a little-known fact that she had two brothers, Batman and Robin. They all had human faces and strange bodies. Because Eva's skin was a leathery black, tough as a motorcycle pants and jacket, she didn't bother with a disguise. Most people don't know that what they think is Batman's cape form is his real self and the human form is the disguise. But that's another story.

Our story begins when Eva decided not to fight nature. She learned how to ride a tricycle by using two pairs of arms on each handlebar. When she was three years old, her parents took advantage of how strong she was and entered her in an international wrestling competition. They didn't have any rules about how many arms or legs you could have, so she bent her way to the top. She took the championship away from a guy who was a motorcycle gang member. His friends stopped her as she was leaving the arena on her tricycle. They surrounded her on their big bikes and rushed her. She grabbed the first one who got to her and used him and his motorcycle as a club to beat on the others. After she had the gang scattered on the street, she bent the motorcycle she'd been using back into shape and rode off on it.

This started Eva on her life task. She had a motorcycle tattooed on her forehead and traveled across nations seeking out ways to end trouble. Eva was always the friend of motorcyclists, despite her rough start. For instance, she was the one who ended the career of another supernatural figure, Harley, the son of a demon (because he was from Norway, he called himself Harley Demonsen). Harley made a habit of eating motorcycles. Eva's strategy was simple. She set herself and her bike out on the road as bait, then rode right into Harley's gullet. She spun a web that froze his mouth permanently open, and then left her tire tracks for others to follow. Now Harley is one more joy ride in an amusement park.

But Eva isn't most famous for her kind acts. Some people just wanted to see her amazing strength, and so she ended up accepting several big challenges in her life. The first was to break the world speed record on the salt flats of the Great Salt Lake. Her speed was so great that she burned ruts into the flats and ruined them for further racing. Her tires were smoking too, so her next task was to ride up Mount Everest. She climbed the mountain with her snow treads and hit the biggest wheelie ever, landing her in China in the middle of the great wall.

This stunt gave people the idea of having Eva jump the Grand Canyon. She picked up speed somewhere in Utah and went up, up, ahh, and over the canyon. She hit a thousand miles an hour, which made her motorcycle so hot it nearly melted.

At the age of 85, Eva faced her greatest task, chasing a dog-monster named Rover. This huge dog was infamous among bikers because he preferred their motorcycles to trees or fire plugs. When Eva went out to ride one morning, she saw Rover lift his leg on her bike. She took off after him and stabbed him to death with one of her knitting needles. This took so long that by the time she got back, her motorcycle was slowly crumbling from the poisonous spray of Rover. Eva died of a broken heart. She was found the next day, lying next to a pile of rust.

Because Eva was a heroine, the other gods came to escort her spirit to the underworld. Eva didn't want to be carried across the river of the dead, so she grabbed a minibike and cleared it in one jump. It gave her a fit of temper, though, because it didn't have a headlight—she was so mad she stripped her gearshift.

What was worse, she realized once she got to hell, was that they had no racetracks for her to ride on. Her engine slowed down, and she realized she was running out of gas. She picked up her minibike and carried it the rest of the way across hell.

About that time, an excavator dug up Eva's skeleton by mistake. After her amazing bones were ground up, she was loaded into a fertilizer-spraying machine. The plane oversprayed, hitting a motorcycle manufacturing plant. Eva's spirit bounded onto a brand-new, souped-up motorcycle and rode into the heavens forever.


COMMENTARY

This story was created as part of a special writing project at Moscow (Idaho) Junior High School in the late 1970s, when the exploits of motorcyclist Bobby "Evil" Kneivel were in the news. Seventh graders in a mythology class were given the five stages in the life of a mythic hero—miraculous birth, first sign of exceptional ability, greatest life task or quest, death, and apotheosis. In five groups of four or five students, with minimal guidance, they filled in the details, taking responsibility for coordinating between writing groups as they proceeded. This story was created in one class session of forty-five minutes. It is recorded here not as an ideal, but as an example of what can be accomplished within a relatively short time. Although I found it amusing and imaginative, I did not believe the experience caused any new growth or awareness in the participants—it was simply an exercise in cleverness, which these bright youngsters had in abundance. This experience led directly to my "no violent solutions of conflict" rule.

## STORY OUTLINE

- Eva is born of Spider Man and a human mother.
- Eva wins a wrestling championship at age three.
- Motorcycle buddies of the former champion attack; Eva wins.
- Eva rides out in defense of good, in search of challenges.
- Eva defeats Harley Demonsen, and turns him into roadside attraction.
- Eva jumps the Grand Canyon.
- In her mid-eighties, Eva faces her last challenge, a monster dog.
- Rover is destroyed, but only after Eva's cycle is turned to rust.
- Eva dies of a broken heart; the gods escort her spirit to the underworld.
- Eva's bones are sprayed over a motorcycle factory, freeing her spirit. She rides to the heavens.

## PERFORMANCE SUGGESTIONS

This can be performed as a shadow-puppet play. Make outlined forms of the characters, glue them to cardboard, cut them out, and glue them to long sticks (bamboo skewers will do). Hang a cloth over a small table so that puppeteers don't project through the curtain. Position lamps behind the puppets, hang a curtain in front, practice holding the puppets close enough to project an image. If you put a joint on the jaw of Harley Demonsen, he can be propped open to allow Eva to ride right through. Use only a giant head for Harley and maybe only big feet for the dog Rover. Prop cliffs for the Grand Canyon work well too.

# SHARING THE WELL

✳

CAST OF CHARACTERS:
    Bouki the hyena
    Leuk the hare
    Kewel the red deer
    Kewel's son
    Leopard
    Fly
    Narrator
    Chorus of animals/audience (can be performers, also)

NARRATOR: Good day!
CHORUS: A fine day!
NARRATOR: For a story?
CHORUS: Yes!
NARRATOR: I'll tell you a story.
CHORUS: We're listening.
NARRATOR: Once upon a thirsty day. . . .
CHORUS: We remember. . . .

NARRATOR: We had a long, dry winter, a warm, dry spring and a hot, hot, dry summer. Most of the water holes and springs disappeared. The animals of the bush had to search so far that they spent most of their day walking, walking many miles for water.

One day they met on a path.

(Leuk *the hare meets* Bouki *the hyena.*)

BOUKI: A good day!

LEUK: A fine day!

BOUKI: How are you, Leuk?

LEUK: Thirsty. And you?

BOUKI: Thirsty.

LEUK: I'm off to a water hole for a drink.

(Bouki *sets down a small gourd.* Kewel *the red deer comes up and picks it up without* Bouki's *noticing.*)

BOUKI: I'm just back from the water hole with my drink.

LEUK: You just came back from the water hole and you're already thirsty?

(Kewel *the red deer and her child quickly drink the water from the gourd behind* Bouki's *back.*)

BOUKI: Yes. It's good that I brought extra water home with me in this gourd.

(Bouki *looks for the gourd;* Kewel *hands the gourd to* Bouki, *who turns it over and sees that it's empty.*)

KEWEL: I'm Kewel, Kewel the red deer, I don't carry water, but you can't stop me from drinking. That goes for my little son too.

(Kewel *and her child run away.*)

(Leopard *and* Fly *come in from different paths.*)

LEOPARD: A good day!

FLY: A fine day!

LEOPARD: Where does Kewel go so quickly?

(Kewel *bounds by again and speaks as she runs through the middle of the animals.*)

KEWEL: For water!

LEUK: We all go for water.

FLY: Unless we have water here.

LEOPARD: A fine idea. How do we do that?

BOUKI: We dig our own!

(Bouki, Leuk, Fly, and Leopard *pantomime digging*.)

NARRATOR: The next day, the animals go early for their water at the distant well. They spend the rest of the day digging to find their own well. Each day they do this.

CHORUS(*looking up*): Each day!

(*As the animals speak, looking at the audience, Kewel sneaks up behind them, takes a sip from a bowl, hands it to her child, who sips.*)

NARRATOR: Everybody works but Kewel. While the others dig clods, carry dirt, pound bricks for the sides of the well, Kewel only causes trouble.

(Leopard *uses big paws to pull out vegetation with a growl*; Bouki *digs furiously; the others use gourd bowls to carry away dirt. As the animals work and wipe their brows, Kewel and her child run through, tipping bowls over and calling out.*)

KEWEL: I'm Kewel, Kewel the red deer. I don't dig for water, but you can't stop me from drinking. And that goes for my little son too.

LEUK: Kewel!

BOUKI: Water, everybody! We've found water!

NARRATOR: Everyone congratulates Bouki and each other and has their first good drink in a long, long time. Then they wash their faces and look down.

LEUK: Good water!

CHORUS: Fine water!

LEOPARD: Not much of it.

FLY: We'll have to post a guard. Or else . . .

(*The animals turn to look at* Kewel, *who stands with her child very close by.*)

CHORUS: Or else.

BOUKI: I'll do it.

LEUK: That's good.

FLY: That's fine.

LEOPARD: Take care you don't fall asleep.

CHORUS: Or else.

LEOPARD: Or else.

(Kewel *dances around the edge of the group of animals, circles the well and animals. The animals leave slowly, watching* Kewel. Bouki *takes her position. At first she is very alert, watching* Kewel's *every move.* Bouki *gets bored, fights sleep, fights sleep very hard, stretches, scratches, stretches—and falls asleep.* Kewel *comes up, walks down to the well, fills a gourd with water, takes a big drink, fills the gourd again, gives her child a drink, washes her face, pours a gourdful over child's face, then goes running over the top of* Bouki, *calling out.*)

KEWEL: I'm Kewel, Kewel the red deer. I don't dig wells but you can't stop me from drinking. And that goes for my little son too.

(Bouki *rolls over, kicks, stretches, goes back to sleep. It's morning. The animals approach with their water gourds, but they get only a little water each.*)

LEOPARD: Look here, Kewel's footsteps.

BOUKI: What the devil!

CHORUS: You slept!

BOUKI: I slept! That Kewel, no one can stop her from drinking.

(*The animals all shake their heads and start to walk away.*)

LEOPARD: Leuk, tonight you watch.

LEUK: I will. Kewel won't catch me sleeping.

BOUKI: That's good.

FLY: That's fine.

(*The animals all leave. Leuk comes back, settles down, watches alertly, looks in every direction, circles around in a small circle, settles down, sinks down slowly, falls asleep in a sitting position. Kewel comes in as before, fills her gourd, drinks, fills her gourd for her child, washes her face, fills the gourd again, and starts to pour it on her child, who shakes her head and takes the gourd. As they leave, the child pours the water on Leuk.*)

KEWEL: I'm Kewel, Kewel the hind. I don't guard wells, but you can't stop me from drinking. And that goes for my little son too.

NARRATOR: The next night Leopard and Fly decide to keep watch together, with Fly waiting down by the well and Leopard hiding some distance away.

(Leopard *and* Fly *take their places.* Fly *buzzes around fiercely, as* Leopard *hunkers down and waits.* Kewel *and her child walk up but don't see anyone at the usual place. They go down to the well.*)

FLY: They're here! Leopard! Leopard! Kewel and her child are here!

(Leopard *growls, jumps out, and blocks the path. All the animals run out,* Kewel *is surrounded.* Kewel *is captured, but her child gets away.*)

FLY: Here's a vine.

LEOPARD: Bouki and I will hold her.

(Leuk *and* Fly *wind the vine around* Kewel *and tie it.*)

LEUK: The child!

FLY: The child got away!

LEOPARD: We'll go looking.

BOUKI: I'll stay here with Kewel.

LEOPARD: Bouki . . .

BOUKI: You can trust me. It's a long time before bed-time.

(*The animals leave to find* Kewel's *child.* Bouki *circles happily around* Kewel, *quite proud of herself.* Kewel *does-n't seem bothered.* Bouki *sits, looks happily at* Kewel, *looks around a bit, looks back at* Kewel, *stretches, realizes this isn't a good idea, sits up straight trying to keep awake.*)

BOUKI: Kewel, sing me your song.

KEWEL: I can't. My leg hurts. I can't sing when my leg is tied up too tight.

(Bouki *loosens one leg a little bit, reluctantly.*)

KEWEL: Ahem. I am Kewel, Kewel. . . . It's still too tight.

(Bouki *loosens the vine a little more.*)

KEWEL: I am Kewel, Kewel, I don't tie vines. . . . Ahem. A little looser, please.

(Bouki *loosens the vine one more time.* Kewel's *child comes up behind* Bouki's *back.* Kewel *smiles and shakes herself.*)

KEWEL: I'm Kewel, Kewel.

(Kewel *jumps out of the vines. The child runs up and distracts* Bouki.)

KEWEL: And nothing can keep me from running.

(Kewel *and her child run away.*)

BOUKI: Hey there, stop!

(*The other animals return, look for* Kewel.)

BOUKI: The devil.

NARRATOR: And that explains why today the animals come to the well for a morning drink and another as the sun sets and as they drink they say:

BOUKI: Drink deep. Kewel comes at night. . . .

LEUK: You can't keep Kewel from drinking.

KEWEL: And that goes for my little son too.

# Commentary

This transcription of a performance combines the homely and the sublime, the ordinary and the tragic, as understood by the actors, after they heard a benign version of "The Foolish Hyena," a tale from Senegal in William I. Kaufman's collection, *UNICEF Book of Children's Legends*.

## Story Outline

- Bouki, Leuk, Fly, and Leopard agree that they need water.
- All the animals but Kewel help dig a well.
- Kewel and her son cause trouble and steal water.
- Bouki is posted to guard the well and falls asleep.
- Kewel and her son steal water.
- Leuk is posted to guard the well and falls asleep.
- Kewel and son steal water.
- Fly and Leopard guard together and catch Kewel.
- Bouki is left to guard as others search for Kewel's son.
- Kewel talks Bouki into loosening her bonds and escapes.
- The animals decide to drink early and expect to share with Kewel.

## Performance Suggestions

Props for this play can be simple: wooden bowls or gourds for digging and holding water; a ribbon to tie Kewel; something to represent the well (we typically use a metal wastepaper basket). Use a convention such as running around the staging area in one complete circle to represent Kewel's escape; Kewel and the son can be watching all the action from the back of the stage. Rehearse with a script only long enough for everyone to master the action, then improvise everyone but the narrator. If you want to save the language of the script, do a puppet play with copies of the script tucked out of sight.

# SAVING STONE MONSTER

✳

CAST OF CHARACTERS:
Attack Brother 1
Attack Brother 2
Fairy
Bumping Turtle

*The* Attack Brothers *enter the Magical Forest carrying cardboard swords and huge bags. They move in quickly, then stop and look around.*

BROTHER 1: Wow.

BROTHER 2: Wow.

BROTHER 1 and BROTHER 2: Look at all this stuff.

(Brother 2 *starts wildly swinging sword around, knocking down "tree branches"—green crepe-paper streamers.*)

BROTHER 2: . . . to kill.

BROTHER 1: . . . to save. Remember?

BROTHER 2: Oh, yeah. To save.

BROTHER 1: For the zoo. The zoo is paying us, remember?

BROTHER 2: Oh, yeah.

BROTHER 1: Yeah, to find the rare Bumping Turtle of Magical Forest!

BROTHER 2: The only Bumping Turtle in the world!

(Brother 2 *starts swinging wildly again and knocks down more green streamers.*)

BROTHER 1: Hey, stop destroying things.

(Brother 2 *takes a swing at* Brother 1.)

BROTHER 2: I'm collecting.

(Brother 2 *stuffs green strips into his bag;* Bumping Turtle *crawls by on the way to the fairy bower, bumps* Brother 1.)

BROTHER 1: Watch it!

BROTHER 2: Watch it! Watch what?

(Brother 2 *bumps into* Brother 1 *trying to see what happened; brothers jostle.* Bumping Turtle *scurries off into the fairy bower, where it disappears from their sight.* Brother 1 *and* Brother 2 *look at each other, amazed.*)

BROTHER 1 and BROTHER 2: The famous Bumping Turtle!!

(*They run after it, stop right before the fairy bower, turn to each other, and shrug shoulders.*)

BROTHER 1: Where did it go?

BROTHER 2: I dunno.

BROTHER 1: I dunno.

(Brother 2 *holds sword in front and searches around the stage.*)

BROTHER 1: The bag!

BROTHER 2: The bag!

(Brother 1 *and* Brother 2 *hold bags open, low, go off-stage in search. After* Attack Brothers *exit,* Fairy *and* Bumping Turtle *emerge from the fairy bower.*)

FAIRY: Speak up, Bumping Turtle. What do you want?

BUMP: The Attack Brothers are after me. They want to put me in a zoo.

FAIRY: Is that who's chopping up my trees?

BUMP: Get them out of here. Please.

FAIRY: You're the one who marked the path. They can follow it.

BUMP: They won't leave until they've captured me. You've got to protect me.

FAIRY: Okay, I'll give you a better shell. Here.

(Fairy *reaches back into the bower for a small cardboard shell.* Bumping *puts it on.*)

BUMP: Thanks.

(Bumping Turtle *crawls off, not as fast as before.* Brother 2 *comes onstage gathering stones, putting them in his bag.* Bumping Turtle *bumps him, and he rolls over just as* Brother 1 *comes onstage and sees his brother, but he doesn't notice the turtle.*)

BROTHER 2: Hey!!

BROTHER 1: What are you doing?

BROTHER 2: Who cares about a stupid turtle? Look at this! Diamonds, rubies, all over the place.

BROTHER 1: The turtle!

(Brother 1 *draws his sword and hits ground near turtle shell as* Bumping Turtle *dives through the fairy bower to safety.*)

BROTHER 1: Oh, well.

(Brother 1 *joins* Brother 2 *gathering stones. They exit stage left.* Fairy *and* Turtle *emerge.*)

FAIRY: A bigger shell?

BUMP: That's right. I need more protection.

(Fairy *reaches back and brings out a larger shell with bumps.*)

FAIRY: These bumps will turn their swords to mush.

BUMP: Good.

(*He puts it on and starts crawling off.* Fairy *goes in her bower.*)

BUMP: Oh, no!

(Fairy *peeks out, head only.*)

FAIRY: Now what?

BUMP: The path! Someone stole my path! Now they'll be stuck here forever.

FAIRY: You have to get rid of them.

BUMP: Me???

FAIRY: You have to lead them out. You know the dangers. I have potions to mix. I have my whole day's work planned out.

BUMP: All right, but I need one more thing.

FAIRY: What's that?

BUMP: I want to be as heavy as a stone if someone tries to pick me up. That way they can't put me in their bag and carry me to the zoo.

FAIRY: Okay, okay.

(Fairy *waves wand over* Bumping Turtle's *head.*)

BUMP: Thanks.

(Bumping Turtle *goes out, stops, sees* Attack Brothers, *who have their bags loaded. They drop the bags and leap.*)

BROTHER 1 and BROTHER 2: Eeyah!!

(Attack Brothers *make a simultaneous leap at* Bumping Turtle, *land on the ground near him, and roll.*)

BROTHER 1: You bumped me!

BROTHER 2: You bumped me!

BUMP: I bumped you.

(Attack Brothers, *one on each side of* Bumping Turtle, *try to lift him up. They can't move him.*)

BROTHER 1: Give up. If you don't come with us, you'll be extinct.

BUMP: Do you want to live in a zoo?

BROTHER 1: Well, no.

BUMP: Neither do I. Not when I have the Magical Forest.

BROTHER 2: Who needs a stone monster? We've got jewels. Let's get out of here.

BROTHER 1: How?

BUMP: I know the way.

BROTHER 1 and BROTHER 2: Great! Great, thanks, Stone Buddy.

BUMP: There's only one problem.

BROTHER 1: Attacking problems is our middle name.

BUMP: How about crawling under Water Fizz?

BROTHER 1 and BROTHER 2: Water what?

BUMP: Water Fizz. A waterfall of burning hot water.

(Attack Brothers *look at each other and shrug.* Fairy *comes out of bower with two turtle shells.*)

FAIRY: Here, take these. After you're gone, we won't need them anyway.

(Attack Brothers *each put shell strap over an arm as a shield and follow* Bumping Turtle. Bumping Turtle *leads them up to the red streamers and points ahead.*)

BUMP: That way.

(Attack Brothers *pass through red "fire" with turtle shields over their heads.*)

BROTHER 1: Ouch! Youch!

BROTHER 2: This isn't so bad.

BROTHER 1: Bye!

BROTHER 2: Bye, Stone Dude!

BUMP: Good-bye!

(Attack Brothers *turn to each other.*)

BROTHER 1: Back to the zoo.

BROTHER 2: With the only living shells of the famous . . .

BROTHER 1 and BROTHER 2: Bumping Turtle.

(*They wave their shells and exit.*)

## COMMENTARY

This was written in collaboration with eight- and six-year-old performers. Two of the children had studied martial arts and could make spectacular simultaneous leaps. We built the story around them and the reactions they produced in others. Folklorists and anthropologists have observed the Celtic fascination with warrior heroes. How do we respond to two charismatic guys in a way that preserves autonomy and a separate capacity for judgment?

## STORY OUTLINE

- Attack Brothers enter Magical Forest looking for Bumping Turtle to take back to the zoo.
- Bumping Turtle runs for protection to Fairy in her bower.
- Fairy gives Bumping Turtle a better shell.
- Attack Brothers fill collector bags with gems.
- Attack Brothers attack Turtle; he escapes.
- Bumping Turtle goes back to Fairy for a stronger shell.
- Bumping Turtle discovers that the gems marking his path have been stolen; he needs to get rid of the Attack Brothers.
- Fairy makes him heavy so that the brothers can't carry him off.
- Bumping Turtle convinces the brothers he won't go with them.
- Fairy gives brothers shells to help them get through dangers.
- Bumping Turtle leads Attack Brothers out of Magical Forest.

## PERFORMANCE SUGGESTIONS

The Attack Brothers speak and act virtually simultaneously. If this isn't achievable, have one "brother" imitate the other as quickly and as closely as possible. The brothers also interrupt each other, push and shove, and bicker constantly.

For Magical Forest, string cord across the staging area and hang blue crepe-paper strips on one side, stapled together at the top for stability, to represent the door to the fairy bower. Loose green crepe-paper streamers in the center of the string represent tree branches that fall when attacked with a cardboard sword. Red streamers on the other side are the Water Fizz, the magical waterfall of hot water. Green crepe paper hangs about waist high on the smaller brother; red and blue hang about twelve inches from the floor, providing enough clearance so that nobody trips. If you hang the cord at a diagonal, the fairy bower is in the back corner, stage right, and the Water Fizz near the front of staging area, stage left. Wads of colored paper or brightly colored bean bags are gems marking the path. The Attack Brothers need no special costume. The fairy wand is a sturdy twig tied with tinsel. Bumping Turtle wears a vest or jacket (we used a green satin Chinese-style jacket) for the soft shell, ovals of two-ply cardboard for the hard shell (cut circles, slash to middle on one side, overlap edges to form a slight cone, staple). One appliance or bicycle box will supply three turtle shells and swords. Use strapping tape to attach cardboard handles on the inside. Tape one handle on each side so that the turtle can wear the shell over his shoulders like a backpack. You could also use duct tape to attach the cardboard shells to lightweight backpacks.

For bumps on the shells, paint or draw circles, cut out half way, and fold cut part upward.

# BACK TO REALITY

✳

CAST OF CHARACTERS:
  Nightingale the Fairy
  Lightning the Unicorn
  Dino Mite Dino
  Punk Poodle
  Dumbo
  Elf
  Snow Queen
  Host 1
  Host 2

*Start with lights dimmed; house lights are flashed, then brought up for entry into Fairy Reality. Center of staging area is the fairy house, with pillows for fairy couch, standing screen or hanging crepe-paper streamers as the walls of the fairy house. Stage left, Dino's bedroom, has a large pillow on the floor and a poster-sized sheet of paper on the wall printed with the title "See! Punk Poodle!" Three card-*

board boxes, covered with plain newsprint paper, decorated with drawings of storybooks, are taped shut and stacked to represent the library. A large pair of cardboard-cutout scissors lies on the floor next to Dino's bed. Dino carries a notebook and pen.

(Hosts enter.)

HOST 1: Welcome to our play. The name of the play is "Back to Reality."

HOST 2: About a month ago, Dino Mite Dino was brought back to life by a scientist. Our story starts after Dino escapes from the scientist and runs to Canada. Because of Dino Mite, our story moves into Fairy Reality.

(Nightingale the Fairy enters, sits on pillow in fairy house. Punk Poodle enters, poses against white sheet of 'poster' on wall. Story characters Elf, Snow Queen, and Dumbo enter, pose by library tower, freeze. Dino Mite enters, looks at story he is writing.)

DINO: President Lincoln's false teeth. Why would I want to write about that? What am I doing here? This is not my era.

(Dino throws down notebook and pencil, lies on bed, snores.)

FAIRY (holding up small blanket): Fairy Reality is nice, but I wish I had a dog I could give this blanket to.

UNICORN: I'll look around for you. I can fly anywhere.

(Unicorn exits toward library.)

(Dino wakes up from nap, fretful.)

DINO: I'm in a bad mood. Where are my five-reality scissors?

(Dino cuts up his poster; as he cuts the paper—tearing it after making a big cutting motion—Punk Poodle screeches and falls into fairyland. Dino cuts up library, kicking boxes over as he makes cutting motion. Dumbo, Snow Queen, and Elf fall into fairyland. )

DINO: That's better.

(Dino *drops his scissors, yawns, lies back down on his bed.*)

FAIRY: Where did you come from? And you? And you?

SNOW QUEEN: I don't know.

ELF: Somebody just cut us out of our books.

POODLE: I know who did it. Dino Mite Dino cut me out of my poster and threw me in the garbage can. Sure enough, when he cut my poster, he cut up my reality too. I fell right through the stage floor. I was acting in front of the President of the United States, and it was pretty embarrassing.

FAIRY (*to storybook characters*): What about the rest of you? Where did you say you came from? And by the way, who are all of you?

SNOW QUEEN: I'm the Snow Queen. I'm from a beautiful story.

ELF: I'm an elf. I work for Santa. I'm sure he's missing me.

DUMBO: Mm, mmn, mmm!

ELF: She can't talk.

FAIRY: I'll fix that. (*waves wand*)

DUMBO: I'm Dumbo. Where's my circus?

FAIRY: I wonder how you got out of your universe.

POODLE: If Dino Mite Dino were here, he could straighten things out. Ever since the professor brought him back to life, he's been in a bad temper.

ELF: How do we get back?

POODLE: Dino could take us. He's got magic scissors. I'm pretty mad at him, actually.

QUEEN: But you were only a poster. I'm in books all over the world.

POODLE: Maybe you haven't heard of me. You only know one story, I guess. I'm a star. I'm more real than a story person.

QUEEN: A story queen.

POODLE: A queen. I'm Punk Poodle, star of posters and stage. I sing, I dance. Awoo! (*She does a twirl.*)

FAIRY: That's wonderful. Wouldn't you like to take a cushion?

POODLE: Thanks. (*sits*)

DUMBO: How are we going to get all the way back?

ELF: I don't know. And only one hundred hammering days until Christmas.

POODLE: Maybe I don't want to go back. I'm tired of prancing around on two legs.

FAIRY: Will you stay and be my dog? I can teach you to fly like Lightning, my unicorn.

POODLE: No doing tricks for dinner?

FAIRY: Not ever.

POODLE: All right, then. Yes, Woof!

ELF: What about the rest of us? Could anything get us back?

FAIRY: There is a magic diamond, but it's a long ways away and is guarded by monsters.

UNICORN (*coming back from behind stage*): Sorry, Fairy, I couldn't find you a—a dog!

POODLE: Not just a dog—Punk Poodle! Awoo! (*does her twirl*)

FAIRY: Lightning, we need Dino Mite Dino here, right now.

POODLE: He's in Canada, hiding from the scientist who brought him back from the Ice Age.

UNICORN: I can fly out of Fairy Reality and get him.

(Unicorn *exits, "flies" over to* Dino, *brings him back*.)

(Dino *slowly enters*.)

POODLE: Woof!

FAIRY: Is that Dino Mite Dino?

POODLE: What were you doing, cutting me down like that? Woof!

(*All but* Fairy *chase* Dino *around the stage,* Poodle *leading the chase, until all are back in center stage again.*)

POODLE: Wait a minute. Maybe he can cut us over to where the diamond is.

DINO: Nope.

POODLE: He can lead a search party for the diamond. And then he can face the wild beasts first. After all, he's a wild beast himself.

DINO: Me?

EVERYONE: Yes!

POODLE: Use your five-reality scissors. We have to find the diamond to get Dumbo and Elf and the Snow Queen back into their stories.

QUEEN: Children are waiting.

DINO: Sorry. I lost my scissors.

ELF: Why did you cut us out of the library in the first place?

DINO: Because I was walking around minding my own business and snipping without thinking.

POODLE: Why did you cut me out of my poster?

DINO: It was only a poster.

POODLE: Oh, yeah? I was actually acting on stage in front of the President of the United States when you cut me out of the poster, and I fell through the stage.

ELF: She says it was very embarrassing.

DINO: Nice special effects, though. Did he enjoy it?

POODLE: I don't know. He probably fired the manager. Actually, I was getting pretty tired of being a star, performing all the time. Ah-woooh! (*howls*) I'm staying here.

FAIRY: Good. (*puts her shawl on* Poodle)

POODLE (*to* Dino): Now that we've actually met, tell me how you got your hairdo.

DINO: When electricity zapped me to bring me back from the Ice Age, I turned this color.

POODLE: It's a cool cut. I mean, it's my style.

(*Both* Dino *and* Poodle *have purple and orange striped hair.*)

DINO: Well, I have purple blood.

POODLE: Purple blood? Coloring your hair?

DINO: I can't explain things. I'm from another era. The brain may be a transplant. A trick of science. Who knows where it's been.

SNOW QUEEN: This is getting complicated.

POODLE: And where did you get the name Dino Mite?

DINO: Doctor Glockenspiel gave it to me when he thawed me out, and I'll have you know, a glockenspiel is a kind of instrument.

FAIRY: You're a very smart monster even if your brain is new. We could use one of those.

ELF: Aren't we going to get the diamond?

DINO: Yeah, I'll go get the diamond.

FAIRY: I'll go with you.

POODLE: You'll need a search party.

FAIRY: Dumbo, do you think you could carry us?

DUMBO: Mm, maybe.

UNICORN: I can carry someone.

POODLE (*does a turn or two around in her new scarf*): I'm going to stay right here where it's nice and safe. I've had enough flying around.

(*All leave following behind* Dumbo *except* Poodle, *who shakes and whimpers while voices of a battle come from behind the scenery. They make several beast/monster noises.*)

FAIRY: Think, everybody, think! Imagine we've won.

ALL (*from behind scenery*): We got it! We got it!

(*All return to stage.*)

FAIRY: Are you ready to go back now that we have the diamond?

DUMBO, ELF, QUEEN: Yes.

FAIRY (*to* Dino): Aren't you going back?

DINO: Well, are there any coke machines here?

POODLE: Oh, Dino Mite Dino. It's better than that. They have water that turns all colors and flavors. They have coke machines if you just imagine it. This is fairyland.

DINO: Where are those machines?

POODLE: Just imagine there's one behind you.

DINO: Hmm. (*Motions with his hands, outlining the shape around it, picks it up, and eats it.*)

I don't really like the metal or the plastic.

ELF: Ate it? You ate it? You're not supposed to eat it. You're supposed to drink what's inside it!

QUEEN: Now you can't have another because you ate the coke machine!

DINO: Now I'm imagining a giant tuna machine.

ELF: A tuna machine!

DINO: A great big tuna can, I'm imagining it right in front me.

QUEEN: Don't eat the can.

ELF: Did you eat the can?

DINO: No, there was some frozen tuna inside, and it tasted horrible.

FAIRY: So who's going back?

ELF: I am.

QUEEN: I am.

FAIRY: What about you, Dumbo, are you going back?

DUMBO: Yes.

FAIRY: Whoever's going back, hold hands. (*She lifts wand.*)

DINO: Bye-bye!

POODLE: Are you staying? Are you staying, please?

DINO: Maybe I can cut up another building here.

FAIRY: You don't have to make such a fuss.

DINO: I'm just imagining a big stick of dynamite on the skyscrapers.

POODLE: Or we can think of something else.

FAIRY: Are you ready, Snow Queen? (Snow Queen, Elf, and Dumbo *join hands*. Fairy *waves wand above their heads.* Dino *and* Poodle *wave good-bye, and* Dumbo, Queen, *and* Elf leave.)

## COMMENTARY

Seven children in a drama class, ages six to eight, developed this play. After agreeing on the beginning, middle action, and ending, each chose a character and character role in the story. I took notes from their rehearsals. After hearing my transcription of their improvisations, they selected favorite lines to memorize, then improvised once more around these lines for their final performance.

## STORY OUTLINE

- Dino Mite Dino is brought back to life by Doctor Glockenspiel, who also gives Dino Mite a brain.
- Dino Mite is tired of being an experiment, escapes with help of his five-reality scissors.
- Dino wakes up in a snit, cuts up his poster of Punk Poodle, and also cuts up the local library with his scissors.
- Punk Poodle and several storybook characters are knocked into Fairy Reality.
- Snow Queen, Elf, and Dumbo want to go back to their books; Fairy sends Unicorn to fetch Dino Mite.
- Unicorn finds Dino Mite, who has lost his scissors. Fairy leads search for the diamond that can take everyone back to their original reality.

- The diamond is rescued; Punk Poodle and Dino Mite decide to stay.
- Snow Queen, Elf, and Dumbo go home.

## Performance Suggestions

Props were created while the story was developing. Elf has an elf hat, Fairy has a headdress/crown and wand, Dumbo has a mask, Unicorn has a mask, and Dino and Punk Poodle have similar pink and purple spiked hair. Face paint could be used. A headband with a single central horn would serve for Unicorn. Actors may prefer headbands with brightly colored crepe-paper streamer hair for Punk Poodle and Dino Mite. Lacking piles of pillows, a chair with a cloth drape will work for Fairy Reality.

With more actors, the monsters could play a larger role in the story and add more dramatic interest—use the staging of "Glooscap" for examples.

# STORYTELLER'S SECRETS

# TELLING TALES

✳

I once heard the poet Robert Bly speak of a poet as grabbing the tail of fancy that sweeps us off our feet and then up, high over the familiar and comfortable. A good poem or a good tale takes us farther than we planned to go. A storyteller is a blend of shaman and poet, swept up in the telling even as listeners hold on for their lives. Are you ready for this? Don't be alarmed. Before you are swept away, you may practice. Here are my collected and tested hints.

If you have an opportunity to read stories to a group before discarding a script, do so. If you photocopy the text, you can use a highlighter to mark the most powerful words and events. Practice looking up from the text and looking at the audience during the most compelling moments of the story. This will give you courage as you look into their amazed, anticipating faces. You can also manipulate your photocopy to make quick reading easier. Cut the text into meaningful sections and mount these story sections on separate pieces of paper, highlighting key words and bracketing paragraphs that go together. Allow a wide left margin; write an outline in this margin in big, readable letters. Wean yourself from the text by using this marginal outline whenever possible.

As a next step, retype the text (in extra-large typeface or all caps, double- or triple-spaced). Highlight, cut apart paragraphs, or bracket as feels appropriate.

Learn how to play your voice like an instrument. Just as classical music can vary tempo, dynamics, and key within a single complex piece, you can play your voice to add interest to the story. The variations in stories, as in music, are endless. You can start with a bright, cheery voice for "I'll Never Be Old," then slow down for emphasis at the end; you can maintain a tone of amazed seriousness for "Ares."

Don't be afraid of dramatic pauses, of speaking more softly right before a much louder surprise, for instance in the shaking voice of Shaydoola just before the thundering pronouncements of Allah. Enjoy every word, every syllable, the way a cellist plays each note. As they say in clown theater, "Make it big."

Some storytellers memorize word by word, but this isn't necessary or even recommended. You can make a brief outline on cards and hold them in your lap or hand for moral support. Practice telling your story from the cards; highlight a key word or two so that your eye can catch each essential element quickly. Time yourself; tell it again, with an audience or into a tape recorder. The tape recorder is especially useful because you can listen for pleasure or pain the first time through, then refer back to your outline as you listen again. Outlines for stories in this book can be your starters. Photocopy or copy and highlight.

What about dialogue? Varying voices? Gestures? Keep dialogue limited for starters—make sure the action carries the storyline, with dialogue for sparkle. Pick a story like "Ares," which allows you to use vocal emphasis or a few gestures. I've included a performance version that gives children a movement for each of the significant parts of the story. It's easier to do something potentially embarrassing as part of a crowd; you can practice along with the audience.

Some storytellers are good at character voices; don't be intimidated. The story is performed in the listener's imagination—you are there to share the experience, not to be the center of attention. You may want to pick one or two movements to emphasize the action; you could use just your shoulders and spine for "Ares," for instance, standing proud and tall when Ares is created, loosening up while poking about with an imaginary stick, then shrinking down when the snake appears. You can stand at a slight angle for one character in a dialogue and turn to the other side for the second character; this works well for the Gypsy creation story "How the Devil Helped." Practice in front of (ouch!) a mirror.

## PROPS AND STAGING

Props are useful. I collect lifelike toy snakes for the story of Adam and Eve. I also have an attractive wooden apple. Masks and soundmakers are fun too. I made an ox mask out of a paper bag for the Gypsy creation story, hidden behind me until the final moment when Ox appears to sweep the Devil off his feet. I've worked backwards, selecting a story to go with an attractive prop. I first told "Of Course" because I had bought a handsome clay whistle in the shape of a bird at a craft sale. When you gain confidence, you can hand simple soundmakers or soundmaking instructions to children in the audience, giving them a cue: "Whenever I say 'Pretty Polly,' you say, 'Of course!'" Making these props and soundmakers can be an important part of a continuing class.

Some storytellers like dressing the stage for their performance. One carries a favorite stool from place to place; another has a fabulous costume. Many have a hat that sets the mood. These are more for the storyteller's benefit than the audience's, but that's reason enough. Go through your hatbox, pull out a neglected favorite, add a big feather, see if it makes you feel more adventurous as you rehearse your story. If so, use it. I've seen one of my favorite storytellers, Myrna Hess, in a genuine Victorian-era blouse and skirt well suited to her delicate storyteller's style.

## Getting Started

Allow yourself some centering and warm-up time before a performance. Vocal warm-ups like those practiced by singers and actors are useful. Stand tall, hang your head, and rotate your head and shoulders slowly. Stretch your arms out, down center, then scoop out and reach up. Sing out the vowels lay-lee-lah-low-loo, breathing from your diaphragm. Shake your arms and hands from the shoulders. Now breathe deeply, mentally recreating the main outline of your story. What mood do you wish to start in? End in? Nerves make us constrict, use a hesitant, small voice and gestures. Pantomime parts of your story, and in this rehearsal make gestures big, as they say in theater. Now, break a leg!

In-gathering and sharing activities before beginning the story are one way to increase involvement. These activities can increase trust and understanding between participants too, which will improve any later story-making activities. One strategy is to create your own opening ritual. Use a focusing convention and a talking convention. I have a story blanket just big enough for about ten children to sit around, and I use the convention of going around the blanket at least once with everyone having the right to pass, no interruptions, and no second contributions until we've gone all around the blanket a first time. A useful exception: Those who pass during their turn can raise their hand and speak out of turn in the circle. This exception is important with mixed ages and very young children; four- and five-year-olds and shy ones may not be able to respond when the pressure is on.

When groups of children are too large for story circle or a story blanket, a convention used by Idaho Theater for Youth is helpful. Have everyone stand where they will be seated, with short people in front. Look around: Is this fair? Good? Then have everyone cross their feet and sit in place. The standing-up time is a good time for adults to rearrange "hot spots" of fidgety friends. The "look-around" encourages each member of the audience to take responsibility for their initial placement and any movement after sitting. It also allows groupings for acting out stories. This method also organizes space fairly and puts audience members in a physical position of alert attention. Need I add that children sitting cross-legged are seated upon two of their more potent weapons?

Be ready with a topic for discussion in smaller groups (usually about ten or so). Start the discussion by posing a question hooking into the everyday experience of most children, then request responses. Your chosen story may suggest discussion topics. In general, Ruth Sawyer's advice to storytellers makes a good guideline for discussion: Learn to feel deeply and see broadly. Encourage your audience's powers of perception: Start where they are; take them someplace else.

One good opener is learning each other's names in a dramatic way. Even the youngest can do the name chant. Children sit in a circle; each one says his or her first name, then others repeat it three times, clapping out the rhythm and accent: "MAR-tha, MAR-tha, MAR-tha." Then make a continuous chant of one name after the other, beating rhythms with hands on the floor.

With many groups of children, I start by introducing them to simple rituals. The first topic of discussion is, "What are the four directions? Which way is east? Where is the sun now?" We go to the nearest window and try to figure out where the sun is . . . not so easy in the average city building. We look at shadows, and I offer a little information on how the sun moves through the sky in our present season, our present hour. They try again. When they agree on the directions, based on the sun's shadows, we come back and position ourselves to face the east, and they bow to the sun, giver of heat and light, then to each other, sources of the light of friendship for each other.

Even large groups can have some interaction before the story if the storyteller establishes conventions for taking turns talking and establishing silence. A "story feather" (or basket or stone) works well for this; whoever holds the object has the right to speak. The person posing the question (or already holding the object) picks the next one to speak by handing off the object that privileges the speaker.

For a religious focus, create a worship center and begin with a simple ceremony. I like to have one volunteer come up to light a candle and give a response to an Important Word. (This is borrowed from the Afro-American holiday, Kwanzaa). The word can be drawn from a stack (I have a box of word cards made by a group of children as a class project) or selected on the spot by the child. My worship focus is portable, a three-part folding cardboard miniscreen made from shallow cardboard boxes taped together and covered with a small curtain.

How do you begin the story? One common strategy is to address the audience with a question. At one storytelling hour, after inviting the children to the front of the sanctuary, storyteller Tom von Alten asked, "Is anyone here a nephew or a niece? . . . Well, I am. I'm a nephew. That's because I have an aunt and an uncle. And this is a story told by a niece, called, 'My Wonderful Aunt.'"

Questions can help children find a hook into the story. "Have you ever taken a walk on the desert? How high were the plants? Did you see many trees? Houses? No, there aren't many, are there." This could lead into the story "Good from Bad" about the brothers Fitzer and Spitzer.

With an active and vocal group, this strategy can take on a life of its own. A very simple opening is always appropriate and helps the storyteller maintain control. Move into place, turn and face the audience deliberately, greet the audience, give your name if appropriate, and state the name of the story. If you want to set the mood more clearly, bring a brass bell or a candle to light or some other mood marker. After saying your name or greeting, ceremoniously lift the bell high and ring it, explaining that this bell marks our entry into story territory. You may want to collect storyteller tag lines, like the one in "Mother of the Dark," taken from

Brazilian lore: "This is a story I heard my Grandmother tell, and she heard it from hers."

## THE AUDIENCE

What about interruptions? The more physical distance between you and the audience, the more formal the situation feels and the fewer problems you will encounter. A high stool also sets you apart. Starting in the style of your story with a tag line like "Long ago, when wishes came true . . ." puts you in charge of the mood.

If you like a more informal, familiar style, prepare yourself to handle interruptions. I prefer to honor a limited number of children's spontaneous contributions, particularly when they are offered in a spirit of sharing and goodwill. When someone starts to speak, I give my full attention, without looking embarrassed or put off. I let my interlocutor speak at least one sentence's worth, then look up and repeat some of it emphatically, incorporating the child's observation and name, if possible, into my story and continuing (also emphatically). "Yes, it is hard to believe, as Jeremy says, that there could be a whole village of people who have never seen a mirror before, but it's true, or at least that's what I was told," and then I continue with my story.

If you get interruptions like this at the beginning of your story, mark it down to your nerves and theirs or to their excitement level. If you get several interruptions or general, large body movements well into the story mercilessly chop your narrative to the bone.

Once in a while I get troublemakers. When this happens, I quickly move to the child, stand as close as I can, turn in a few degrees, and address the story directly to the mischievous face. I establish eye contact and I don't let go. Or I'll physically move the child up by my chair, plant a heavy arm around small shoulders, all without a break in the story, which causes no end of amusement to the rest of the children but generally controls any further outbreaks. My actions are performed, by the way, in a spirit of having discovered a potential talent, not a troublemaker. Then, if we are performing the story, I immediately assign a role to the child. Once I tied a scarf around a particular child's head and addressed him as grandmother. Most such children enjoy the attention, are amazed to escape punishment, and like to perform.

## Explorations and Participation

When should we bring audiences to their feet and have them act out stories we have told? This depends on the situation, the reason for the story, and the nerve of the storyteller. Storytelling is often used as entertainment for large groups; few tale-tellers care to create a spontaneous performance with fifty or a hundred children. But it can be done and is worth doing. Performing a story as song, dance, ritual, or created theatric is energizing and inspiring. Participation reinforces memory. It makes the story personal as it increases a feeling of belonging to a community. And it's an opportunity to do things we wouldn't do otherwise. Acting is an excuse to experience divine folly or a hero's adventure.

The simplest form of audience involvement is a repetitive simple movement or choral response as the story is told. Remember the old American melodramas, with their convention of cheering the hero and booing the stage entrance of the villain? Pick a story with a stock phrase or situation or character, and assign a line, a movement to the audience. For the story "Of Course," all audience members can join in repeating the one phrase spoken by Polly the parrot. Limit the number of such enhancements to five or six per story so that they don't interrupt the movement of the action.

Awareness-building activities can improve the quality of stories. These are active equivalents of workbook practice, of selecting one skill and practicing. To help the group become more observant of sights, smells, and sounds, ask each person to select a soundmaker. In groups of eight or so, take turns, each making his or her special sound. Then stand in order from loudest to softest sound, highest to lowest, or some other categorizing system agreed upon by the group. Use movement activities. You can perform familiar nursery rhymes, inventing your own simple actions. Use easy postures and a jump or two for "Little Robin Redbreast sat upon a tree. Up went Pussycat, down went he. Down came Pussycat, away Robin ran. Says little Robin Redbreast, 'Catch me if you can!'"

For a nursery-age class, story cushions and squares of carpet strategically spaced on the floor can convert to lily pads, and each child can be a frog jumping each time they hear a *glunk* in the song "Glunk-glunk went the little green frog one day."

With little children, you can pantomime the events of an ordinary day—petting a cat, comforting and drying a wet pup. Then pick an animal: Become a happy poodle or a kitten in a pet store. Pantomime a familiar holiday or other special event—a day at the beach, a visit to grandmother's apartment, or the first day of school.

The game of "Who Am I?" gives each child the experience of being in command of a dramatic situation, if only for a moment. It increases the importance of magical creatures in stories like "Glooscap." Set up a chair-table or bench-chair combination so that the children can step up onto the bench or table, walk across it, and step down. Children line up before the first stool or chair; the teacher stands by the opposite end. The teacher approaches the table or bench as the child walks across. The teacher says, "Who am I?" and the child invents a creature. The teacher adjusts gestures, then asks, "What's my name?" The child invents a name, like Sad-mouth, or Four-noses. The teacher answers with the name just assigned, "Four-noses. Yes, that's me. Who's taller, you or me?" and the child picks an answer. The teacher either crouches or stands very tall, according to the child's description, and agrees with whatever the child said, walks in character in a small circle, comes back in neutral character, ready to be transformed by the next child. This can be varied by questions or by having children take turns doing transformations for each other.

Elements from a story can be teased out and used for movement experiences. Chinese theater conventions are excellent resources for many dance/chant/rhythm-band activities. Twirling ribbons can represent sun, wind, rain, thunder and lightning, rivers calm or boiling.

I've turned a Chinese folk story about two old sillies into a sedate, mysterious dance. The sillies seek advice on how to make the mountain move; they must put their belongings on their head and walk backwards, says the sage. If this story is performed in winter, children can fold their coats into a pack, balance it on their head, and step backwards to a sedate rhythm—without collisions. This makes a good awareness activity too.

Children ages eight through ten can work on an actual scene, with a beginning, middle, and end. To avoid the static, didactic look of much adult, talk-driven drama, seek out moments of challenge to dramatize. "Sharing the Well" is a story with nonstop action and response and opportunities to turn the animal characters into animals of choice. This story also benefits from a study of African wildlife and the tradition of the trickster character less familiar to many children.

Concepts can be explored through story. The Afro-American holiday Kwanzaa is especially well suited for this. Kwanzaa brings together symbols and principles of living found in many countries—candles, a communal cup, corn, fruit, and other vegetables—to celebrate unity, self-determination, collective work and responsibility, cooperative economics, purpose, creativity, faith. Each of these could be illustrated by an improvised scene chosen by the children.

After older children have mastered the performance of a simple story, have them create their own. Then use development time for new dramatic elements. For instance, have them add an unexpected and unwelcome intrusion to their scene. This could be a runaway train, a fire, or a person. One group had a totally inappropriate superhero burst in on a friendly lion-taming scene. This was so successful that it became the center of a satisfyingly goofy short play.

Stylized theatrics and conventions are another way to enter a story and another culture. Watch a video of dance performance in Thailand, then read stories from the *Ramayana* and practice walking like Hanuman, the monkey king. Have participants talk about their own cultural roots; use these as source material for performance styles and stories to retell. The story outlines of commedia dell'arte are fun to modernize. I have used the nineteenth-century etchings of Le Brun to lead children in imitation of the conventions of emotional expression in early American theater.

Life cycles make interesting developmental activities. Pick an animal a plant from a sourcebook or let each child pick one. Use the stages of this plant's or animal's life or a series of events in a particular day as prompts for performance.

Five-, six-, and seven-year-olds like the seed exercise, here given the addition of a magic gardener. Start on the floor as a seed. Push out one root, then another. Stretch up a tender stalk above ground; slowly stand, push out leaves. Your leaves grow strong and move in the rain and in the wind; they turn to the sun. Now you are mature and produce a flower; your flower is ripe enough to toss its seeds. Your stalk is old and stiff now; gradually you shrivel in the frost and die or freeze standing up. You can avoid the death scene or extend and modify it as long as it holds interest. A magic gardener can come by with a special water that allows the plants to pull up roots and fly; this could accompany the story "Water of Life." A small group can be a tableau of a single plant. Four girls can crouch down. Two can stand slowly, back to back, with their arms pushing out; the other two can stretch out their legs and arms as roots, then bring their arms together for potatoes. Finally, a farmer can come along and dig, sending potatoes flying. Another group of five children can plan how to be an iris planting. They stand and bloom sequentially, only two blooming at any one time; the first ones shrivel and go back to the ground. Use discussion time to talk about flowers they like and remember; save your old seed catalogs for reference.

This age also likes to perform as favorite animals. Find out who eats what—and who eats who—then illustrate the food chain by having plants, rabbits, wildcats, humans (ours was an eight-year-old hunter with his six-year-old friend as his dog) — all coming out in appropriate order. This exercise was refined into a performance by a group of children ages six through fifteen.

## Performing for an Audience

Start with an overall plan. If you intend to have children respond to a narrator only with pantomime movement, then a quick rehearsal of movement before the performance is enough. The story of "Ares" works well for this. A large group of children can be divided up so that groups can be assigned to a role, as snake, toad, angel, cloud, or Ares. A smaller group can walk in a circle, shifting movement and role as the narrator speaks. For the snake, arms extend straight out from body, then twist, hands move like a snake's head. For the toad, arms reach down at sides, then elbows curve out and pulsate to simulate toad's big, heaving stomach. For a cloud, arms make big, floaty circles in front of the child's body.

Allow plenty of time for rehearsals if you will be performing a more elaborate play before an audience. It will be more interesting for children if they can switch roles from time to time. Rather than work with a formal script, you can work from an outline and help each person have a gesture or body position for each emotion, then let them find their own words to express their feelings and purpose. Let the story refine itself through rehearsal. Ask questions along the way. For example, in "Sharing the Well," ask, "What do you want to do now, Kewel? How do you feel when your baby is captured? How do you want to show us that?" The basic pattern is

(1) something happens, (2) character reacts, then (3) character responds.

As you rehearse, you can mention a few staging instructions. Bring your most important scenes up close to the audience. Be sure to face the audience when you speak or use your face to show what you are thinking. An eighteenth- and nineteenth-century convention is handy—with your body, with a gesture, show us what you are thinking, what you are about to do or say.

If you have a class full of enthusiasts, you'll have to establish a convention that eliminates long, riotous chase scenes. Use an object or a place in the room, and give instructions: "Moses, you run over to here. These four people holding ribbons are the Red Sea. They step apart and let you pass. Soldiers, you run only as far as the Red Sea." I save directive language for moments like this.

Finally, script out crucial lines of dialogue. For four- to six-year-olds doing "Glooscap and Baby," the lines could be as follows: Glooscap enters, Baby crawls out and lies on a blanket (our story blanket). Glooscap looks down and says, "Baby, come here!" Baby gurgles. Glooscap frowns, points toward the camp of monsters, and says, "All right then, monsters, come here!" Glooscap waits for Baby's response, then says, "Monsters, go away!" This pattern is varied by changing the name of each group of spirit people; Baby only stares at monsters, cries for stick people, and then gurgles, coos, and crawls up to the rainbow people, reaching for their "hair." At this, Glooscap says, "All right, Baby, I give up. You're the strongest," and makes an exit. Everyone then comes back on stage and lines up for the inevitable applause.

From school performances, some children have become accustomed to using narrators. A narrator is a shortcut; it's more interesting to see than hear about most events. Talk about what a narrator might say, and whenever possible find a way to perform it instead. This may mean changes or additions to the story as originally told. As often as possible, let it become their story to modify and inhabit.

For children who are entering into the story, stage properties and scenery should support the imagination and enhance the story, not overwhelm it. Provide a few materials with many uses rather than an abundance of finished props. Have the usual crayons, marking pens, paper, scissors, and glue available; add stacks of newspaper, old curtains, fabric glue, cardboard boxes, and other materials.

Bring an abundant quantity of one new material to each class. Newspapers stapled together and painted or marked over can become one-time costumes, for instance. Cut big scallops around the bottom edge of newspaper pages, pleat with a stapler, and you have person-sized flower skirts, collars, or hats. Start newspaper tree branches by laying out three large sheets, overlapped for several inches each. Roll up into a large tube and tape the tube together from middle to bottom. Then with a good pair of scissors, make three or four vertical cuts through the tube, from the top to about one-fourth of the way down. Now, taking hold of the inner strips you have formed, pull up and twist the strips. This will form fernlike cascades of "leaves."

You can also draw and cut out scenery, then tape it to the wall. Cardboard boxes can be covered with plain newsprint or butcher paper and stacked to form walls or buildings.

A guest mime can demonstrate techniques for using imaginary props and building imaginary walls.

The Paper Bag Players of New York developed a number of skits and costume ideas using big sheets of corrugated cardboard. Cut the cardboard into person-sized mountains, toads, angels, or other story characters. Cut a hole for the head, hold the prop cardboard body in front of you, and start talking.

Headbands are a good way to establish character without getting in the way of movement or vision. All manner of stuff, from paper ears to crepe-paper hair and feathers, can be stapled on by even the youngest actors.

Dance ribbons are an important part of Chinese theater and lend themselves to many stories. They can be made of materials simple or glamorous, from crepe-paper streamers left over from a party to genuine ribbon or long scarves. Cut a strip of ribbon that is from one to one and one-half times as long as the child is tall. Wrap and glue to the end of a cardboard or wood handle (tongue depressor, popsicle stick, or triple-folded shirtboard). Decorate as desired; glitter is a nice addition. Glue leftover gift ribbon to the handle; leave a few strands hanging for flair. Now practice twirling the ribbon: An arm extended straight out, twirled in a circle, is the sun; a zig-zagging motion up and down or in a large S is rain; a big S aimed at the floor is a turbulent river; a big S overhead is storm clouds or big fat cumulus, depending on technique. You can integrate these movements into many stories, adding weather factors to tales of adventure or travel, for instance. This is a good role for small, shy children who don't wish to perform as actors. Ribbons can express emotions and energy, even the violence of battle in a symbolic fashion, as in the *Ramayana*.

### Soundmakers

Soundmakers have a multitude of uses in storytelling and story performance. Children are accustomed to a range of sounds from their experience with television cartoons. Those who are too shy to perform can act as a sound orchestra or sound effects. Or performers can make their own sounds, holding a shaker, rain stick, sand drum, or drumming sticks for dramatic emphasis or for rain/storm effects.

Make your own sounds and soundmakers. Nail soda bottle caps in pairs to strips of wood (enlarge the nail holes so that the caps rattle a bit). Decorate the handles by wrapping them with yarn. Collect old keys and dangle them by strings in groups of four or five; they make lovely chimes. Pairs of sticks or wooden spoons clack together as timekeepers.

Drums are too resonant for most classrooms. If you have the space, by all means experiment with sticks or wooden spoons on the bottoms of bowls, pans, or large empty cans. I purchase high-quality parchment paper to become bottoms for sand drums, rain sticks, and shakers. (Parchment and rice paper create a lovely sound and are stronger than standard paper, they can also be moistened and stretched into place.)

For rain sticks, stick straight pins into cardboard tubes (centers of paper towel rolls, for instance). Glue a circle of parchment across one end, add a few grains of rice, then glue another circle of parchment across the other end to close. Cut and decorate a sheet of paper to cover the tube and its pinheads. Turning the stick over and over creates a lovely soft sound. Leave out the pins and use rice, pebbles, or beans inside smaller tubes (toilet paper size) for shakers. Film canisters and plastic aspirin jars also work fine, with their own lids as built-in means of closure. A larger hoop of cardboard with parchment covers on the ends and a small fistful of sand creates another versatile sound instrument that won't disrupt everyone else in the building.

*Masks*

Masks and headdresses can greatly expand the range of drama. They allow children to take parts otherwise beyond their range of characterization as old people, animals, and other beings. They can extend the child's emotional range, too, as a way to take on powers and larger-than-life qualities. They create instant atmosphere and encourage ritualized action. They also shift attention from the face to the body, from voice to gesture, allowing the action to be exaggerated without embarrassment. They can cover shyness and deemphasize the personality of the actor, allowing for an emphasis on the story rather than the performer. They are especially helpful in the classroom, allowing different children to try on a particular character. Masks also tie together art, literature, and cultural studies, giving children a chance to try on another point of view.

The taking-on of powers has a negative connotation in our culture; masks are associated with bank robbers, Halloween pranksters, Mardi Gras revelers discarding the rules they were raised by, and worse. Without guidance, some children will use masks to act out aggressive behaviors.

Orient your children to the positive potential of masks with developmental exercises. Agree on a positive powerful figure from literature or history and create a mask of this person. Pick a contemporary situation and have this historic character enter it and help solve a contemporary problem.

Masks can be used with adolescents to explore hidden realities or misleading appearances. A Hopi story by Ekkehart Malotki, "How Maasaw and the People of Oraibi Got Scared to Death Once," has the people frightened by a particularly ugly but kindly protector-god, Maasaw. (We don't always recognize the sacred when we run into it!) And the opposite is possible. Dangers and threats can be hidden behind an attractive visage. The Japanese had two-faced puppets of a beautiful girl who changed into a fox; the Kwakiutl created masks-within-a-mask. Masks for young adults can represent abstractions, like the characters in medieval miracle plays who gave physical form to Indulgence, Cynicism, and Despair. Teenagers could talk about the dangers they face, create masks to represent the earth and its present dangers, then create a modern pilgrimage through danger to paradise in an update of *Pilgrim's Progress*. The discussion of what action should be taken in the face of each temptation is worthwhile in itself.

Some children become mask fanatics and want to make masks for every story, just for the pleasure of recreating the character. I run every class through one mask-making experience, often using inexpensive paper plates plus yarn ties as base materials. Then more mask-making is incorporated on demand, with different materials, such as crepe-paper, yarn, string, paint, glitter, feathers, paper cups, and egg cartons to make goggle-eyes.

Adults can make use of masks too. If you have a subject you wish to discuss, try dramatizing your point with the help of a simple mask. One preschool teacher wanted to talk about tolerance, a very abstract notion for a four year old. He made a simple paper-plate mask with long pointed nose and purple skin, set the mask outside the class door, and told the children that there was someone new joining their class. He then exited, returning in the mask, and sat close to the children, asking questions. "Will you share your snack with me? Can I stay in this class? Will you be my friend?" And so on. After they responded, he took off the mask and led the brief discussion. If he had asked the same questions without the dramatization—how they would respond to someone different, maybe someone with purple skin—they might not have known.

### The Stage

Where is the stage? The elevated stage is a useful convention when you have an audience. For story-making, where the value is in the experience, any feature of a space can take on new meaning. A radiator can be a monster or a refrigerator; a window ledge wide and sturdy enough to walk on can be the ledge around the castle. A table can be a mountain, home of the gods, or roof. Decide what spaces can be used for play and performance; decide together how to assign the space between groups or within groups. Old blankets and curtains work well to establish a lake or an island.

If there will eventually be a recital or performance, set up a few chairs to represent the audience. Children can take turns watching the action from these seats and offer comments on sound and visual qualities during "notes." See Closings on page 247.

### Puppetry

Puppetry is another favorite way of performing for some children. It has a long history in religious observance, starting with animal skulls used in ancient cave ceremonies. In a museum in

New Delhi, there is a terra-cotta monkey on a string estimated to be four thousand years old. A jointed jackal puppet on display in the Louvre is from Egypt, about the same period. Ingeniously joined puppets and faces-within-faces of masks have been used to bring the spirits of gods and ancestors into the drama being enacted by people of many cultures.

Puppetry can be as simple as mounting cutout drawings of characters on popsicle sticks or tongue depressors. For recycled puppets, draw figures on the backs of used envelopes, then push a pencil into each envelope and tape it in place. Small figures drawn by the children can be glued to another piece of paper for strength, and then fixed to a strap of paper that can be taped around the finger for finger puppets. One imaginative teacher of puppetry, purchases inexpensive cotton gloves of the type used by artists to protect their work as they paint. She has children draw a character on each finger for a story on a glove!

Flannel boards aren't used as often as they could be. I made mine by covering a cork board with flannel. Keep scraps of flannel or felt to glue on the backs of children's own drawings of characters, or create your own. If you have access to a photocopier, children can create these together. Start by dividing the characters between children, each drawn in outline form. Photocopy a set for everyone. Color and mount them on cardboard or heavy paper, then glue them with sticky fabric glue to a hunk of nappy fabric. Each person can set up a box for such puppet characters and add to it from time to time.

Scrap cloth works also. I gather up odd bits of plain, cream-colored cloth for puppetry. Each child is given two rectangles about six inches by eight inches and draws a character on one rectangle using permanent markers, crayons, or fabric paints. Put two rectangles together with the drawn side on the inside, sew around three sides, and pull it inside out so that the drawing shows. The sewing time is a good time to talk about how you wish to perform your story. If there are more characters than children, put another character on the other side of the "puppet." Now slip the hand inside this puppet-pocket for performance.

I've used these puppet-pockets for a two-class performance of the exodus from Egypt. Our first class period was used to hear the story and to start making the puppets, which were completed and used in a second class. These puppets were more than characters in the usual sense; they depicted each of the ten plagues, as well as the figures of Moses and Pharaoh.

This classroom performance added another delightful dramatic element that required a glass of juice per child and a modification from the Seder ceremony. Put a finger into your glass, and flick out a drop of juice for each plague to remember the pain and loss of that event. In this case the teacher narrated, but a child could also act as narrator. Here the children did not use a stage, but sat in a circle and held up their puppets at the appropriate mention in the story.

A surprising number of nine-year-olds will get their first sewing experience this way, so it is a good idea to have one helper as sewing-table resource person ready to cut cloth, thread needles, make knots, and demonstrate stitches.

Staging for puppetry can be an arrangement of props for added pleasure and invention rather than for performance before an audience. Chair backs and tabletops, especially with a blanket thrown over the top, are sufficient. A collection of cardboard boxes that nest together for storage can have many uses. A stack of boxes can be a tree, a mountain, or a city. Use boxes big enough for puppet-holders to sit in, or use smaller boxes, with tops open and many windows and doors cut out, on a tabletop. Puppeteers stand around the table, reach in and improvise their own stories or versions of ones told to them. These box stages will suggest many opportunities for decoration and elaboration. Shoe boxes are just right for finger puppets.

Libraries have many books of instruction for more elaborate puppets, including sock puppets and jointed ones with papier-mâché heads. Ordinary balloons, lightly inflated, make the base of the head. Use three parts water to two parts flour in proportions, with a toss of salt or a squirt of white glue for additional strength. Dip strips of paper in the mix, and spread in layers over the base. Use small paper balls for noses and bulging eyes, cutouts of cardboard for lips, held down with more gooey paper strips. Allow plenty of time, at least one day, for drying before painting with tempera or acrylics.

## CLOSINGS

"Notes" are a useful convention from the theater world. This works especially well if performers work together in groups so that everyone has the chance to be audience for others. At the end of each performance, no matter how brief or spontaneous, everyone, audience members and performers, describes (1) what they saw, (2) what they liked, and (3) any confusion experienced. This establishes the habits of careful watching and responsible criticism and puts positives before negatives. Adults need to model "notes" only a couple of times, then they can step back and encourage children to speak first.

Closing rituals shift everyone back to the real world. They give shape and meaning to experience, reinforcing the feeling of community. Openings say, "Something important to all of us is about to happen." Closings say, "Something important to all of us is concluding." They can be informal, the passing-around of a basket of treats. They can be slightly more formalized, the lighting of a candle, asking one person to say what was the best part of the time just spent together while everyone eats treats. Or they can be a closing activity. Gathering in a circle makes everyone feel equally valued.

Here's a circle closing that requires only one soundmaker per person; I call it the sound-around. This can be performed with shakers made by the children or items from a ready-made rhythm instrument box, or even with rocks and sticks picked up around the campsite at an outdoors retreat. You can use the well-known children's song "When you're happy and you know it," make up your own words, or have sounds only. Participants position themselves in a circle, standing next to each other or scattered about the room. One person is the sound conductor and points. Participants make their sound only when the conductor points to them. I've had clumps of participants who create their own simple instruments, then organize their sound pattern and sound combination. This particular sound-around was used with great success as part of an adult-child church service. Since it was an outdoor service, the children selected positions behind rocks and trees or hidden in grass, but the basic pattern was a circle of sound used to close the service.

Another circle closing is an easy expansion of a closing reading. Write a short reading or prayer on butcher paper that is posted where all can read. Form a circle and walk in a circle while reciting the words together. Prayers from the Navajo "beauty-way" ceremony are particularly appropriate, to paraphrase, "May we walk in beauty, may we walk in harmony, may we walk in peace."

The close can be integrated into story performance. I'll give two examples, a simple one good for all ages, including the very young, and one primarily for older children.

The story for this close came from the Snohomish (recorded in *American Indian Myths and Legends* by Erdoes and Ortiz). It's a tale of the need for cooperation. The sky is dangerously low and can be raised only by a mighty effort from people of many languages and tribes. One person thinks of a solution: Everyone must make a sky-pusher and learn the signal word—"Yah-Ho!" After hearing the story, each child made and decorated a sky-pusher stick, beginning with a rolled piece of butcher paper. When all sky-pushers were done, we acted out the final triumphant sky-pushing effort. Children milled around the room, as one person passed on the signal word to another, then muttered the signal word to each other meaningfully while practicing their pushing. When everyone had heard the word, they joined the teacher in a loud finale—"One, two, three, Yah-Ho!"—and pushed up together.

Another story for a close came out of a telling of the *Ramayana*, an excerpt taken from the great story cycle of southern Asia. The version used here was from the Tibetan Buddhist tradition, which declares that as soon as warriors of the demon army were defeated, they became loyal defenders of the forces of Buddha. We acted out the battle in entirely ritual fashion, as two lines facing each other, two menacing steps forward, two steps back, to the sound of Balinese puppet-show music. Since demons are magical creatures that can fly, they had the privilege of "fighting" by twirling dance ribbons while standing on classroom chair seats. When the battle was won (and music ended), all demons jumped down and joined a celebratory circle dance.

## SELECTING AGE-APPROPRIATE STORIES

Babies like rhythmic sounds and the feeling of rhythmic sounds emitted by a loving adult voice. Nursery rhymes and songs make use of nonsense words for good reason. You can prepare a child for stories with repetitive sounds and actions: Clap your hands, click your tongue, puff out your cheeks, and imitate the baby's sounds and moves. Do deliberate variations, with soft mouth noises, increasingly louder ones, then adding meaning to sounds:"Let's bounce like a bunny! Let's make a big hop like a kangaroo!" Add the expression of emotion; when out strolling with a three-year-old, you can say, "Here's my happy walk. Here's my sad walk."

Listening to stories (as part of a small audience) can start a year or two after the child's socialization process has begun. Also, children who hear and then tell their own stories make better listeners (and later, better readers). A few three-year-olds can listen; many four-year-olds can.

Very young children like stories with recognizable characters and events. Parents and preschool teachers who keep a costume box and play pretend games are developing the imagination and sequential association that is required in a good listener. Young listeners like rituals and repetitions, as well as participations such as showing off how well they know the days of the week. "Glooscap and Baby" and "Ares" use magical events for empowerment of the child. First child Ares, happily poking an insect with a stick, amuses children because he is so natural. And the Creator provides instant protection from the threatening elements with an enormous guardian angel who leads listeners into a secure everyday world. The Arawak story "What Sun Wanted" also has humor suited to four-year-olds.

Although young children like a simple story line and a limited number of characters and events, this does not mean that stories must be pedestrian. The line between what might be and what is blurs pleasantly for preschoolers. In "Good from Bad" Fitzer and Spitzer each visit the cave of the ants, with many parallels of language and events. In "Glooscap and Baby" Glooscap calls in three kinds of magical beings to intimidate the baby.

Five- and six-year-olds enjoy exercising their sense of humor, their recognition of the ridiculous and the extreme. They like tales of stupids, of comic mistakes, and of foolery. They are also getting interested in adventure, magical gifts, and powers. This is the age of obsessions and fixations; one girl will like only stories of seals, one boy will sit still only for dinosaurs. I modify stories to suit audience and story-making participants. This age willingly jumps over the limitations of sex roles too; in a mixed-age group performance of "Ares" two girls decided to act together as Creator, communing on each act of creation, then splitting apart, one descending to earth to serve as Angel when an angel was needed.

Even for this age I prefer stories that put the genii back into the bottle. I treat supernatural powers with great care. Consider Hopi and Navajo traditions of a distant dwelling place for supernatural beings and particular times and ceremonies that bring such powers into the midst of the folk. Even in story, I believe we should not call upon magical powers to satisfy our urge for quick, absolute solutions to dilemmas.

Animal tales are good for five- and six-year-olds, who attach to and empathize with their pets. "How Wisdom Scattered" gives them a chance to recognize the stubbornness of Tortoise and appreciate the personalities of the various animals Tortoise encounters. This story also lends itself to adaptation, allowing the child to select a favorite animal role for acting out. Having children write their own kind of wisdom on paper, hiding it, and holding a search for wisdom honors the child's sense of what is good.

The Chinese story "Of Course" is well suited to this age also. They can be a Polly-chorus of parrots who anticipate and share the comeuppance of the landlord. Children at this age still prefer characters with simple motives and actions, but that doesn't mean resorting to the violence-charged stories of good guys versus bad guys that are too often marketed for this age. Although Bruno Bettelheim makes a case for this dichotomizing of good and bad and there may be a short-term emotional benefit in identifying with a hero or heroine who defeats an evil power, I believe that any lasting improvement in a child's sense of control and personal power will come from life experiences, not fantasy. Learning to identify and face down that which is truly harmful is the work of older children; nearly all societies are still highly protective of children of this younger age. For this reason, the story of Etana was selected from our oldest traditions to show a youthful hero triumphing without violent confrontation.

Seven- through ten-year-olds are lovers of fantasy and adventure. They like excitement, suspense, and surprises, a trip entirely away from recognizable reality. The flight of Etana and the Pretty Girl's escape from her family in "I'll Never Be Old" are especially provocative for this age. "Water of Life" was designed to incorporate marvelous adventure with a clear separation of magical and ordinary worlds for the benefit of younger children. They will like the courage of Brave John.

It's a stretch for children of this age to appreciate stories of renunciation and sacrifice, such as "Na Ha Calls Down the Storm" and the tale of "The Chicken Stars" from Thailand. Still, they appreciate the terrible truth that sometimes sacrifice is essential for a larger good. Boys respond to the determination of Na Ha; given several volunteer heroes, I've created a family of brothers to fight off the sea monsters and find the Keeper of Animals. Girls like "The Chicken Stars." One group of seven- and eight-year-old girls improvised a front-yard scene of chicks at play, teasing their protective, indulgent mother hen in a way that is reminiscent of Juliet and her nurse in Shakespeare's *Romeo and Juliet*. Another group of mixed-age children recreated "The Chicken Stars" as paper puppet theater, with separate puppets for three stages in the transformation of chicks into stars. "Seven Most Obedient Sons" fits this age or younger.

Abstract ideas must still be embedded in action. The stones paralyzed by envy and greed in "Water of Life," Rude leading a ritual to free the soul of her mother in "Better Rude Than Sorry," and the bittersweet ending of "I'll Never Be Old" are as close to moralizing as is appropriate for this age. The drama of "Lady Green of the Speaking Tree," with its metaphor of wisdom growing out of community, comes to focus on one lonely woman and a happy child.

After age ten, children are ready to draw their own moral from a story and appreciate being allowed to do this themselves. The Mayan creation story, in its expanded version, could be told for them. Older children appreciate the story of "Shaydoola" because they recognize some justice in the outcome and also understand that this is a story reflecting a culture quite different from the dominant Western European one. Adolescents hearing "The

Quarrel" can think of acquaintances and family members with personalities like those in the story. They recognize the truth that the power of the mirror is the way it can change attitudes among the villagers. "Mother of the Dark" has an unexpected explanation for the world as we know it. The story of Rude could be used to lead into a discussion of how cycles of revenge and violence are perpetuated—and ended.

## STORYTELLING WITH ADULTS

Theatrical explorations can be valuable for adults too. One example of this is using masks to experience the sacred. Start with the many ceremonies in other cultures used to remind mask-wearers of the dangers involved in the taking on of powers. Agreeing to wear the mask means agreeing to great responsibility. Ron Jenkins, in an article in *Parabola* entitled "Two-Way Mirrors," tells us that in Bali the mask is a mediator between opposing worlds, past and present, spirit and flesh, king and servant. Masks can be living archetypes that move between myth and fact, giving new meaning to both. "The power of the mask is rooted in paradox, in the fusion of opposites . . . enabling us to look at the world through someone else's face . . . a potent metaphor for disguise and revelation." A person in a mask is something quite different from person or mask, a conscious, entirely new persona.

As adults we realize that we are all born into a play we didn't write. As feminist and actress Estelle Signet wryly says, "The bad news is that I always play victim parts. The good news is that I have my lines memorized." Drama gives us a chance to see larger patterns; masks give impersonal forces a face. Whereas much of the theater we see plays on our sense of powerlessness and magnifies our vulnerability to random dangers, we can recreate a more healing, sacred drama that emphasizes our capacity to make choices. Sacred drama can remind us that our footsteps fall on a broader path and connect us back into community. We can enrich the basics of motivation (be careful what you ask for—you may get it) and purpose. We know how habit defeats ideals. We recognize the myths of our culture and the limitations of worldly expectations and rewards. We can explore these even if we aren't ready to create a new, coherent story out of our lives.

I'll give an example of a sacred drama exercise using masks. A supply table was set up before class. Attendees were given a task: Create a mask of power, name the power or powers contained therein, and name your mask-spirit. Make a card for others to read: "I am _____, who is _____ and _____ and can _____." These can be actual historical figures or inventions, depending on the class choice.

After masks were made and set up for display, each with its card underneath, each person took a stack of cards and meditated on unanswered questions and unmet needs in his or her own life. Each question or need had its own card. One at a time, each person sat in a chair facing the rest of the class and spoke through a mask as that power or character. Classmates by turns changed one of their need cards into a question and addressed it to the masked power-spirit for an answer. As an alternative, a set of prepared questions can be available. Some questions:

- What is worth knowing? Can any knowledge save me?
- Show me the way to a more satisfying life.
- I am afraid. Can you comfort me?
- I have tried so many times and failed. Where is the courage to try again?
- I am angry. How can I forgive those who have offended me?
- What are the rewards of following your path? The costs?
- How will I know I am living the right way?

Experiences like this are excellent sources of ideas for workshop activities or further group studies. They can also lead to other creative activities. One group entered into a six-week series on "sacred arts," focusing each week on a different art form seen for its spiritual potential—dance, chant, painting, weaving, mask-making, and improvisational story performance.

# CREATE YOUR OWN STORY

✳

How do you invent a story? Begin with a grain of sand and build your pearl. Stories that take a hold on us, the ones that glow, accumulate layers, often over time. They are true in several ways, often as a response to a difficult, troublesome question. So watch for your irritants, name them, and build a story around them.

Where should you look for your own best grain of sand, and what will you layer over it? Here are some starting points. You can work within folklore traditions or invent your own story. I'll supply a variety of strategies to add color and detail. You can craft something from your own life or share someone else's story. Start anywhere. Don't wait for the perfect idea. I once heard the poet William Stafford say the reason he could write so many poems is that he didn't expect too much from any one of them. So express, explore, surprise yourself.

## STORY STARTERS

Keep a notebook of sayings, quotations, and overheard words. Include bumper stickers and T-shirt slogans, advertisements, riddles and jokes, memorabilia and ephemera of all kinds, whatever sticks to you after you've seen or heard it. Photographs, proverbs, riddles, jokes, songs, games, dance performances, festival and holiday traditions, family sayings, charms and talismans are all rich with story possibilities. Children's lore is a rich source. At a family gathering, join the cousins table and listen in. Games, insults, jokes, even clothing choices can be the starting point for a story.

Use your journal to identify meaningful props. Imagine that you are walking through a room of your past; pick up a favorite or otherwise meaningful object, a pansy from your walkway, perhaps, or a tattered baby blanket. Now discover something with negative associations. For each object, use all senses to describe it. Now integrate one or more into a story format or build a story around it.

Folksingers often retain the ancient tradition of storyteller, using rhyme and repetition with variation to enhance the emotional impact of the story. If you are lucky enough to have a musician in the family, ask for a few songs. If you ask well before a family event, they will have time to practice and remember more.

Often, two or more sources can be combined to make an even better story. In my file on Afghanistan, for instance, I have several folk tales, a book of interviews with Afghan women, newspaper clippings, and proverbs found at an Afghan site on the Internet. (Example: "A tilted load will not reach market".) I also have an analysis of the patterns of rugs woven by tribal women. Collector Christopher Alexander interprets rug patterns as overlapping realities in the lives of the weavers, each motif reflecting the perfection of Allah. The rugs suggest that village life has many balances that must be maintained at once.

To turn a proverb into a story, first translate its language into a situation that is familiar to you. Then ask yourself some basic questions to develop the story. For example, who might have experienced this? Many cultural traditions have a kind of 'first fool,' one who makes mistakes or is victim of misfortune and copes more or less successfully. Mulla Nasrudin stories are told in many Muslim cultures. Coyote plays this role for many Native American people. Boukee or Bouki the hyena serves that role in African stories and in Caribbean collections. As a child, Joel Chandler Harris heard many such cautionary proverbs, anecdotes, and tales. His retellings, featuring a variety of animal characters, are now a permanent part of American story lore.

Now tell your own story of exactly what load is being delivered to market, how it got off center in the first place, how the problem grew worse, and why your hero or heroine was oblivious to the problem.

### *Build or Borrow a Motif List*

The reference section of a library contains motif indexes that list story types or story elements. These story elements can be found in innumerable stories. One of the first and best, the Thompson-Aarne *Type and Motif Index*, was a resource for early Walt Disney productions. You can use motifs for your own story variants. Here are a few I have used.

- You have been given a traveling cap that carries its wearer anywhere.
- Your longed-for child has been born; she is no bigger than a thumb.
- The beautiful cloak you inherited comes from the land of the dead.
- Yours is a magic fiddle. Or, your ring will grant wishes.
- What you seek is on the other side of an impenetrable forest.
- The lamp you are holding reveals what is hidden.
- The crown you just put on your head is in fact a serpent's crown.
- Your sweetheart has just made an unreasonable demand on you.
- Love leads you to commit a foolish act.

- You have just stepped through the gates of hell.
- The stranger you just met on the road was born of iron.
- You need to find your way out of a bad bargain.
- Is the Sun your father? How will you find out?
- You have been unfairly banished. An adventure awaits.
- That which others have ignored turns out to be important.
- The demon spirit who threatens you isn't as clever or powerful as he thinks he is.
- You are in a bad spot, yet can escape with a good bluff.
- What looks like a monster is a person under an enchantment. Will you help?
- A beautiful wife feels trapped and yearns to take back her animal form and escape.
- You experience the happy consequences of doing a favor for the Devil.

## Story Theme Ideas

Story themes are everywhere in our word- and image-drenched culture. I have an envelope of clippings from various sources, including magazine illustrations. Start your own with an older magazine, cutting out illustrations you find provocative. Cut away slogans and save them separately. Tape the image to a larger sheet of paper and create your own slogan or outline suggesting a new story behind the image. Write two or three paragraphs.

A group can use a game approach to respond to a story starter. Write a single sentence or tape a classified advertisement from a newspaper to the top of a sheet of paper. One at a time each player writes at the bottom of the sheet what could be the story behind the given starter. The writer folds the paper up so that the next person can respond without reading what has been written.

Prequels and sequels are ways of exploring a given story's potential. Use one of your own or any other story you like. You can also use an illustration, a painting, or a photo. For prequels, tell what led up to the existing story or image. For sequels, tell what came after. "Happily ever after?" can also be a gambit for a group exercise. Agree on a story, everyone write for 20 minutes or so, then compare versions.

"Wriggles" is a similar strategy with younger children. Each child has a sheet of paper and access to colored markers. They make a squiggly fast design or image at the top of the page, then pass it around and say what the squiggle is all about at the bottom of each sheet. For very young children, have helpers do the writing. These ideas can be reorganized into a group story or poem.

### Explore the Idea of Conflict

There are as many kinds of struggle in stories as there are in life. We can simplify this to humans against each other, humans against the larger forces of nature, humans against the rules and pressures of culture, and humans facing the unexpected, chance, or fate. We can struggle toward goals of control over destiny, achievements, respect of others, use of one's gifts, love, and acceptance. Much folklore expresses this in terms of a quest, a search with tests along the way. Find a new metaphor by placing your conflict in a contemporary environment rich with implications—an enormous shopping mall, factory, carnival, banquet, ball game, zoo.

One way to explore conflict in a group is to have two or more people act out parts of or aspects of a single person. Make each aspect of the person a separate character. Look for the emotions that a situation is likely to produce and give character to the hidden, that which cannot be immediately recognized or that we typically try to suppress. Imagine Fear awakening an old warrior, Joy awakening a youth.

Popular culture, including folkways, often neglected the consequences of conflict. This is one of the dividing lines between folklore and what we call the fine arts. To add depth to your writing, set up an exploratory exercise. Begin with an object that represents what a character loses or gives up as a result of conflict. This is a powerful activity to mime with or without mask. A group exercise from Seattle's Umo theater company includes this in its role-play of a day in the life of a medieval beggar who lives outside the city walls. A similar kind of incident could be added to any story in development. What if _____ lost her most precious possession? What would it be, and what would she do about it? Look at "Most Precious" in this collection for an example.

## Interruptions

Drama begins when the usual order and ways are interrupted. It can be a fictional device when combined with journal-keeping. Take some moment from your daily routine, write it at the top of a sheet of paper. "I was driving down the freeway at seven-thirty in the morning, when. . . ." Now interrupt the everyday with something entirely unexpected, and imagine how you would respond.

I've used interruptions to explore the idea of superheroes with children. They form into small groups and agree on an everyday action, appoint one of their own to be a self-important superhero, determined to fix something that may or may not be broken. This produced storylines that wouldn't have emerged any other way. There's an interesting philosophical issue behind this, which I didn't raise with the children.

## Action or Object and Response

Here are more improvisations to see the potential in any moment. The exchange of an ordinary object can be the focus of action in a story, as in any drama. You will need two or more people, one object (a book or cup or apple will do), and a set of cards. The first person in the pair is holding the object or picks it up and hands it to the second person, who responds as the card suggests. The first person amplifies and adds to this. Here are my card prompts to stimulate you to create your own.

- Your response: "Get rid of this!"
- Your response: "Thanks for a job well done!"
- Your response: "Are you asking for my help with this?"
- Your response: "Are you done with that already?"
- Your response: "I have no idea why you are handing me this."
- Your response: "You should not be giving me this."
- Your response: "I never thought I'd see this again. Where did you find it?"
- Your response: "I can't accept this, really. It's too much."

You can add to your story bones with a bag of assorted objects (mine had small stones, pine cones, shells, feathers, a bit of rope, ribbon, a comb, clothespin, driftwood, and small toys) and homemade idea cards. These cards are much like those used in board games. Here's a set I quickly assembled for a storyteller workshop:

- Two characters are on a quest for a gift.
- Your character is searching for a cure or remedy for a dreadful illness.
- You are a bystander; describe how one of the other characters looks to you.
- Describe the place where another character is standing: what sights, smells, sounds?
- Draw an object from the bag and listen to it speak. What is it saying to you?
- Draw an object from the bag. It is trying to warn you of something. What?
- Draw an object from the bag. It can help the person on a quest for a cure. How?
- Draw an object from the bag. It will obstruct another character from achieving a goal. How?

*Alphabet*

This is a standard theater game, easy, fun, and different every time. Two people sit in front of a group. They tell a story, creating it on the spot, each person using what has already been said and adding to it, taking turns, with one rule: Each person begins with the next letter of the alphabet. So the first person begins their story with the letter "A." This is a good icebreaker for a party or meeting of storytellers.

*Creating with Masks*

Masks and other animal props allow us to exaggerate both comedy and danger. I have a "wolf" consisting of a paper wolf mask, a plastic headband with attached felt ears, a tie-on tail, and tie-on ruffs of raw wool for ankles and wrists. I also have a collection of latex animal noses on elastic strings, the kind that are available for a small price at party outlets. Put a pile of noses in the center of the room. Each person selects a nose, puts it on, and then by turns brings their character into the story.

Beginning storytellers are often self-conscious about gestures. How much helps and when is it too much? One interesting way to explore gesture is to pantomime a simple story for others, wearing blank masks. These can be made of cardboard, plaster tape or papier-mâché.

Two people, each wearing a mask, start from different doorways or sides of a room and "discover" each other. A third person tells them what they will be doing before the masked ones move. The stories can be very simple. Remember, no dialogue as performers move to a resolution. My examples are gleaned from various theater workshops.

- Search for something precious to you that you have lost. Try to tell us about it by gesture.
- The most important person in your life is late meeting you. Very late.

- You don't want to be seen. Try to blend into your environment.
- You are in a crowd at a concert looking for a friend. Something terrible happens.
- You are alone, dejected. Something good happens.
- You are lost in a strange town, looking for signs of where you might be without being obvious.

Here are exercises for two masked people.

- One person is out front, working at something (Sawing wood? Building a wall? Reading? Or use any of the search ideas, above). The second one emerges, discovers Person 1. Our Person 2 has never seen anyone the least like Person 1 before. Person 2 approaches and looks at length before Person 1 notices.
- Again, Person 1 is out front, doing something intently. Person 2 approaches and warns Person 1 of a danger. Person 1 is gradually convinced.
- Person 1 moves cautiously out front and begins doing something. Person 2 discovers Person 1, and remembers that Person 1 has done something bad. Person 2 struggles with ways to apologize.
- Person 1 and Person 2 move out at about the same time and meet for the first time. They try to discover if the other is dangerous. Eventually, one offers food to the other.
- Person 1 is working on something; Person 2 finds Person 1 and tries to get Person 1 to play a game.
- When they meet, one character likes the other, who is frightened.

## CHARACTERS

Where a novel can be panoramic, sweeping across centuries and whole communities, a story is meant to be read or told, absorbing and entirely satisfying, in one sitting. Thus, the characters in a story are sharply drawn, emphasizing characteristics directly related to the theme and direction of the story. Compare this to a photograph that holds two or three subjects in focus while backgrounds soften into general contours. There are no incidental characters or events in a traditional-style tale.

## Traditional Character Types

This is a sampling of traditional characters. Put these or your own on cards, shuffle and deal out an arrangement that must be fitted together into an impromptu story.

- a helpful ghost or spirit
- an angel in disguise of a poor pilgrim
- a talking horse with power to fly
- a powerful old woman with a terrible temper
- a youth mistaken as a fool
- the fool who finds a solution others miss
- the Bears have a wondrous child
- a cruel parent
- an orphan girl is looking for help
- a young person being chased transforms into an animal and escapes
- a demanding ruler
- a mischievous imp
- a stranger who is not what he seems
- a jealous sibling

Add a motivation for each character. In a group, pantomime the action with vocalizations such as grunts and exclamations of glee, but no words. Then do it again, adding words.

- dig in a garden, discover treasure
- look through hallways, hear sounds through doors; look through keyholes, show what you find

- go into a cold tent, crawl into a sleeping bag, try to warm up; hear strange sounds
- make your bed while: sad; happy; angry; distracted

A group exercise to follow this: Individuals walk in all directions around the room. One person is appointed wizard. The wizard affects the movements of everyone else, by waving a wand or hands. Take turns being wizard, and practice having the group move all together, attracted to or pushed away by one source.

## Stages of Life of a Mythological Character

My list is adapted from that of David Adams Leeming in his book, *Mythology: The Voyage of the Hero*.

1. The miraculous birth of the hero or heroine: This may be a remarkable combination of parents, a break from the limitations of the past, a crack in the cosmic egg, which produces an individual with potential unlike that known for any previous being. This prepares the listener for large events with great importance.

2. A threat or danger to the infant: This must be overcome before the infant has achieved her or his own powers. Metaphorically, I suspect that a Herod-like king or father represents the resistance we all feel toward the truly new and powerful, even that which promises us something better.

3. Early signs of remarkable gifts and/or importance of the hero/heroine: This increases our sense of conflict to come if we also see how disturbing these gifts may be for those invested in the way things are.

4. A time of decision when the hero/heroine recognizes the challenge or quest that can or should be taken: This is a time of reflection and self-doubt, an important quality that will sustain the hero later. It is a reminder of how remarkable deeds require a strength that begins with self-inventory.

5. Acceptance and beginning of the quest: This often includes the first serious test of the hero's will, abilities, and wisdom.
6. Challenges and tests: These may be few or many.
7. The final struggle, which is lost; death of the hero/heroine.
8. Descent to an underworld; loss, then atonement or transformation, the reappearance of the hero in another form.

The world after the death is a different place, one with new possibilities or new ways of seeing things. Notice that pop-culture films often have simplified versions of this outline, without apotheosis or a changed world. Perhaps that's to leave room for a sequel. One result of the pop-culture style is that the end of the story leaves us uneasy; evil can emerge again because only one extraordinary figure was able to contain it.

## STORY DEVELOPMENT

Whether you work alone or with others in a class, workshop, or writer's group, you can improve and expand your stories with a variety of writer's strategies.

### Story Bones

1. Start by placing the story in a time and place. This could be yesterday, of course. To free yourself and allow magical events, alternate realities, set your story in a time before the world operated by the rules we accept today. This could even be the beginning of creation, before the separation of the elements or before humans appeared. Look back at my collection or at Greek or Native American tales for examples. In myth this could be a time before rivers were tamed, a time when evildoers were not stopped, or a time before evil. It could be a time when demons regularly came down from the mountains or a paradise when angels walked among us.

2. Introduce a character with a goal.

3. Suggest a major problem or obstacle, something that would deter most if not all characters.

4. Introduce a helper. This can be a wisdom source (look at African and Native American stories to see how often this wisdom figure is a creature easily overlooked or dismissed). This can be a magical person or an object.

5. Suggest a direction, set off on a quest for a solution. This is a metaphor for the way we must take ownership for finding our own solutions and not wallow in our misfortunes.

6. Bring in a complication. Long, dangerous quests; objects of mysterious power; and powerful, magical characters are introduced to test the mettle and skill of the protagonist.

7. Now add a twist, a new direction, an unexpected element that has to be dealt with.

8. Pile on something else, another complication or an action responding to item 7 above, which will have its own consequences.

9. Describe the climactic events that lead to a conclusion of the story. In northern European lore, this is often a great conflict with winners and losers. In less momentous European folktales, a young protagonist marries well and inherits a kingdom, a metaphor, I believe, for being a fully autonomous adult, able to rule one's own life. Cultures that put high value on finding a place in community have acts of cooperation as the climactic event. Asian stories often have acts of self-sacrifice for the greater good as the most important event.

10. Tragedy and serious mythology have one more element: an end to the cycle of events that produces momentous change yet keeps the spirit of the hero available to influence or assist us. Naha becomes a tall cliff from which his people can see danger coming from the sea. In folktales, two intertwining plants may emerge from the graves of the lovers. In comic tales, the world goes back to pretty much the way it was before; the world is disturbed but not fundamentally changed.

## Five W's and an H

This stalwart set of reminders from journalism continues to be a good working tool for writers. They are: Who, What, When, Where, Why, and How. Label an index card or half sheet of paper with each of these words, then brainstorm. For the Who and What, imagine that you have an intelligent but baffled visitor from the distant past standing in front of you. Kindly explain what to you is obvious. For Where, apply all five senses, treating them as paragraph labels that you must fill in. After some practice at this, you will find yourself adding sensory details more easily as you write a draft or revise.

Exaggeration and playful variation are good ways to gain insight into your characters and their actions. It's not an accident that many cultures give the power of speech and assign human motives to animals other than humans. Use this yourself; assign likely animal characteristics to a person in your start on a story. Use five or six words to characterize your animal's personality before you set them back into a story outline or incident.

Here's another simple way to see a story in a new way. Shift from third person to a first person narrative. Or tell your story from the point of view of a minor character or a biased bystander (let's say, the wife of the Wolf or the Wolf himself in Red Riding Hood).

What happens in a story? Joseph Campbell's work in the area of mythology led to useful outlines of the main events in a myth. Outlines of traditional tales are good starting places for many stories, especially those out of European traditions.

## Change Your Perspective

This can be a journal exploration for an individual or a group exercise, with each person writing a response, then sharing.

"The Land of Opposites" is a simple one for younger children. Gather names of animals, real or fictional. Prepare this ahead, use a reference source, or solicit ideas from the children. Then ask them to complete the sentence "I saw a _____ so _____ (fat, huge, tall, small . . .) that _____." This could be combined with acting out the Disney story of Dumbo.

"Whose Rules" is another exercise. Write the ten commandments (or five or so most important rules) of your household as observed through the perspective of a family pet, a small child, or an observer from another planet. This is a list provided by a young teenaged male in a workshop:

- Do not eat Master's KFC.
- Defoliating gardens is not appreciated.
- Nor is eating potted plants.
- Sharpening claws on furniture gets a pillow in the face.
- Attacking the rotating apple on a black plastic disk (something about beetles) is forbidden.
- Slurping Nils's catnip tea is not the way to his heart.

Such a list can lead easily to a story from the perspective of the pet.

Here's an exercise from a storyteller's development group. Everyone agrees ahead of time to bring a personal object to the meeting. Set these in the center of the table. Now each person takes ten minutes or so to write on the subject "The Secret Life of _____." Compare afterward. An alternative is to have each participant contribute the names of familiar personalities, fictional or not, on chits of paper, which are laid face down in a bowl or on the table. Each person draws a name and proceeds in the same way.

This is a story invention activity for very young children. Do a variation of "Follow the Leader" by having the first child in line invent something to fit into the format, "I am a _____ who can _____. Follow me!" It can be a slug that can climb over clouds or an elephant that can squeeze through keyholes. Assign properties as needed (pillows can represent clouds or two sides of a keyhole), and circle the room once before changing leaders.

For older youths and adults, do "Progressions." Divide a group in half; one half remains seated, the other half moves. For the first five minutes, the initial pair starts a story of its own choice. Then a bell rings and the movers sit down with someone else. The seated give a brief starter clue and then the mover picks up the story (of course, without knowing the details). Clever movers will try to provoke the seated one to offer more clues. Keep moving, as long as time allows, then seated ones summarize the story. The goal is to see how much the movers can contribute within the rule: Each person incorporates what is known of the story so far and advances the story in some way.

### Challenge Chorus

The ancient Greek chorus can be updated in a provocative way. I've found this especially productive with adolescents, who are beginning to question everything on their own. It's a way of legitimizing this while making them responsible for their offhand statements and helps them place themselves within a larger story, literally. I start with a published story or a known story outline, something conventional, generally accepted. I've used the Old Testament account of the great flood, for instance. The plagues of Egypt work as well. Appoint a narrator and recorder; everyone else participates as chorus. To gather material for the chorus, the original text is read slowly, one sentence at a time. The chorus brainstorms by offering questions, arguments, and challenges for each sentence. They may ask for more information or proof.

Record everything. Then go back as a group and highlight especially good chorus ideas. Rewrite as narrator and chorus, selecting in a way that is dramatic and effective. Decide how the chorus comes to its own ending, and whether they make a final judgment on the action, agreeing that it was necessary or right or important. This should be an active discussion. Perform this on tape or for an audience.

## Backstory

As dramatists remind us, a significant part of any story takes place in the imagination of the writer behind the stage and before the curtains open. Here is a set of backstory cards that I've used after a story has its basic bones. They are fun to use to revise a familiar fairy tale in performance. I created them for a storyteller's development group. They could be used alone, after crafting a story outline, as a story improvement tool. Use them by yourself or with a group for improv or story invention by putting two or three of these characters together.

- Your character has a serious toothache. (fang ache?)
- You are ferociously hungry.
- You lack confidence. You speak softly, and every statement is a kind of question?
- You are a take-charge kind of person.
- You have been on your quest all day, and your feet hurt.
- You want people to think you are a regular fellow, so you cuss a lot. You make up your own cuss words.
- When-you-are-nervous-or-scared-you-talk-fast-and-run-everything-together.
- You don't listen well. You interrupt.
- You aren't sure anyone understands what you say, so you say it twice. Twice. At least. Twice.
- You are blinded by love.
- This experience is wounding your feelings.
- Someone else's enthusiasm or eagerness is making you suspicious.
- You have *no* respect for the person speaking to you, but can't show it.
- You once had a bad dream about a place like this.
- You love danger.

## Magical Egg

Magic, as contemporary pagans remind us, is a way of explaining the unexpected. Magical events carry us beyond our assumptions and expectations. I have a favorite exercise for myself and for groups to introduce possibilities. I begin with a papier-mâché egg, large enough to sit in the palm of an ordinary hand. It is brightly painted to suggest its contents, and it opens to reveal a collection of odd bits: an agate marble, a chip from an ancient Japanese tile, small shells, a ball of sand hardened into a round stone, a feather, a stamp featuring Amelia Earhart, a mound of polished quartz, ocean-washed green bottle glass, a turtle glued up from tiny shells, a rubber frog, an eraser in the shape of a miniature angel . . . you get the idea.

After a group has developed a basic story using elements of a myth or the story bones or something similar, I pass around the egg. Each person must select one object, lift it up to show others, and with great seriousness describe the magical qualities of this object. Nearly everyone is surprised by what comes out of their mouth, and the accumulated revelations have a powerful effect, one that is, well, magical. Here are suggestions that I saved from a workshop:

"This piece of glass has been across the ocean floor. It was washed up and back so many times that it can look backwards in time and into the future."

"This ball of sand came from God's sandal. It knows many secrets."

"This tile chip can complete the picture on the floor of the Taj Mahal."

"This ball of sand is a curdle of the sky from the moment that earth and sky separated. Whoever finds it can call up a storm."

"This shell hears the agony of the ocean."

"This stamp delivers mail to heaven."

"This stone will hit whatever it is aimed at."

"Hold this flat black stone between your palms, and you can travel anywhere."

"This little hunk of amber perfectly preserves the past."

"This remnant of butterfly wing will fill you with energy and wisdom if you blow on it."

"This frog floated in the original primordial soup."

Next, each person wrote a very short story (given five minutes) that incorporated any of these magical elements. Here is one:

"A forest fire drives Grasshopper to the river. She is alone, except for the whizzing, buzzing, over-heated water bugs. Frightened, she falls in the water, sinks, and lands on a large, half-submerged shell. She hears a murmuring. With some effort she picks the shell out of the mud and carries it to the surface. The shell tells her it will protect her. She sets it on the water, then floats safely inside, as the shell comforts her with sad songs of the ocean. All around, the fire burns everything it can reach, until eventually it is gone."

Here is a unique creation story:

"Our first mother, Frog, was a greedy eater. She ate everything in sight. She took bites of volcano flowing into the ocean and gave birth to bright-colored fishes. She ate falling stars and gave birth to starfish. She ate fish in a bad mood and gave birth to sharks. When she was teased by the Devil for being so fat and wrinkled, she took a bite out of him and gave birth to humans."

### Use the Yellow Pages

Your telephone directory's Yellow Pages contain invaluable sources of ideas for characters. They and a clipboard were all I brought to a workshop for teenagers (with several adult advisors) from rural communities with many fixed ideas about a topic of interest at that time: logging national forest land. I set up a situation: "We are part of a community dependent on farming and the logging mill. Environmentalists are concerned about an upcoming logging contract that is next door to a park that is a favorite place to go around here. They plan some kind of local action. Rumors suggest that if the logging company isn't allowed to go in for the cut here, the mill will close."

Instructions were for participants to take turns opening the phone book's business advertisements at random, selecting a business, and creating a character who owned or worked for that business. Then they took turns introducing their character, telling how the mill closure might affect them. An example: "I'm Karen Johnson, a single parent with three children under the age of twelve. I'm hard-working and stable, but struggle with all my family obligations. I work as a court reporter. I know that the actions of these environmentalists will have legal consequences, and I'll have a lot of pressure on me. I don't look forward to the stress of legal actions that pit one family against another in my town." Another: "I'm Sally Smith, a hairdresser. Women won't get their hair done if the mill closes."

Most of the teenagers gave fairly short character descriptions. They were amazed when an older woman created this role for herself: "I'm Louisa Carpenter, a widow eighty-two years old. I love to garden and have the young neighbor kids over for tea and cookies. I've lived in this town since I was married, sixty-two years ago. My husband retired from the mill in his sixties; I have one son who still works there. He has three children. My other son owns the hardware store on Main Street, and that will certainly be affected by the mill closing. I've known the mill owner and his family for years. They have always done good things for this community. They buy our band uniforms."

Using the directory broadened the sense of how real people would be affected by an introduced conflict. We expanded on this by having everyone stand in a line. First person in line acted as an environmentalist trying to get townspeople to sign a petition outside of the town market. Each person walked up to this environmentalist and improvised from their character's perspective. When they were done, they took the clipboard and became the environmentalist.

The interactions were so gripping that I had to intervene and change characters. Playing both sides of the conflict produced some of the best story ideas I've ever seen.

## Stories Based on Life Experiences

Every family has its challenges, losses, and triumphs, its dramatic moments, as well as an assortment of habits, anecdotes, traditions. Yet much that was endured as well as treasured by one generation is lost to the next. Who would not enjoy a description of a journey through an ordinary day in the life of a great grandparent? You can save such a record for yourself, as a way to understand your experiences and to make a gift to the future.

Look back at times when you made a choice (or fate chose for you) with serious consequences. Whose advice, whose influence, made a difference in your life? Begin by keeping a personal journal that explores the mundane as well as emotionally charged moments.

Go around your rooms with a notepad, describing objects, arrangements, any evidence of personal or family style. Do you show family photographs on the piano, as my mother and I have both done? Mine are snapshots, while my mother displayed high-school graduation portraits of her six children, in identical frames—formal, idealized mementos of the year we stepped into what we believed to be adulthood.

Select one object or several, and write about them. Then go through a family photo collection, writing captions. Now assemble a group of objects or photographs that relate to a particular day or event, a holiday, perhaps, or a picnic or family outing. Write as if describing this event, what led up to it, the event itself, and what followed, as if writing a letter to a dear friend.

Interview someone in your family. For a close relative, a photo album is a good story starter. Bring a selection of photographs and a tape recorder. You may be surprised at how a direct, specific question and follow-up question can provoke details that are entirely new to you. You could ask, "Where was this picture taken? How often did you and Dad go on picnics like this? Were you already married?"

I learned about my father's youthful participation in the North Dakota Farmers Holiday Association only by asking pointed questions. What was slightly disreputable to my mother was fascinating to me. In your interviews, be sure to ask about ordinary days as well as special ones. When I asked about going to church as a child, my mother described services in a little Lutheran community church where men and women sat on opposite sides of the center isle. No musical instruments were allowed. My mother's mother had the strongest voice of the women; she sat, by common agreement, at the front seat closest to the isle, directly across from the man with the best voice. These two would look at each other, nod, strike a pitch, and lead the hymns without turning around.

Family get-togethers are good times to collect stories as well as tell them. Ask permission of the group, and if you get it, place a tape recorder inconspicuously near you. Set a microphone in the middle where everyone can see it, and turn it on. Announce the event and names of participants. Remember that if you don't have a separate directional microphone, extraneous sounds like traffic or a dishwasher will be more noticeable on tape, and moving the microphone while it is recording will make a rumble. Be ready to turn off the recorder or change the tape.

When you conduct an interview in a family setting, with people who know you well, you may hear multiple and conflicting stories. Encourage these; record them all. It is the nature of memory to mutate. Your job isn't to find the truth, if such can be found in this situation, but to hear stories.

After the event, write down your observations of the event itself. Who cooked the turkey or ham? Who carved it? Did you hear stories during the meal? Any repetitions, with or without variation? Who does cleanup, and is there talk associated with this? Equally important is the issue of who doesn't join the events and what isn't discussed.

If you leave a wide left column for these notes, you can go back over them with a highlighter and mark notes to yourself for follow-up interviews. Then call or visit family members separately for more complete versions of stories.

You can also make a note of stories out of your community or region, from historic records, newspapers, or conversations. Carefully document each source, with dates and contact information.

Here's a story that I adapted from *Owyhee Outpost*, June 1978. Lola Blossom found the original account, filled with exciting detail, from an undated newspaper story published in the *Times News* of Twin Falls, sometime before the turn of the twentieth-century. The story speaks of the real life of the south Idaho cowboy and the kind of cooperation that allowed families to survive.

### A Cowboy's Ride for Help

Word came to a young cowboy, A. H. Brailsford, from the neighboring Owens place. Charlie Owens's daughter, little Emma, needed a doctor, and the nearest doctor was sixty-five miles away, in Mountain Home. It was 9 P.M. on a frosty January evening, and there were no telephones, no autos, and no roads that deserved the name. A. H. Brailsford's friend found him a horse, while A. H. put on a warm coat and tied a muffler over his head. A. H. jumped on a big sorrel with long legs and rode off into the night on a trail that took him over icy ledges, frozen creek bottoms, and gullies loaded with belly-deep snow on his way to his first stop, Clover Flat.

It was very late by now, and the ranch house at Clover Flat was dark and quiet. A. H. knocked at the door, explained his mission, and within minutes kerosene lanterns guided him to the corrals where a cow pony was soon saddled, a little bay from the 71st outfit that came up from Texas. A.H. rode on through the dark and cold, only the creak of the saddle for company, for four more dark hours to Art Pence's place at the head of the Bruneau valley. Art's hired hands came out of the bunkhouse. Art was a state senator meeting with the legislature in Boise just then, but they knew he'd surely want to help. The hands saddled up Art's big black mare and A.H. rode off once more.

Daylight came with a surprise, an unseasonable thaw. The foot of snow A.H. had been riding over turned to slippery muck. The ice ledges he had to climb on his way out of creek bottoms were melting to sludge as he rode up to the Loveridge ferry on the Snake River. Loveridge was sympathetic. He knew that A.H. still had hours to go, without another place to stop for a fresh mount before he reached town. Loveridge did have a gray mustang available; the nag was ornery but tough, said the ferryman. If you can stay on, he'll get you to Mountain Home! Loveridge held the bridle as A.H. mounted- that mustang took off like a shot! Hours later a tired mustang carried the cowboy slowly into Mountain Home.

A.H. found the doctor, who luckily was in. A.H. was ready to hand over responsibility and take a well-deserved rest for himself and the mustang before heading back. "The Owens baby is sick! Grab your bag and a good horse," he blurted out. But Doc was unwilling to make the ride. He fixed up a batch of medicine to send to the Owens ranch as both the mustang and A.H. ate a quick meal before starting back. Doc handed the cowboy a small bottle of whiskey for the ride along with the medicine; A.H. had a pocketful of cigars to keep himself awake too.

On the way back the acrid smoke and taste of the cigars helped keep A.H. going, but the whiskey made him sleepy, and he tossed it, bottle and all, to the side of the trail. The mustang, not quite as skittish now, moved steadily through the mud toward Loveridge ferry. This was lucky for A.H. because the long journey was wearing on him.

At each stop, someone had hot food and the mount the cowboy had left behind half a day earlier. He left the ornery mustang with Loveridge, then the black mare at Art Pence's place, where they had the cow pony ready to ride to Clover Flat. By this time A. H. didn't take time to eat.

It was midnight when he rode the sorrel in to the Owens place. Someone took the medicine out of his pocket and helped him down. The insides of his legs were raw, but he didn't notice yet. He slept nearly thirty hours. Somebody shook him awake to eat a bit, a couple of times, before he slept again.

Emma Owens lived to tell the story to her grandchildren, and A. H. himself told a newspaper reporter many years later that he couldn't have done it without good neighbors and dependable horses. His favorite, he allowed, was the mustang. It was mean, all right, but it carried him through.

## Interviewing

I use interview procedures recommended by Troy Reeves, oral historian for the Idaho State Historical Society. Troy urges using a sixty-minute tape (shorter tapes hold up better) and a tape recorder with an external microphone. Built-in microphones try to equalize all sounds and can exaggerate traffic and other environmental sounds.

For the first visit, bring a form your interviewee can fill out. Request basic information as full names of your interviewee and family, including parents, grandparents, siblings, spouse(s), and children, if any. This information also helps you form questions more accurately. While your interviewee records names of family and dates of birth and marriages, set up the tape recorder. Announce that you are about to do a test, and have each person speak briefly. Turn on the tape and give your own name, the date, and the place where the interview is taking place. Then ask the interviewee to give her or his name. Immediately play back that part of the tape to verify that it's working.

While conducting the interview, say as little as possible your-self. Ask one question at a time, for one particular piece of infor-mation, and keep a balance of specific and more general requests. Use your information sheet to ask follow-up questions, or repeat questions that seem worth exploring further ("You say that your mother died when you were six. Can you tell me how this changed your life?") If you return for another interview after a time gap, ask if there's anything that could be added to the topic covered last time. Some interviewers take a break after an hour or so, but leave the tape running to catch any informal talk. I prefer to leave the tape off for breaks and return for another visit. I also honor any requests to turn off the tape and keep some comments off the record.

At the end of your interview, agree upon a topic for a follow-up meeting. Review your notes in the meantime, and identify areas to explore again. Details and better stories can follow a time of reflecting on the earlier interview. Ask, "Is there anything you'd like to add on this subject?" "Have you thought more about your army years since we last talked?"

Ask about typical life events and relationships, about grandpar-ents, parents, childhood, adolescence, courtship, marriage, birth and development of children, work and career, family life, retire-ment. Keeping in mind dates and places where your narrator has lived, ask about participation in historical movements and events. Remembering an important public event can trigger memories you wouldn't get any other way and can help you tie down dates ("How old were you when the veterans of the Great War marched from the train to the state Capitol building?"). As you gain the trust of your interviewee, ask about the inevitable difficulties of life and how they were overcome or lived through. With older people—those who have had time and reason to reflect—ask questions about beliefs and values and how they have changed over time. What is this person most proud of achieving? Surviving?

Finally, try to videotape and photograph at least one session. Use a tripod; sit beside the camera facing your subjects so that they can look at you while you stay out of the shot. Describe your question, pause, repeat it, with the understanding that they begin their response after you push the start button.

Interview questions might include:

- How old are you now?
- When were you born? Where? Can you describe this place?
- What were your parents' names? Any stepparents? Your grandparents?
- Do you know the history behind family names?
- Do you know where your parents grew up? Do you have photos of them in their younger years?
- What kind of work did the adults in your family do? The children? Who had what chores?
- What are your memories of siblings? When were they born? What did you do for fun? Any sibling conflicts? What has become of your siblings? Are you close today?
- Recall typical meals, who cooked what. What were favorite foods, treats, feasts? Any holiday traditions?
- School experiences: best, first, worst, friends, subjects studied, school activities
- Family hobbies, habits, recreation, crafts, talents? Describe the family environment: strict or casual, orderly or disorderly, silent or lots of joking or dancing or singing? Magazines, books, movies, games together, socializing? Stories of humor, of temper? Tension?
- Any family sayings, aphorisms, proverbs, moral lessons, songs, bedtime stories? What were your family ten/five "commandments"?
- Any special abilities in your family? Strengths? Failings? What kind of person was your mother or father? Do you find any of these qualities in yourself?
- What kinds of places did you visit together? Did you visit relatives or entertain them? Any memorable visits?
- What were some of the major events that occurred while you

grew up? How did this affect your family? What disappointments, tragedies, regrets: what followed any misfortune? What lessons learned from this?

- What was the general health of family members? Any major illnesses, deaths?
- What caused family difficulties? What was the style of family discipline, for what behavior?
- What of your family's physical legacy: any heirlooms, documents, photos, possessions? Who has them now?
- Any odd or notorious characters in the family? Tales of lost wealth? Any gifts of healing? Anyone famous? Any adventures or funny stories passed through the family?
- How would you describe your family's place in the community? How did this affect you?
- What community involvement, clubs, activities in your family: what social life, by whom?
- Was there someone who was not a family member who was important to you as a child?
- What affect has your home town or community had upon you?
- What were your childhood dreams, ambitions?
- Were you part of any groups or cliques as a teen? Describe your appearance then. What styles, fads did you participate in? What heroes and idols? Typical recreation, special interests, jobs, religious activity?
- Describe influential friends, teachers, activities, classes, troubles, ambitions, graduation memories.
- How did you socialize? Did you have a special friend? Did you date? Where did you go for fun?
- Did you experience problems with your family at this time? How was conflict resolved?
- How did you become independent? What job plans? What jobs? How about college?
- Did you form new sustained, stable relationships as an adult?
- Did you marry? How did this happen? What was response of your family?

- Describe your wedding ceremony, honeymoon, or early marriage stories. What surprises, challenges here?
- What was your expectation of the future then?
- Recall the births of any children you had and their major life events.
- Did you enter military service? Which branch, why? Where were you trained and how? What rank achieved?
- Where were you sent after basic training? Where did you serve? Did you see combat?
- Are any of your war memories still painful? Do you think of war times now?
- What are your favorite stories, the best and worst of military years?
- Did you have friends in service? Any nicknames? Are you still in touch?
- What did you have to adjust to, once home? How did you do this?
- What was best about coming back? What was worst?
- Do you remember feeling depressed, out of place? How did you find work after you came back?
- How has your military service affected your life since? What about your feelings about war as policy?
- Describe your first full-time job and how you got it. How about changes in employment?
- Describe your most memorable work experience. What have you enjoyed most about this part of your life?
- What has helped you in your work? What held you back? Did you have role models, mentors?
- What gives your life pleasure now? Where do you go to relax, to get away if you need to?
- Describe your friendships, organizations that matter to you, volunteer work, sports and other outdoor activities, family connections. Whose company do you seek? How has this changed with time?

- Describe any hobbies, crafts, arts, or performance arts that you enjoy as participant or observer.
- What were your earliest religious experiences? Earliest beliefs? Have these changed? How?
- What do you consider your life's turning points? What problems have you faced; how did you overcome them?
- What sacrifices have you made and why? What achievements are you most proud of?
- What shows, programs, performances, or literary works matter to you? Who do you admire?
- What do you consider your dumbest financial decision?
- Have you ever been really poor? What did you do about it? Learn from it?
- Were you in any scrapes? Trouble? Have you been hurt, injured in any significant way?
- Have you had an enemy, someone who wished you harm? Who have you forgiven?
- Is it important to you to work for a cause?
- Do you have favorite places or sources of comfort?
- Some say the first forty years are about stability, the next about reconnecting to the best of your past as well as finding new goals and meaning in life. What was your biggest change in middle life?
- Do you regret the loss of youth? Yearn for a last chance? Any strengths or pleasures of midlife? Concerns? What are the annoyances of old age? Any health limits? Regrets?
- Any gifts that have come with advancing age?
- What keeps you going now, what keeps you interested? What strengths do you now rely upon?
- What advice might you offer to today's young people?

Here's an example of a true story, as recalled by a man who refers to himself, modestly, as a retired farmer. Frank Blick grew up hearing his family's stories. His knack for observation and love of reading, encouraged by a high-school teacher, led him to enroll in the prestigious writing program at the University of Iowa after he served in World War II. Then he caught a family disease: pioneer fever. He came back to Owyhee County to farm his father's homestead with his older brother, Arthur. Evenings when work was done, he continued to write stories in his blend of down-home and elegant, almost Elizabethan, cadence. He drew upon both family history and community stories for his self-published book, *A Walk to Walla Walla and the Anvil Chorus*, published in 1999 by Vantage Press.

I interviewed Frank several times at the home he shares with his younger sister, Trudy. One meeting was spent correcting and editing this version of an incident in his early life. I selected this incident from many in Frank's narrative because I felt that it could be interpreted as a modern quest story, one in which the object of the quest has to change with the times. Our country began with many immigrants like the Blicks, settling on their own piece of land, connected to the seasons and the animals they depended upon. Now we are pragmatic town dwellers who mostly work for someone else and live in structures and rhythms we have not created and only partially control. Frank's family made this transition to the land and back twice, and they managed it by helping each other. In this story Harry, Frank's father, understands horses but not cars. Arthur, the oldest boy, not only contributes to the family budget, but takes responsibility for driving after Harry gives it up.

### One Wheel Off

My father, Harry A. Blick, was born 1877 in Winston Salem, North Carolina. His family was from central Europe, the old Austria-Hungary empire. My dad came west with his parents to Farmington, in eastern Washington State, when he was four years old. His stepmother's parents owned a bakery in old Salem; she started a thriving business baking bread on her kitchen stove. A railroad was coming through, with plenty of hungry workers. At the age of eight, my dad carried wood to the store and made deliveries. By the 1890s, when he was still a teenager, he'd left home and taken up working with horses.

Dad was running a livery stable in Durkee, Oregon, when he met Eugenia Gertrude Moore at the Baker County Fair. Eugenia, my mother, came from true pioneer stock also. Her father had come to Walla Walla country in 1859, when he was fifteen. Eugenia had been born in Baker City in 1886 and was a high-school graduate when she and my father met. Completing high school was unusual in those days.

My father was known for his care of animals, his own and everyone else's. Mom told us stories of how good he was with them. My father understood horses, and they understood him. Then cars came along, everywhere, and that was the end of the livery business. Shortly after they married, in 1906, Mom and Dad moved to Boise, Idaho. He worked on the streetcar system in Boise, in maintenance, I believe, and he and Mom were buying a house. But they hadn't given up on the idea of getting a place out of town, raising horses and kids. Evenings, after dinner dishes, they would sit around the table and talk about it. They already had one son, Arthur, when dad heard from a real estate man, a friend of his, that a piece of land on the banks of the Snake River was available, ten miles upstream from Marsing. My folks traded their equity in the house for the land and moved in 1911. That's where I was born in 1919.

It wasn't a farm really; it was an acreage with sagebrush and a small flowing well. We just got by. We could catch fish. There were some pretty big fish in the river at that time, sturgeon. One of our neighbors made a living catching those sturgeon. The prosperity that came with World War One allowed Dad to borrow money to drill a deeper well. That supplied enough water for a two-acre garden and hay for a cow and a couple of horses. Mom filled our root cellar with sacks of potatoes and half-gallon jars packed with sweet corn, beans, and peas. She knew how to make do and do without. She understood that farming was a family enterprise, and she was a real boss too, I'll tell you.

School was only a mile away, an easy walk to Enterprise, a town no longer in existence. Givens Springs School, named for the resort nearby, was a building with four or five grades in one room, only eight or so students.

Families didn't run around then the way we do today. Twice a year my folks would hitch their team of horses to the farm wagon and take us children along to get supplies. The nearest city, Nampa, was a thirty-mile round trip by the ferry route. It took half a day, and my parents were always concerned about getting an early start so that the horses could pull the steep Snake River grade before the heat of the day.

The farm depression of the 1920s was hard times. By 1923 my folks were starved out of the farm. We moved by train to Tillamook County, which is on the coast, west of Portland. We had family there who were certain Dad could find work. That's where the youngest of us, my sister Gertrude was born, in Nehalem. My father worked in logging, and Arthur, who had graduated from high school by this time, took a job in a foundry in Tillamook.

Soon after we arrived, Dad bought a Model T Ford. In those days you could buy a car for a few dollars; Henry Ford put the whole country on wheels. Logging jobs moved around, and Arthur's job was twenty miles from the house we were renting. And in some weather Dad thought I needed a ride. Out there, if it isn't raining, it's trying to.

One morning Dad was taking me to school on his way to work. They didn't have oiled roads, they had plank roads wide enough for two cars to pass. Timber was cheap in those days, and the ground was soggy from all the rain. It wasn't like the desert country we were accustomed to; the coast had all kinds of trees, underbrush every place. You couldn't see very far ahead, and the planks were slick when they were wet, which was most of the time. While Dad was driving along the road on this morning, I felt one wheel drop over the plank. I knew we were heading for the ditch; you couldn't get back on once a wheel went off.

My dad just sort of froze. He didn't touch the brake or nothin'. He sat there frozen, with his feet stuck out in front of him and his hands gripping the wheel, shouting, "Whoah, whooah!" We slid entirely off the road and kept going until we were stopped by the bushes. My dad just sat there, kind of dazed. I got out and walked the rest of the way. When I got out of school that afternoon, my brother Arthur was waiting for me in the Model T. He said that Dad had left the car where it stopped and walked to work. Someone passed on the word to Arthur. Dad never talked about this again; Arthur did all the driving for the family after that.

## CONCLUSION

I will bid you farewell and urge you on to your own storytelling and storymaking adventures with an anecdote from my friend Renee Johns, recalling something that happened in the last week of her three years teaching high school in Chad.

"Just before I was leaving my home in Mongo, Chad, some women I knew from the leprosy village asked to have lunch with me. Hanana and Am-Hissein were women I had interviewed a few months earlier and enjoyed a cup of tea with. We met for lunch at the home of our mutual friend, Riska, a Dutch nurse. While Riska was inside, the three of us tried to have a conversation. My Arabic is minimal, and they did not speak French, so we quickly went through a few greetings, then struggled with my limited vocabulary. Hanana asked, 'Amiki inti?' I could not get the last word. She was asking, 'Does your mother have . . . ?' but I had no idea what the final word was. Nor had we been talking about my mother or my family at all. Just as Riska hollered out the word in English, Hanana reached into her tattered blouse and brought out her breast. 'Does your mother have breasts,' she was asking.

"I was taken aback. No one had ever asked me that before! It took me months to understand that interchange. Part of the question was a simple question of biology. These women with leprosy had been isolated and had never been to school, met few foreigners, and really didn't know if a woman from another land, with another skin color, had the same anatomy. So on one level the question was, 'Do you give birth like we do? Do you nurse your children as we do?'

"But I have concluded that the more important question was, 'Are you like us? Do you laugh? Do you cry? Do you prepare meals for your family? Do you worry about your children? Do you grieve for those who die? Do you find hope in the sunrise?' And through all those layers of cultural difference, all those layers of opposing worldviews, I answer Hanana each day now. Yes, our mothers have breasts. Yes, Hanana, we are like you. Yes, Hanana, we too dream of a world of justice, equity, and compassion, a world at peace.'"

# SELECTED BIBLIOGRAPHY

Abrahams, Roger D., ed. *Afro-American Folktales*. New York: Pantheon Fairy Tale and Folklore Library, 1985.

Afanas'ev, Alexander. *Russian Fairy Tales*. Translated by Norbert Guterman. New York: Pantheon Fairy Tale and Folklore Library, 1973.

Alexander, Hartley Burr. Summary of Adrian Recinos's translation of Mayan codex, in *Latin American*. Vol. 11 of *The Mythology of All Races*. Boston: Marshall Jones Company, 1931.

Blick, Frank. *A Walk to Walla Walla and the Anvil Chorus*. New York: Vantage Press, 1999.

Blossom, Lola. "Three Creek, Idaho." *Owyhee Outpost*, no. 9 (June 1978). Murphy, Idaho: Owyhee County Historical Society.

Boas, Franz, ed. *Folktales of the Salishan and Sahaptin Tribes*. New York: American Folklore Society, 1917.

Bulatkin, I. F., trans. *Eurasian Folk and Fairy Tales*. New York: Criterion Books, 1965.

Burton, Richard F., trans. and annot. *The Book of the Thousand Nights and a Night*. New York: The Heritage Press, 1962.

Bushnaq, Inea, trans. and ed. *Arab Folktales*. New York: Pantheon Books, 1986.

Cabell, James Branch. *Jurgen*. 1921. Reprint, New York: Dover Publications, 1977.

Calvino, Italo. *Italian Folktales*. Translated by George Martin. New York: Pantheon Fairy Tale and Folklore Library, 1980.

Campbell, Joseph. *The Masks of God: Primitive Mythology, Occidental Mythology, Oriental Mythology, Creative Mythology*. New York: Viking, 1976.

Campbell, Joseph. *The Flight of the Wild Gander*. Chicago: Henry Regnery, 1969.

Champion, Selwyn Gurney, and Dorothy Short, comps. *Readings from World Religions*. Greenwich, CT.: Faucett Publications, 1959.

Clark, Ella E. *Indian Legends of the Pacific Northwest*. Berkeley: University of California Press, 1958.

Coho, Grey. "Ancestors." In *The Whispering Wind: Poetry by Young American Indians*. New York: Doubleday, 1972.

Confucius. *The Sayings of Confucius*. Translated by James R. Ware. New York: Mentor Religious Classics, 1955.

Curtis, Natalie, ed. *The Indians' Book*. 1923. Reprint, New York: Dover Publications, 1960.

Davidson, H. R. Ellis. *Gods and Myths of Northern Europe*. Baltimore, MD: Penguin Books, 1968.

Duling, D. C., trans. "Testament of Solomon." In *The Old Testament Pseudepigrapha: Apocalyptic Literature and Testaments*. Vol. 1. Edited by James H. Charlesworth. New York: Doubleday, 1983.

Eberhard, Wolfram, ed. *Folktales of China*. Foreword by Richard M. Dorson. Chicago: University of Chicago Press, 1965.

Emerson, Ellen Russell. *Indian Myths or Legends*. Minneapolis: Ross and Haines, 1965.

Erdoes, Richard, and Alfonso Ortiz, eds. *American Indian Myths and Legends*. New York: Pantheon Books, 1984.

Estes, Clarissa Pinkola. *Women Who Run With the Wolves*. New York: Ballantine Books, 1992.

Fletcher, William. *Recording Your Family History*. New York: Dodd, Mead, 1986.

Franck, Frederick. *Days with Albert Schweitzer*. New York: Henry Holt, 1960.

Greenberg, Joel. "In Israel, a Saint Brings a Ghost to a Minority." *New York Times*, February 14, 1993.

Grinnell, George Bird. *Blackfoot Lodge Tales*. Lincoln: University of Nebraska Press, 1962.

Grinnell, George Bird. *Pawnee Hero Stories and Folk Tales*. Lincoln: University of Nebraska Press, 1961.

Hamilton, Edith. *The Greek Way to Western Civilization*. New York: The New American Library, 1954.

Harris, Joel Chandler. *Nights with Uncle Remus*. Boston: Houghton Mifflin, 1883.

In-sob, Zong, trans., collector. *Folk Tales from Korea*. New York: Grove Press, 1979.

Jameson, Michael H. "Mythology of Ancient Greece."In *Mythologies of the Ancient World*. Edited by Samuel Noah Kramer. New York: Doubleday, 1961.

Jenkins, Ron. "Two-Way Mirrors." *Parabola* 6, no. 3 (August 1981): 17.

Jordan-Smith, Paul. "The Serpent and the Eagle." *Parabola* 14, no. 3 (Fall 1989): 64.

Jordan-Smith, Paul. "The Two Hunchbacks." *Parabola* 7, no. 3 (August 1982): 47.

Kaufman, William I., comp. *UNICEF Book of Children's Legends*. Harrisburg, PA: Stackpole Books, 1970.

Kingsland, Mrs. Burton. *The Book of In and Out Door Games*. New York: Doubleday, Page and Co., 1904.

La Barre, Weston. *The Ghost Dance: Origins of Religion*. Garden City, NY: Doubleday, 1970.

Langdon, Stephen. *Semitic*. Vol. 5 of *The Mythology of All Races*. Boston: Marshall Jones Company, 1931.

Lannoy, Richard. *The Speaking Tree: A Study of Indian Culture and Society*. Oxford, England: Oxford University Press, 1971.

Leeming, David Adams. *Mythology: The Voyage of the Hero*. New York: J. B. Lippincott, 1937, reprinted 1973.

Leon-Portilla, Miguel. "Mythology of Ancient Mexico." In *Mythologies of the Ancient World*. Edited by Samuel Noah Kramer. New York: Doubleday, 1961.

Linderman, Frank. *Plenty-Coups, Chief of the Crows*. 1930. Reprint, Lincoln: University of Nebraska Press, 1962.

Lummis, Charles F. *The Man Who Married the Moon*. New York: The Century Company, 1894.

MacDonald, Margaret Read, and Brian W. Sturm. *The Storyteller's Sourcebook: A Subject, Title, and Motif Index to Folklore Collections for Children*. Farmington Hills, MI: Gale Group, 2001.

MacCulloch, John A. *Celtic / Slavic*. Vol. 3 of *The Mythology of All Races*. Boston: Marshall Jones Company, 1931.

Malotki, Ekkehart. *Hopi Coyote Tales*. Lincoln: University of Nebraska Press, 1984.

Mead, Margaret. *The Rainbow Book of People and Places*. New York: World Publications, 1972.

Miedzinski, Charles. "Spiritual Geometry: Turkish Carpets at the de Young Museum." *Artweek*, January 10, 1991.

Minford, John, trans. *Favourite Folktales of China*. Beijing: New World Press, 1983.

Monteil, Charles. "God and Pride." Translated by Anne Twitty. *Parabola* 9, no. 1 (January 1984): 48.

Mourning Dove. *Coyote Stories*. Caldwell, ID: Caxton Printers, 1934.

Munsch, R. *The Paper Bag Princess*. New York: Firefly Books, 1986.

Narayan, R. K. *The Ramayana* (Tamil version). New York: Penguin Books, 1981.

Neihardt, John. *Black Elk Speaks*. Lincoln: University of Nebraska Press, 1960.

Nemcová, Bozena. *Fairy Tales from Czechoslovakia*. Vol. 1. Translated by Ludmila Ondrujova. First Limited and Numbered Edition. Rockville, MD: Kabel Publishers, 1987.

Nobleman, Roberta. *Mime and Masks*. Rowayton, Conn.: New Play Books, 1979.

Ogunmola, Kola. *The Palmwine Drinkard*, opera libretto. Stanford, CA: Stanford University Music Library, 1969.

Pont, Anna M. *Blind Chickens and Social Animals: Creating Spaces for Afghan Women's Narratives under the Taliban*. Portland, OR: Mercy Corps, 2001.

Reichard, Gladys. *Navajo Medicine Man Sandpaintings*. New York: Dover Publications, 1977.

Rouse, W. H. D. *Gods, Heroes and Men of Ancient Greece*. New York: New American Library, 1957.

Schultz, J. W. *My Life as an Indian*. Lewiston, MN: Confluence Press, 1983.

Seki, Keigo. "The Quarrel." *Parabola* 11, no. 2 (May 1986): 75.

Sproul, Barbara C., ed. *Primal Myths: Creating Myths Around the World*. New York: Harper Collins, 1991.

Squire, Charles. *Celtic Myth and Legend*. Newcastle, England: Newcastle Publishing Co., 1975.

Storm, Hyemeyohsts. *Seven Arrows*. New York: Ballantine Books, 1972.

Synge, Ursula. *Land of Heroes: A Retelling of the Kalevala*. New York: Atheneum, 1978.

Talashoma, Herschel. *Hopi Tales*. Translated by Ekkehart Malotki. Tucson: University of Arizona Press, 1983.

Thompson, Stith. *Tales of the North American Indians*. Bloomington: Indiana University Press, 1971.

Thompson, Stith. *The Folktale*. New York: Dryden Press, 1946.

Toelken, Barre. *The Dynamics of Folklore*. Logan: Utah State University Press, 1996.

Tong, Diane. "How the Devil Helped God Create the World," told by

Vladislav Kornel. In *Gypsy Folk Tales*. New York: Harcourt Brace Jovanovich, 1989.

Tutuola, Amos. *Palmwine Drinkard*. New York: Grove Press, 1984.

United States Committee to UNICEF. *Hi Neighbors*, Volumes 1-5.

Vinton, Iris. *The Folkways Omnibus of Children's Games*. New York: Hawthorne Books, 1970.

Von Puttkamer, W. Jesco. "Stone Age Present Meets Stone Age Past." *National Geographic* (January 1983): 69.

Walker, Deward E., Jr. *Myths of Idaho Indians*. Moscow, ID: University Press of Idaho, 1980.

Watt, Homer, trans. "The Second Shepherd's Play." In *The Literature of England*. Vol 1. Chicago: Scott Foresman, 1966.

West, John O. *Mexican-American Folklore: Legends, Songs, Festivals, Proverbs, Crafts, Tales of Saints, of Revolutionaries, and More*. Little Rock, AR: August House, 1988.

Williamson, Ray A., and Claire R. Farrer, eds. *Earth and Sky: Visions of the Cosmos in Native American Folklore*. Albuquerque: University of New Mexico Press, 1992.

Wolkstein, Diane. "The Seer of Lublin's Shirt." *Parabola* 9, no. 2 (April 1984): 82.

Wright, G. Ernest, and Reginald H. Fuller. *The Book of the Acts of God: Contemporary Scholarship Interprets the Bible*. New York: Doubleday, 1960.

Yep, Lawrence. *The Rainbow People*. New York: Harper and Row, 1989.

Zong In-Sob, trans. and ed. *Folk Tales from Korea*. New York: Grove Press, 1979.

# ACKNOWLEDGMENTS

I am indebted to the children and young at heart who have informed and enriched my stories for many years. Helen Langworthy helped me incorporate still-alive legends of eastern Europe into "Better Rude than Sorry." Those participating in classes and workshops who substantially contributed toward this collection include Kristy Clark, Tammy Lowe, Trista Jacobsen, April Jackson, Andrea Penick, and Mellisa Cox, who came up with the idea for how blondes came to be known as airheads. Heather Bartlett, Kirstan Davidson, Amy Howell, Will Hudson, Soly Lyons, and Jennifer Thibodeau developed "Sharing the Well." Will Hudson, Jennifer Thibodeau, and Austin and Dylan Reedy created and performed "Saving Stone Monster." Nicholas Bock, Radha and Revati McNamara, Sara Spink, Mandy Dressor, Seth Loughmiller, and Yola Owens developed "Saving Stone Monster" in response to the five-reality scissors of Nicholas Bock.